*New Casebooks*

# PHILIP LARKIN

# NEW CASEBOOKS

Further titles are in preparation

New Casebooks

# Philip Larkin

Edited by

Stephen Regan

St. Martin's Press
New York

St. Martin's Press, Scholarly and Reference Division,
175 Fifth Avenue, New York, N.Y. 10010

First published in the United States of America in 1997

This book is printed on paper suitable for recycling and
made from fully managed and sustained forest sources.

Printed in Hong Kong

ISBN 0–312–17348–2
ISBN 0–312–17349–0

Library of Congress Cataloging-in-Publication Data
Philip Larkin / edited by Stephen Regan.
p.   cm. — (New casebooks)
Includes bibliographical references and index.   ·
ISBN 0–312–17348–2 (cloth). — ISBN 0–312–17349–0 (pbk.)
1. Larkin, Philip—Criticism and interpretation.   I. Regan,
Stephen, 1957–   .  II. Series.
PR6023.A66Z8  1997
821'.914—dc21                                          97–911
                                                        CIP

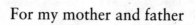
For my mother and father

# Contents

# Acknowledgements

The editor and publishers wish to thank the following for permission to use copyright material:

Alan Bennett, for 'Alas! Deceived' in *Writing Home* (1994), pp. 357–78. Copyright © 1995 by Forelake Ltd, by permission of Faber and Faber Ltd and Random House, Inc.; James Booth, for 'Philip Larkin: Lyricism, Englishness and Postcoloniality', by permission of the English Association; Steve Clark, for 'Get Out As Early As You Can: Larkin's Sexual Politics' in *Philip Larkin: A Tribute 1922–1985*, ed. George Hartley (1988), amended and included in Steve Clark, *Sordid Images: The Poetry of Masculine Desire*, Routledge (1994), by permission of Marvell Press and Routledge; Barbara Everett, for 'Philip Larkin: After Symbolism', *Essays in Criticism*, XXX (1980), by permission of *Essays in Criticism*; Seamus Heaney, for 'The Main of Light' from *The Government of the Tongue: Selected Prose 1978–1987* (1988). Copyright © 1989 by Seamus Heaney, by permission of Faber and Faber Ltd and Farrar Straus & Giroux, Inc.; Graham Holderness, for 'Reading "Deceptions"', *Critical Survey*, 1 (1989), by permission of *Critical Survey*; David Lodge, for 'Philip Larkin: the Metonymic Muse' in *The Modes of Modern Writing*, Edward Arnold (1977). Copyright © David Lodge 1977, by permission of Curtis Brown on behalf of the author; Andrew Motion, for 'Philip Larkin and Symbolism' in *Philip Larkin*, Methuen and Co (1982), by permission of Routledge; Tom Paulin, for 'Into the Heart of Englishness', first published in *The Times Literary Supplement*, 20–26 July 1990 and reprinted as 'She Did Not Change' in *Minotaur: Poetry and the Nation State* (1992). Copyright © 1992 by Tom Paulin, by permission of Faber and Faber Ltd and Harvard

University Press; Janice Rossen, for 'Difficulties With Girls' in *Philip Larkin: His Life's Work* (1989). Copyright © 1990 by Janice Rossen, by permission of Harvester Wheatsheaf and University of Iowa Press; Stan Smith, for 'Margins of Tolerance' in *Inviolable Voice: History and Twentieth-Century Poetry* (1982), by permission of Gill & Macmillan Publishers; Andrew Swarbrick, for 'Larkin's Identities' in *Out of Reach: The Poetry of Philip Larkin* (1994), Copyright © Andrew Swarbrick, by permission of Macmillan Ltd and St. Martin's Press, Inc.

For copyright material included in the above essays:

Faber & Faber Ltd for extracts from Philip Larkin's poetry included in *Collected Poems*, ed. Anthony Thwaite (1988). [Quotations from the poems will be prefaced by the abbreviation *CP* and accompanied by the relevant page number in *Collected Poems*]; The Marvell Press for 'Deceptions' and extracts from 'Whatever Happened', 'Poetry of Departures', 'Toads', 'At Grass', 'Dry-Point', 'I Remember, I Remember', 'Next, Please', 'Church Going', 'Myxomatosis', 'Reason for Attendance' and 'Lines on a Young Lady's Photograph Album' from *The Less Deceived* (1974).

Quotations from unpublished manuscripts held in the Philip Larkin archive at the Brynmor Jones Library, University of Hull, may not be reproduced without permission from the Estate of Philip Larkin.

Every effort has been made to trace the copyright holders but if any have been inadvertently overlooked the publishers will be pleased to make the necessary arrangement at the first opportunity.

# General Editors' Preface

The purpose of this series of New Casebooks is to reveal some of the ways in which contemporary criticism has changed our understanding of commonly studied texts and writers and, indeed, of the nature of criticism itself. Central to the series is a concern with modern critical theory and its effect on current approaches to the study of literature. Each New Casebook editor has been asked to select a sequence of essays which will introduce the reader to the new critical approaches to the text or texts being discussed in the volume and also illuminate the rich interchange between critical theory and critical practice that characterises so much current writing about literature.

In this focus on modern critical thinking and practice New Casebooks aim not only to inform but also to stimulate, with volumes seeking to reflect both the controversy and the excitement of current criticism. Because much of this criticism is difficult and often employs an unfamiliar critical language, editors have been asked to give the reader as much help as they feel is appropriate, but without simplifying the essays or the issues they raise. Again, editors have been asked to supply a list of further reading which will enable readers to follow up issues raised by the essays in the volume.

The project of New Casebooks, then, is to bring together in an illuminating way those critics who best illustrate the ways in which contemporary criticism has established new methods of analysing texts and who have reinvigorated the important debate about how we 'read' literature. The hope is, of course, that New Casebooks will not only open up this debate to a wider audience, but will also encourage students to extend their own ideas, and think afresh about their responses to the texts they are studying.

*John Peck and Martin Coyle*
University of Wales, Cardiff

# Introduction

*STEPHEN REGAN*

I

At the time of his death in 1985, Philip Larkin's reputation as a writer seemed unblemished and secure. Although his high esteem rested largely on three slim volumes of poetry – *The Less Deceived* (1955), *The Whitsun Weddings* (1964) and *High Windows* (1974) – Larkin enjoyed both critical acclaim and immense popularity. Widely acknowledged as the nation's unofficial Poet Laureate, Larkin came to be identified with an essential and enduring Englishness. The formal achievements of his verse – its colloquial tenor, its ironic humour and its clear-sighted realism – were construed as civic virtues. Even those aspects of the poetry that some critics found wanting – its wry circumspection and parochial outlook – seemed to encapsulate the authentic experience of a drab and disillusioned England. Larkin's wistful, lyrical grasp of life's shortcomings was considered in keeping with the quietistic mood of the post-war years.

In Larkin, the poetry and the personality were unusually compact, so that many readers claimed an intimacy in which the poet seemed to address them personally or speak on their behalf. Larkin himself did little to dispel the image of the poet as 'the man next door', writing a poetry that would articulate the changed ideals and experiences of post-war society: a rational, vigilant poetry, responsive to a new physical and mental landscape. A comfortable critical consensus settled around a poetry that was perceived to be English in its self-restraint and ironic reserve, but English, too, in its fundamental decency and tolerance. Even the more jaundiced, conservative vision of *High Windows* could be seen to be tempered by a recognition and acceptance of communal instincts and obligations. The vehemence and outrage of 'This Be The Verse' or 'Going, Going' were surely dramatic gestures, concealing a more composed and humanitarian outlook. Larkin's poetic ideals were sometimes questioned, especially when his work was compared with the more 'adventurous' work of contemporary American writers, but his status as the representative spokesman of respectable, mainstream English culture was never seriously contested.

In the decade following his death, however, Larkin's reputation underwent a profound and dramatic transformation. With the publication of the *Collected Poems* in 1988, *Selected Letters* in 1992 and the authorised biography, *Philip Larkin: A Writer's Life*, in 1993, the abiding interests and concerns of Larkin scholarship were radically and decisively altered. The two-part chronological arrangement of the *Collected Poems*, edited by Anthony Thwaite, had a significant effect on the critical perception of Larkin's development as a writer. Eighty-three poems appeared in print for the first time, almost doubling the number of poems that had previously represented Larkin's 'output'. A quite substantial *Collected Poems* immediately contradicted the notion that Larkin's 'spareness' and 'sparseness' were defining characteristics of his art. More important, though, was the overall perspective which the *Collected Poems* afforded, especially the clear indication it gave of a writer striving for his own distinctive style and reaching ambitiously, poem by poem, for the most felicitous use of metre, deployment of rhyme, and choice of vocabulary.

As well as showing the steady progression of Larkin's mature work from 1946 to 1985, the *Collected Poems* assembled a remarkably precocious group of 'Early Poems' composed between 1938 and 1945. With such an arrangement, it was possible to reconstruct the contents of a projected volume, *In the Grip of Light*, which Larkin conceived in 1947 but failed to publish. Along with the combined and persistent influence of Thomas Hardy and W. B. Yeats, there emerged a very different set of tugs and tensions which were set in sway by the powerful appeal of W. H. Auden and Louis MacNeice. The poems written between 1938 and 1945 could be viewed together for the first time as a body of wartime writing worthy of serious critical attention.[1] The precise dating of individual compositions in the *Collected Poems* considerably eased the critical task of contextualising the poems, providing new opportunities for socio-historical enquiry, but also encouraged an unhealthy biographical speculation that impatiently awaited the publication of Andrew Motion's *Philip Larkin: A Writer's Life* (1993). The dating showed, among other things, that some months and years in Larkin's life were highly productive, while others – most noticeably between 1946 and 1950 – were relatively barren.

Clearly, there were gaps and silences that hinted at deep and unresolved conflicts in the writer's private life. Blake Morrison's incisive review of the *Collected Poems*, appropriately titled 'In the Grip of Darkness', commented revealingly on 'how often the knots and blockages in Larkin's work have to do with sex, not always distinguishable in his mind from death'. Much of the new material, in Morrison's view, suggested 'how far an obsessive guilt and fear governed Larkin's attitude to sex', so that Larkin remained 'tormented by sex, seeing it as something enclosing and destructive and hostile to artistic ambition'.[2] One of the poems that most obviously supported such a conjecture (and one frequently cited by both sympathetic and hostile reviewers) was the brutally confessional 'Love Again', in which personal failure is vaguely and enigmatically construed as 'Something to do with violence / A long way back, and wrong rewards, / And arrogant eternity'. This painfully candid exposure, unrelieved by any sense of ironic detachment or compensating tenderness, could only fuel the mounting biographical speculation.

Defenders and detractors alike suspected that the speaker in such poems was hardly a guise at all, and the problem of disengaging 'art' from 'life' was inevitably extended to the rest of Larkin's work. Germaine Greer, reviewing the *Collected Poems* in the *Guardian*, disputed the idea that Larkin's poems were essentially dramatic monologues: 'This is a difficult argument to sustain, for, despite Larkin's virtuoso manipulation of tone and colloquial ellipsis, the reader is seldom allowed any role other than complicity in what is being confided.' In equating the 'expression' of the poems with the 'negativity' of their author's 'feelings', she anticipated much of the controversy that attended the publication of Larkin's biography: 'His verse is deceptively simple, demotic, colloquial: the attitudes it expresses are also anti-intellectual, racist, sexist, and rotten with class-consciousness.'[3] Although these charges were to be frequently levelled against Larkin's *Selected Letters*, very few critics at this point had explicitly condemned Larkin's verse in such terms. These were serious claims which made the earlier charges of 'narrowness' and 'parochialism' look very slight.

Larkin's *Selected Letters*, edited by Anthony Thwaite and published in 1992, met with very mixed reviews. There was much that was genuinely interesting and revealing in the letters, but also much that was offensive and disturbing. Anthony Thwaite's concern with the complexity of Larkin's personality seemed designed to cushion the impact of the letters: 'They are an informed account of the lonely, gregarious, exuberant, desolate, close-fisted, generous, intolerant, compassionate, eloquent, foul-mouthed, harsh and humorous Philip Larkin.'[4] An early letter to J. B. Sutton in December 1940 sets the tone of Larkin's continuing repartee with a number of male colleagues and friends: 'Dear Jim, I'm beginning a letter to you because there's fuck all to do & I'm tired of doing it.' The style is often amusing, but the attitudes are vile. Larkin's complaint to Kingsley Amis in 1943 that 'all women are stupid beings' and his encouragement to Amis in 1978 to 'keep up the cracks about niggers and wogs' are characteristic of his cheap, relentless jibes.[5] Thwaite's selection of letters was meant to be 'a first presentation rather than a complete and exhaustive archive', and deliberately omitted a large amount of correspondence, including all of Larkin's letters to his parents, because this would have 'swelled the book to unmanageable proportions'.[6] The letters chosen for publication did not appear in their entirety either, which made some readers suspicious. Tom Paulin voiced his concern in the *Times Literary Supplement* that Thwaite's omissions were perhaps 'designed to protect Larkin by cutting short his prejudiced utterances'. He concluded: 'For the present, this selection stands as a distressing and in many ways revolting compilation which imperfectly reveals and conceals the sewer under the national monument Larkin became.'[7]

Future critics of Larkin's work were unlikely to pass judgement on the poetry without some recourse to the letters. A few critics and reviewers tried to excuse or explain the letters in terms of their author's habitual self-dramatisation, but Larkin's reputation *as a poet* continued to be questioned. Tom Paulin's metaphor was an apt one, for it seemed that some foul contagion had leaked from the letters and infected the poems. At no point, however, did Paulin condone the idea that either the letters or the poems should be censored. On the contrary, he argued that Larkin's letters should be published in full, with an introduction that 'sought to place, analyse and understand – socially and psychologically – Larkin's racism, misogyny and quasi-fascist views'.[8] Other critics raised equally un-comfortable questions about the extent to which the letters made explicit a set of assumptions already at play in the poems, and about the extent to which this undermined Larkin's 'centrality' in modern British culture. Lisa Jardine questioned 'the place Larkin's poetry occupies at the heart of the traditional canon of English Literature'. For Jardine, the furore over Larkin's 'reputation' was essentially about 'cherished values' and about the ideas and senti-ments traditionally associated with British culture. 'Can we', she asked, 'continue to present the poetic writings of Larkin as self-evidently "humane" when the student who consults the selected Larkin letters in the college library confronts a steady stream of casual obscenity, throwaway derogatory remarks about women, and arrogant disdain for those of different skin colour or national-ity?' While not explicitly advocating censorship, Jardine confided that Larkin's poetry was no longer a set text in her department of English at Queen Mary and Westfield College, University of London, and recommended that 'we must stop teaching the old canon as the repository of authentically "British values" and as a monument to a precious "British way of life" '.[9] Jardine assumed too readily, however, that this was how 'we' all taught Larkin's poetry elsewhere. Her brief intervention in the Larkin 'furore' met with deep disdain in many places for simplifying the relationship between the letters and the poems, and for seeming to make 'politi-cal correctness' the only criterion of value.

By the time Andrew Motion's biography of Larkin was published in 1993, the terms of the ensuing critical debate were already estab-lished. In his preface to *Philip Larkin: A Writer's Life*, Motion ex-plained that his own difficult task of describing the 'dismal ground' from which the poetry blossomed would 'necessarily alter the image of Larkin that he [Larkin] prepared so carefully for his readers'.[10] Many of the reviews that followed seemed intent on relegating Larkin to the league of minor poets. For James Wood, Larkin was 'a minor registrar of disappointment, a bureaucrat of frustration'. For Peter Ackroyd, he was not only 'a rancid and insidious' philis-tine and 'a foul-mouthed bigot', but 'essentially a minor poet who acquired a large reputation'. Bryan Appleyard began his outraged 'Comment' in the *Independent* by asking 'why is this provincial grotesque now so adored, edited, biographied and generally elevated to the highest ranks of Eng Lit?' For Appleyard, Larkin was 'the dreary laureate of our provincialism ... a minor poet raised to undeserved monumentality'.[11]

There were others, including Andrew Motion, for whom Larkin's greatness as a poet was undiminished. Motion recorded his own view that 'the vast majority of Larkin's work magnificently floats free of its surrounding material'. On several occasions after the publication of the biography, Motion intervened in the controversy to insist that 'art is not a convulsive expression of personality. It is much more subtle than that'.[12] In the United States there were positive reviews of the biography that helped to enhance rather than undermine Larkin's reputation. Dana Gioia's discerning review in the *Washington Post* acknowledged Larkin as one of the century's 'indisputably great poets', whose writings withstood comparison with those of Thomas Hardy, W. B. Yeats and W. H. Auden. Among critics writing for the British press, Ian Hamilton was bold enough to call Larkin 'the best poet we have had since Auden', but recognised a severe shift in the popular view of Larkin's work: 'A few years ago, "Larkinesque" suggested qualities both lovable and glum. Today, it means four-letter words and hateful views.' In the same spirit, Martin Amis registered his dismay that 'the word Larkinesque used to evoke the wistful, the provincial, the crepuscular, the sad ... Now [in 1993] Larkin is something like a pariah, or an untouchable.'[13]

To Martin Amis it seemed that Larkin's life was being exposed to the sanctimonious judgements of a 'newer, cleaner, braver, saner world'. At the same time, though, it was clear that while Larkin was being denounced as 'a casual, habitual racist, and an easy misogynist' (Jardine), there was little that was new or enlightening in the criticism of Larkin's poetry. Perhaps the most depressing aspect of the critical debate accompanying the Larkin letters and the biography was its simple-minded reversion to an assessment of the poetry that was commonplace at least thirty years earlier. All the tired clichés of Larkin criticism came rolling back, as if words like 'philistine', 'parochial' and 'suburban' were the only available critical vocabulary. Much of this negative criticism had to do with the assumed 'Englishness' of Larkin's poetry, and with national ideals that were clearly found wanting once Larkin's personal code of conduct had been so thoroughly discredited.

## II

The critique of Larkin's poetry in terms of national character began as early as 1955, with the publication of *The Less Deceived*. Charles Tomlinson complained in 1957 that 'Larkin's narrowness suits the English perfectly. They recognise their own abysmal urban landscapes, skilfully caught with just a whiff of English films *circa* 1950. The stepped-down version of human possibilities ... the joke that hesitates just on this side of nihilism, are national vices.' Similarly, Al Alvarez, introducing *The New Poetry* anthology in 1962, berated the limiting effects of Larkin's 'gentility', which he felt was best summed up in terms of those familiar English virtues, 'politeness' and 'decency'. For both critics, Larkin's neatly ordered verse compared unfavourably with the more 'urgent', experimental poetry being produced by American writers.[14] When Donald Davie spoke for the defence, it was to insist that Larkin was 'a very Hardyesque poet' with a thoroughly English soul, a writer who stoically accepted the way things were: 'The England in his poems is the England we have inhabited.'[15] From the outset, Larkin's critical reception was finely tuned to a set of assumptions – often very questionable assumptions – that had to do with England and the English national character.

It was not until the 1970s that the old critical consensus based on Larkin's cautiously empirical and narrowly English assessment of 'the way things are' was effectively challenged. In 1976 J. R. Watson wrote an article, appropriately titled 'The Other Larkin', in which he claimed that Larkin's poetry was much deeper and more complex than Alvarez had suggested. He found in the poetry moments of 'epiphany' and 'deeply felt longings for sacred time and sacred space'.[16] The idea of a 'transcendental' element in Larkin's work began to emerge in critical essays, along with the related idea of a 'symbolist' dimension in the poetry. Watson's essay coincided with a changing horizon of expectations among readers of Larkin's poetry, many of whom were dissatisfied with traditional critical methods and increasingly swayed by the newer critical practices loosely identified as 'literary theory'. From the mid-1970s onwards, new attitudes to Larkin's poetry came into play, along with new critical procedures. This New Casebook on Larkin takes that significant moment in Larkin criticism as its starting point.

The opening essay by Seamus Heaney has been highly influential in challenging established critical perspectives and promoting a more positive, affirmative view of Larkin's poetry. While acknowledging that the poetry is firmly rooted in a long tradition of English lyricism, Heaney nevertheless perceives a visionary, transcendental quality that recalls the experimental modernism of James Joyce and W. B. Yeats. Heaney acknowledges the symbolist potential in Larkin's work and finds ample evidence of this tendency in the brilliant images which illuminate so many poems. Much of the appeal of Heaney's essay derives from one poet's candid appreciation of another poet's work, and from a sympathetic concern that such work is not 'sold short' by a criticism that fails to recognise its value *as poetry*. The essay effectively breaks with the earlier critical consensus on Larkin's work by repeatedly drawing attention to the 'reach and longing' of the poems. Countering the suggestion that Larkin's poems are cynically withdrawn and sedulously empirical, the essay asks us to consider those moments when consciousness is pushed towards 'an exposed condition' and the poems come close to 'revelation'. If Larkin's poetry inhabits a dull and dreary terrain, it also strives for something more 'serene' and 'crystalline'.[17]

The idea of a symbolist dimension in Larkin's poetry is further developed in Andrew Motion's *Philip Larkin* (1982, reprinted in part as essay 2). Here, there is strong evidence that Larkin, despite his declared lack of interest in 'foreign' poetry, was well acquainted with the work of French symbolist poets. Like Heaney, however, Motion attributes much of the symbolist potential in Larkin's work to the enduring influence of W. B. Yeats. He disputes Larkin's claim in the 1966 preface to *The North Ship* that the influence of Yeats had been displaced by that of Thomas Hardy, and shows how the continuing presence of *both* poets produced in Larkin's work a fierce debate between hope and hopelessness, fulfilment and disappointment. Although the identification of Yeats as predominantly 'symbolist' and Hardy as predominantly 'empirical' is too neatly drawn, Motion succeeds in showing how the dislocations and illogicalities of symbolism complicate the form and structure of the poetry, but also infuse it with moments of intense aspiration. Symbolist devices provide 'release from the empirically observed world, and its attendant disappointments, into one of transcendent imaginative fulfilment'.[18] This recognition doesn't help us to understand the source of 'disappointment' in the poems (it takes the 'circumscribed' world as a given condition), but it nevertheless points to an unmistakably affirmative aspect of Larkin's work. Like Heaney, then, Motion questions the familiar assumption that Larkin's poetry is inflexibly pessimistic and uniformly depressed.

Although Andrew Motion detects the influence of French symbolism in one of Larkin's earliest poems, 'Femmes Damnées' (1943), he claims that *High Windows* contains the most 'purely symbolist' poetry in Larkin's *oeuvre*. This perception finds confirmation in some of the baffled reviews that followed the publication of *High Windows* in 1974. Clive James was among those readers who pointed to the unnerving obscurity and allusiveness of the poems in *High Windows*, memorably bestowing on Larkin the title 'poet of the void'. What James finds most intriguing is the obvious disparity between Larkin's allegedly despairing outlook and the powerful imaginative intensity and sheer 'beauty' of the writing.[19] These observations by Clive James provide the starting point for Barbara Everett in her highly illuminating essay (3), 'Philip Larkin: After Symbolism' (1980). Commenting on Larkin's 'new style of ferocious lucidity', Everett offers an impressive and persuasive account of Larkin's intense engagement with modernist and symbolist art. The most valuable and original aspect of her argument is that Larkin both employs and rejects the themes and techniques of French symbolist poetry. By insisting that Larkin's involvement with symbolism is essentially ironic and playful, Everett can claim very plausibly that Larkin is not simply *anti-modernist* but in many respects *post-modernist*. In other words, Larkin's work engages with symbolism while simultaneously providing a critique of its basic assumptions and ideals. Larkin's 'Sympathy in White Major', for example, is seen as a highly elaborate parody of Théophile Gautier's 'Symphonie en blanc majeure', while 'High Windows' is considered as an ironic response to Stéphane Mallarmé's 'Les Fenêtres'. Where Everett differs from Heaney and Motion is in her suggestion that Larkin employs symbolism *critically*, often doing so as a way of denying the spiritual fulfilment and transcendental idealism associated with symbolism. Nevertheless, her scholarly elucidation of Larkin's obscurities and obliquities leaves the old charges of English 'gentility' and 'suburbanism' far behind.

### III

The growing popularity and appeal of linguistic criticism, especially from the 1970s onwards, helped to promote a more favourable climate of reception for Larkin's poetry. By focusing on issues of style and structure, linguists were able to show that Larkin's poetry was neither transparently 'realist' nor narrowly 'expressive' of its author's attitudes and opinions. David Lodge's brief but instructive essay (4) shows how a particular set of structuralist ideas and methodologies can yield significant insights when applied to Larkin's poetry. In this essay Lodge draws heavily on the distinction between *metaphor* and *metonymy* proposed by Roman Jakobson, and on the kind of structuralist analysis associated with the 1930s Prague school of poetics and linguistics. Lodge begins with the principles of *selection* and *combination* typical of any system of signs. He takes as his example the sentence 'ships crossed the sea', and explains that if he selected the word 'ploughed' as a substitute for 'crossed' he would create a *metaphor* based on a perceived similarity between two otherwise different things. In substituting 'keels' for 'ships' he offers an example of *synecdoche* (part standing for whole, or whole for part), and in substituting 'deep' for 'sea' he employs *metonymy* (an attribute or aspect of a thing standing for the thing itself). Lodge also adopts Jakobson's 'typology' or classification of literary 'types', claiming that Romantic writing is essentially metaphoric and realist writing metonymic. He identifies Larkin's work as predominantly realistic and metonymic, and points out how Larkin employs techniques usually associated with the realist novel, including the extensive scenic detail that characterises poems such as 'The Whitsun Weddings'. Despite their predominantly metonymic function, Larkin's poems sometimes shift unexpectedly into a metaphoric mode, such as the sudden appearance of the rain shower at the end of 'The Whitsun Weddings'.

There is clearly much in common between Lodge's recognition of a 'transcendent' metaphoric activity in Larkin's work and the perception of its symbolist leanings by Heaney, Motion and others. This point is not missed by Guido Latré, who develops Lodge's argument into a lengthy structuralist study of Larkin's poetry in *Locking Earth to the Sky* (1985).[20] As well as adding a third 'symbolic' mode to Lodge's metonymic and metaphoric types, Latré looks closely at the structure of syntax in the poems and also shows how the structuralist anthropology of Claude Lévi-Strauss might be applied to the underlying myths and archetypes in many of Larkin's poems. Structuralist criticism can be valuable in discouraging a vague and impressionistic response to literary works, but it runs the risk of becoming a sterile exercise in recognising patterns and systems. Of much greater potential is that variety of linguistic criticism that understands poetic language as 'social discourse' or 'rhetoric'.

An encouraging start to a discourse analysis of Larkin's poetry was made by Jonathan Raban in his discussion of 'Mr Bleaney' in *The Society of the Poem* (1971). Raban's method is to 'map out the social geography' of poetry, asking if poetic structures correspond in any way to social structures. His analysis of 'Mr Bleaney' shows how the poem's conflation of different voices and linguistic registers is closely related to the economic and political structures of class society in the post-war period.[21] This kind of discourse analysis has become extremely popular in recent years, largely because of the impact of Mikhail Bakhtin's insistence on the 'dialogic' nature of literary works. Katie Wales, for instance, looks at the dramatic interplay of Larkin's 'dual-voiced, split personalities' in 'Church Going', and shows how Bakhtin's understanding of dialogue as 'dialectic' or 'internal polemic' can greatly assist rhetorical analysis.[22] The same resourceful use of Bakhtinian theory is evident in Andrew Swarbrick's *Out of Reach: The Poetry of Philip Larkin* (1985, essay 11), which explores the persistent question of 'identity' in Larkin's poetry in terms of its 'polyphonic' qualities.[23]

## IV

Modern literary theory ought to find much of interest in Larkin's work, and yet the poems have remained curiously impervious to some of the newer critical methodologies such as feminism, psychoanalysis and deconstruction. Graham Holderness, however, puts theory to work (essay 5) by staging an imaginary debate on Larkin's poetry among four critics of different theoretical persuasions: Cleanth (a formalist in the practical criticism / new criticism mode); Raymond (a Marxist); Kate (a feminist); and Colin (a poststructuralist). Concentrating on a single poem, 'Deceptions', Holderness shows how critical theory can 'open up' Larkin's writing to a variety of illuminating, if not always reconcilable, viewpoints. Cleanth is very much concerned with the atmosphere, mood and imagery of the poem and with its 'enacted realisation of a wholly imaginary experience'. Raymond insists that the poverty and exploitation that the poem depicts are 'continuing realities', and that the poem's true value is to be found in its historical grasp of a general social condition: 'every member of that oppressed Victorian underclass ... was a victim of deception, blinded by ideological illusions to the real conditions of their lives'. For Kate, the poem is incontrovertibly about 'a woman who has suffered at the hands of a man'. Significantly, though, the woman's story is told by a man, so that 'female experience is densely encoded into varying registers of masculine discourse'. What the poem presents us with is essentially a masculine view of rape. Colin begs to differ: 'What the poem is about is language.' In 'Deceptions' the poet 'recognises that the reality of experience he has been pursuing is simply not there: just as the woman's existence has been obliterated, so the effort to capture a reality beyond language is doomed to failure'.[24] Holderness makes no attempt to prioritise one set of meanings over another, but instead reveals a set of reading methods or 'interpretive strategies', each with its own distinctive values and assumptions.

As the imaginary debate on 'Deceptions' makes clear, the issue of sexual politics in Larkin's poetry is difficult to ignore, especially when it appears in such a painfully explicit and starkly confrontational way. Much of Larkin's poetry is concerned explicitly with sexual desire and sexual disillusionment, yet remarkably few critics have seriously addressed these concerns. Steve Clark, however, draws impressively on the insights of feminism and psychoanalysis in his highly revealing essay (6) on Larkin's sexual politics. Like other critics represented here, Clark takes issue with the idea that Larkin is essentially 'a wry commentator' on the straitened circumstances of contemporary Britain. He feels that there is far less 'settling for' in Larkin's work than the old critical consensus suggested. What interests him is the persistent concern in Larkin's poetry with sexual identity and with the paradoxes of involvement in desire. Larkin's speakers appear to be uncompromising advocates of male celibacy, and Clark links this impression to what he terms 'the epistemological Larkin, whose unsparing meditation on ageing, death, "endless extinction" aspires to a kind of agnostic sainthood'.[25] The seemingly selfish, monadic behaviour of Larkin's speakers might seem worthy of contempt, but Clark argues that there is much to value in their unillusioned abstention from sex and in their dramatised refusal to conform to contemporary sexual 'norms'.

Janice Rossen's *Philip Larkin: His Life's Work* provides a good introduction to some of the principal concerns of feminist criticism, concentrating on the different 'kinds' of women and the different 'versions' of femininity that Larkin's poems depict. Rossen shows how women are habitually presented in terms that are either negative and hostile or romanticised and idealistic. She argues that this polarity of viewpoints typifies the dilemma of a generation of men who were educated apart from 'the girls', and who consequently viewed the opposite sex as 'mysterious and inaccessible'. Other feminist critics might find Rossen's approach to Larkin's poems too moderate and restrained, but she doesn't flinch from 'the problem of the misogyny his work expresses'. Of particular interest in her chapter, 'Difficulties with Girls' (here reprinted as essay 7), is her emphasis on the perspective of distance that Larkin's speakers adopt towards women. In the case of 'Deceptions', for instance, she finds the speaker's attitude 'detached almost to the point of sadism'. Like Clark, though, she finds something redeeming in Larkin's sexual politics, insisting that Larkin doesn't simply endorse the negative attitudes his poems convey, but often satirises such views and shows that 'women ought to be treated less as objects and more as people in their own right'.[26]

## V

Tom Paulin's review (essay 8) of Janice Rossen's *Philip Larkin: His Life's Work* was quickly recognised as a major critical statement when it appeared in the *Times Literary Supplement* in 1990. It has been both widely admired and strongly castigated for its provocative political critique of Larkin's work. Like Clark and Rossen, Paulin acknowledges Larkin's refusal of sexual obligations, but associates this preservation of male autonomy with a particular sector of English class society. Larkin, he claims, 'speaks for the English male, middle-class, professional, outwardly confident, controlled and in control'. This calm demeanour, however, is a mask for deeply repressed desires and instincts: 'Angry at not being allowed to show emotion, he writhes with anxiety inside that sealed bunker which is the English ethic of privacy.'[27] In Paulin's estimation, Larkin's melancholy lyricism issues from a deep distaste for many aspects of England's modern social democracy, including the loss of cultural and social prestige that accompanied the end of empire.

Larkin's real theme, he insists, is national decline. As well as encouraging a postcolonial reading of seemingly 'innocent' poems such as 'At Grass', Paulin also reveals the depth of nostalgic, nationalist sentiment in the relatively unknown poem 'The March Past' (written in Belfast in 1951).

Tom Paulin's historical, postcolonial critique of Larkin's poems was anticipated, to some extent, by Blake Morrison's impressive pioneering study of the Movement writers. Morrison's book contains an acute analysis of class and culture in the post-war years, and shows how the Movement writers were deeply ambivalent towards the changing balance of power after 1945. While appearing to represent and promote the democratic ideals of a new society, some Movement writers harboured a sense of nostalgia and regret in the face of Britain's decline as a world power. Morrison claims that the reason Larkin's 'At Grass' became one of the most popular post-war poems is that 'by allowing the horses to symbolise loss of power, Larkin manages to tap nostalgia for a past "glory that was England"'. He identifies 'At Grass' as 'a poem of post-imperial *tristesse*'.[28]

Stan Smith's essay (9) in this volume is one of the most trenchant historicist readings of Larkin's poems. Like Paulin and Morrison, Smith explores the extent to which the poems both respond to and evoke a general sense of national and cultural decline. His method, however, involves a rigorous application of Marxist critical theory, especially the historical materialism of Walter Benjamin, with its recognition of the 'duplicity' of every work of art. The title of Smith's book, *Inviolable Voice*, is an echo of Benjamin's memorable statement that a work of art is 'at once an inviolable voice, proclaiming "beauty is truth, truth beauty", and a testament to the violations and barbarities of a class society'. 'Most poetry', Smith comments, 'seems to function at a level remote from history, where a dissociated mind confronts a landscape innocent of social meaning.' 'This illusion', he adds, 'is one of the most powerful enchantments poetry weaves.'[29] He shows how Larkin's poems emerge from and are shaped by a precise historical experience, despite their common impression of distance and displacement from the events they depict. Smith demonstrates very forcefully how Larkin's preoccupation with distance and disengagement manifests itself as class consciousness in 'The Whitsun Weddings', and how it also produces a distortion and simplification of Britain's colonial legacy in 'Homage to a Government'.

Not surprisingly, the critics who have been most sensitive to the question of 'Englishness' in Larkin's poetry are those who, like Tom Paulin, have cultural allegiances with Ireland as well as with England. Both Seamus Heaney and Neil Corcoran have written impressively and revealingly about the postcolonial consciousness that informs Larkin's poetry. In 'Englands of the Mind', a lecture given at the University of California, Berkeley, in 1976, Heaney considers Ted Hughes, Geoffrey Hill and Philip Larkin as 'poets of the mother culture ... now possessed of that defensive love of their territory which was once shared only by those poets whom we might call colonial ...' In the language of each of these poets, Heaney finds traces of continuity with English ways and customs that are rapidly disappearing. Each poet occupies and preserves his own imaginative geographical terrain. Larkin's 'England of the Mind' shares its ancestry with Rupert Brooke's 'Grantchester' and Edward Thomas's 'Adlestrop', but at the same time Larkin possesses his own distinctive post-war English sensibility, which seems less rooted and less secure than the Englishness of his predecessors:

> He sees England from train windows, fleeting past and away. He is urban modern man, the insular Englishman, responding to the tones of his own clan, ill at ease when out of his environment. He is a poet, indeed, of a composed and tempered English nationalism, and his voice is the not untrue, not unkind voice of post-war England, where the cloth cap and the royal crown have both lost some of their potent symbolism ... .

In this essay, Heaney astutely identifies the political origins and ramifications of the backward-looking, nostalgic pastoralism in such poems as 'Going, Going'. In this respect, he is probably the first critic to acknowledge the shaping effects of postcolonial history on Larkin's poetry: 'The loss of imperial power, the failure of economic nerve, the diminished influence of Britain inside Europe, all this has led to a new sense of the shires, a new valuing of the native English experience.'[30]

Neil Corcoran explores the idea of 'post-imperial pastoral' as it manifests itself in such poems as 'Church Going', 'The Whitsun Weddings', 'MCMXIV', 'To the Sea', 'The Explosion' and 'Show Saturday'. In all these poems, a close attachment to English 'nature' or English landscape begets 'a dream of thwarted potential or desired persistence'. Like Tom Paulin, Corcoran believes that Larkin's dejection is a form of cultural melancholy that issues, in part, from the end of empire and the subsequent loss of power. He hints at a subtle connection in Larkin's poetry between the perception of England's national decline and the frequent suggestion of sexual disappointment: 'Larkin's idea of England is as deeply and intimately wounded by such post-imperial withdrawals as some of the personae of his poems are wounded by sexual impotence, incompetence, anxiety or distress.'[31] Corcoran's impressive readings of such poems as 'The March Past' suggest the extent to which 'Englishness' became for Larkin a repository of tradition and identity that outweighed all other sources of potential value.

## VI

James Booth and Andrew Swarbrick (essays 10 and 11) are among those critics who have objected strongly to the kind of historicist criticism discussed above. In the wake of such criticism, however, there can be no going back to some innocent 'traditional' reading of the poems. What has ensued is the liveliest critical debate on Larkin's work since Alvarez formulated his 'gentility principle' in 1962. Booth and Swarbrick have an obvious advantage over earlier critics of Larkin's poetry in having access to revealing biographical information, including Larkin's letters. At the same time, in their shared sense of opposition to strong political readings of Larkin's poetry, they practise what might aptly be described as new formalism or aesthetic criticism.

James Booth is one of the most ardent defenders of 'the universal commonplaces of lyric poetry'. In *Philip Larkin: Writer* (1992) he argues strongly that Larkin's poetry resists any attempt to 'reduce' it to an ideological programme. Accordingly, he takes a dim view of those 'over-committed' readings which interpret Larkin's work as 'conscious or unconscious political ideology'. Booth is adamant that 'neither his own [Larkin's] strident political remarks nor the social context of post-war England offers the key to his art'. The method in *Philip Larkin: Writer* is one of skilful stylistic analysis, and one of its most valuable insights is its recognition of Larkin's 'negative sublime': the way in which the rhetoric in poems like 'High Windows' 'contrives a sublime emotional elevation out of negatives'.[32] In the essay printed in this volume, Booth returns to the battle between 'aestheticist' and 'ideological' readings of the poems, insisting that the prejudices of writers are separate from, and irrelevant to, their artistic achievement: 'Intensely English though he was, Larkin's lyricism is profoundly at odds with his nationalism.'[33] The argument he adopts here immediately comes into conflict with the political, historicist readings of Tom Paulin and others.

Much of the hostility directed at Larkin's work after the publication of Andrew Motion's biography of the poet was based on a naïvely expressive idea that what the poems 'said' or appeared to 'say' was entirely coterminous with what was known of their author's beliefs and opinions. Andrew Swarbrick's *Out of Reach: The Poetry of Philip Larkin* (1995) has been extremely valuable in dispelling some of this simple-minded biographical speculation. Insisting from the outset on a careful distinction between the personality of the writer and the personae in the poems, the book shows how the development of Larkin's poetry is intricately related to the creation of fictional identities and repeated experiments in dramatising different 'voices'. The 'selves' who inhabit the poetry are essentially rhetorical constructions, the products of language, and what the poems aspire to is some imagined fullness of being or complete selfhood which remains forever 'out of reach'. Swarbrick's method, then, is one of rhetorical analysis, in which the poems are regarded as dramatised speech acts. He remains sceptical of any critical attempt to impose upon the poems a single, unified identity consistent with that of Larkin himself. Gathering support from the critical writings of Mikhail Bakhtin, he detects in Larkin's poetry a multiplicity of tonal registers which undermines authorial stability. Like Booth, Swarbrick resists those readings of the poems which seek to uncover a dominant ideology such as 'Englishness'.

Even so, the question of national identity in Larkin's poetry will not disappear. However much we might try to isolate some pure, transcendent lyric element in the poetry, Larkin's Englishness seems palpable. As Seamus Heaney explains, words are not just 'articulate noise', but a 'symptom of human history, memory and attachments'.[34] It is not just in the physical geography of the poems but in their diction and syntax that Larkin's Englishness manifests itself. For many readers, the Englishness of Larkin's poetry is a complex and intriguing part of its substance and appeal, a point that has been made repeatedly in such books as *Literary Englands* by David Gervais and *Edwardian Poetry* by Kenneth Millard.[35] Larkin was the obvious Poet Laureate, an appointment he declined in December 1984.

As with the work of Thomas Gray and William Wordsworth, Larkin's poetry came to maturity at a point when private communings found a familiar, social discourse, and when solitary introspection could be turned outwards and invested in a recognisable English landscape. England is 'there' unobtrusively but securely in the poems in *The Less Deceived* (1955), and it seems so appropriate that Larkin's autobiographical musings in 'I Remember, I Remember' should take place 'Coming up England by a different line'. It is still there, though seemingly about to disappear, in the elegiac 'Going, Going' in *High Windows* (1974): 'And that will be England gone.' The process of fracture can be seen in *The Whitsun Weddings* (1964). Part of the appeal and popularity of the title poem is the vivid impression it creates of a known community – 'the fish-dock', 'canals with floating of industrial froth', 'dismantled cars', 'an Odeon', a cricket match – and yet the speaker's relationship with the newly married couples climbing aboard the train suggests that this community is not *entirely* known. The pulsating energy of 'The Whitsun Weddings' is generated by the search for a shared sense of endeavour, a shared sense of human identity and a shared sense of place. A deeply felt need for social coherence and continuity is evident in Larkin's instinctive plea for the preservation of national customs and rituals such as the English agricultural show: 'Let it always be there.' The need is such that Larkin's speakers turn ruefully and ironically to an England that is patently mythic. David Gervais comments on Larkin's later poems that 'what the word "England" conjured up most potently for him was another England that was absent', an England of 'guildhalls' and 'carved choirs' and 'the pubs wide open all day'.[36]

Both Tom Paulin and James Booth refer to a little-known quatrain, published in Larkin's *Collected Poems* in 1988:

> In times when nothing stood
> But worsened, or grew strange,
>   there was one constant good:
>     she did not change.
>         (*CP*, 210)

That anonymous 'she' is not unusual in Larkin's work, and these lines might easily be construed as a fragment of love poetry casually composed and then quietly dismissed by Larkin. James Booth is not inclined to treat these lines very seriously as poetry. This is a very peculiar love poem, however, because it appears to be addressed to Her Majesty the Queen. The date of composition coincides with the Queen's Silver Jubilee in 1978, inviting us, perhaps, to stress with some reverence the pronoun in the closing line: '*she* did not change'. These lines might please the monarchist and dismay the republican, but whether we share their sentiments or not, they afford us a valuable insight into a moment of deep cultural disaffection in Larkin's poetry. Larkin's view of 'times when nothing stood' might not be as dramatic as Yeats's perception that 'things fall apart', but it nevertheless issues from a deep-seated anxiety about the nature and direction of Britain's civic life and cultural institutions. Only the monarch herself seems to afford any guarantee of goodness. Larkin's quatrain coincided with the release of that great classic of punk rock, 'God Save the Queen', by the Sex Pistols, and the comparison is instructive. Where Larkin's lines are reverentially royalist, the Sex Pistols' lyrics are anarchic and sardonic, but both issue from a profound sense of lost value and a perception of national decline, and both deny any secure future.

One reason, perhaps, for the enduring interest in Larkin's 'Englishness' is not that his poems dutifully parade some ideal, conservative vision of the nation, but that they prove in the end to be so responsive to the fractures and collisions in post-war English culture. *High Windows*, in particular, is riven with a sense of break-up between classes and generations. The friction is registered in the growing stylistic tendency in Larkin's poetry to shift abruptly between a calm, reflective lyricism and a harsh, demotic idiom. The challenge facing Larkin's readers is whether to locate the value of the poems in some purely aesthetic, transcendental realm or whether to admit to their reading of the poems some account of the shaping influence of specific biographical and historical circumstances. For Tom Paulin, 'there are no imaginative exits from history', and for Stan Smith, 'there is no such thing as an "innocent" poem', since: 'All poetry, at its deepest levels, is structured by the precise historical experience from which it emerged, those conjunctures in which its author was formed, came to consciousness, and found a voice.'[37]

In *Philip Larkin: A Writer's Life*, Andrew Motion relates the poems as closely as possible to the biographical information he has at his disposal, and in doing so provides a valuable historical context for the study of Larkin's work. For Motion, however, 'it's clear that his writing transcends his time rather than merely encapsulating it'.[38] It's clear, too, that the way in which history and

biography inform imaginative writing, and the extent to which we
should admit these factors in literary criticism, will continue to
provoke debate. A volume of this kind can give only a fleeting indication of the impact of Motion's biography of Larkin and the controversy that ensued. Alan Bennett's review is reprinted here (essay
12) because it is neither sanctimonious nor exculpatory in its attitude to Larkin's life. It will briefly acquaint new readers of Larkin's
work with the revelations contained in the biography, but it will
also send them back to the poems. Bennett says of the poems in relationship to the biography, 'I could not see how they would
emerge unscathed. But I have read them again and they do.'[39] What
he returns us to is a poetry of far-reaching insights and resounding
virtuosity, a poetry to learn from and be thankful for.

## NOTES

Quotations from the poetry of Philip Larkin are taken from *Collected
Poems*, ed. Anthony Thwaite (London, 1988). The abbreviation *CP* will be
followed by the relevant page number.

1. See 'Larkin's Wartime Writings', in Stephen Regan, *Philip Larkin*
(Basingstoke, 1992), pp. 66–77.

2. Blake Morrison, 'In the Grip of Darkness', *Times Literary Supplement*,
14–20 October 1988, pp. 1151–2.

3. Germaine Greer, 'A Very British Misery', *Guardian*, 14 October 1988,
p. 27.

4. Anthony Thwaite (ed.), *Selected Letters of Philip Larkin 1940–1985*
(London and Boston, 1992), p. xv.

5. Ibid., pp. 5, 63.

6. Ibid., p. xi.

7. Tom Paulin, in a letter to the *Times Literary Supplement*, 6 November
1992, p. 15.

8. Ibid.

9. Lisa Jardine, 'Saxon Violence', *Guardian*, 8 December 1992, Section 2,
p. 4.

10. Andrew Motion, *Philip Larkin: A Writer's Life* (London, 1993), p. xx.

11. James Wood, 'Want Not, Write Not', *Guardian*, 30 March 1993,
p. 20; Peter Ackroyd, 'Poet Hands on Misery to Man', *Times*, 1 April

1993, p. 35; Bryan Appleyard, 'The Dreary Laureate of our Provincialism', *Independent*, 18 March 1993, p. 27.

12. Andrew Motion, in an interview with Sebastian Faulkes, 'Too Close for Comfort', *Guardian*, 31 March 1993, Section 2, p. 2.

13. Dana Gioia, 'The Still, Sad Music of Philip Larkin', *Washington Post Book World*, 15 August 1993, pp. 1, 9. Ian Hamilton, 'Self's the Man', *Times Literary Supplement*, 2 April 1993, p. 3; Martin Amis, 'Don Juan in Hull', *New Yorker*, 12 July 1993, p. 74 (reprinted as 'A Poetic Injustice', *Guardian Weekend*, 21 August 1993, p. 6).

14. Charles Tomlinson, 'The Middlebrow Muse', *Essays in Criticism*, 7 (1957), 208–17. Reprinted in 'Poetry Today', in Boris Ford (ed.), *The Pelican Guide to English Literature*, Vol. 7: *The Modern Age* (Harmondsworth, 1973), pp. 471, 478–9. Al Alvarez (ed.), *The New Poetry* (Harmondsworth, 1962; 1966), p. 25.

15. Donald Davie, 'Landscapes of Larkin', in *Thomas Hardy and British Poetry* (London, 1973), p. 64.

16. J. R. Watson, 'The Other Larkin', *Critical Quarterly*, 17 (1975), pp. 348, 354.

17. See pp. 23–31 below.

18. See pp. 32–54 below.

19. Clive James, 'Don Juan in Hull: Philip Larkin', in *At the Pillars of Hercules* (London, 1979), p. 61.

20. Guido Latré, *Locking Earth to the Sky: A Structuralist Approach to Philip Larkin's Poetry* (Frankfurt am Main, 1985).

21. Jonathan Raban, *The Society of the Poem* (London, 1971), pp. 29–30.

22. Katie Wales, 'Teach Yourself "Rhetoric": An Analysis of Philip Larkin's "Church Going"', in Peter Verdonk (ed.), *Twentieth-Century Poetry: From Text to Context* (London, 1993), pp. 86–99.

23. See pp. 211–25 below.

24. See pp. 83–93 below.

25. See pp. 94–134 below.

26. See pp. 135–59 below.

27. See pp. 160–77 below.

28. Blake Morrison, *The Movement: English Poetry and Fiction of the 1950s* (Oxford, 1980), p. 82.

29. Stan Smith, *Inviolable Voice: History and Twentieth-Century Poetry* (Dublin, 1982), p. 1.

30. Seamus Heaney, 'Englands of the Mind', in *Preoccupations: Selected Prose 1968–1978* (London and Boston, 1980), pp. 150–1, 167, 169.

31. Neil Corcoran, 'A Movement Pursued: Philip Larkin', in *English Poetry Since 1940* (London, 1993), p. 87.

32. James Booth, *Philip Larkin: Writer* (Hemel Hempstead, 1992), pp. 3, 168.

33. See pp. 187–210 below.

34. Heaney, 'Englands of the Mind', p. 150.

35. David Gervais, *Literary Englands: Versions of 'Englishness' in Modern Writing* (Cambridge, 1993); Kenneth Millard, *Edwardian Poetry* (Oxford, 1991).

36. Gervais, *Literary Englands*, p. 215.

37. Tom Paulin, *Minotaur: Poetry and the Nation State* (London and Boston, 1992), p. 5; Smith, *Inviolable Voice: History and Twentieth-Century Poetry*, p. 1.

38. Motion, *Philip Larkin: A Writer's Life*, p. xix.

39. See pp. 226–49 below.

# 1

# The Main of Light

*SEAMUS HEANEY*

E. M. Forster once said that he envisaged *A Passage to India* as a
book with a hole in the middle of it. Some poems are like that too.
They have openings at their centre which take the reader through
and beyond. Shakespeare's Sonnet 60, for example:

> Like as the waves make towards the pebbled shore,
> So do our minutes hasten to their end;
> Each changing place with that which goes before,
> In sequent toil all forwards do contend.
> Nativity, once in the main of light,
> Crawls to maturity, wherewith being crowned,
> Crooked eclipses 'gainst his glory fight,
> And Time that gave doth now his gift confound.

Something visionary happens there in the fifth line. 'Nativity', an abstract noun housed in a wavering body of sound, sets up a warning
tremor just before the mind's eye gets dazzled by 'the main of light',
and for a split second, we are in the world of the *Paradiso*. The rest
of the poem lives melodiously in a world of discourse but it is this
unpredictable strike into the realm of pure being that marks the
sonnet with Shakespeare's extravagant genius.

In so far as it is a poem alert to the sadness of life's changes but
haunted too by a longing for some adjacent 'pure serene', the sonnet
rehearses in miniature the whole poignant score of Philip Larkin's
poetry. With Larkin, we respond constantly to the melody of intelligence, to a verse that is as much commentary as it is presentation,
and it is this encounter between a compassionate, unfoolable mind

23

and its own predicaments – which we are forced to recognise as our predicaments too – that gives his poetry its first appeal. Yet while Larkin is exemplary in the way he sifts the conditions of contemporary life, refuses alibis and pushes consciousness towards an exposed condition that is neither cynicism nor despair, there survives in him a repining for a more crystalline reality to which he might give allegiance. When that repining finds expression, something opens and moments occur which deserve to be called visionary. Because he is suspicious of any easy consolation, he is sparing of such moments, yet when they come they stream into the discursive and exacting world of his poetry with such trustworthy force that they call for attention.

In his introduction to the reissue of *The North Ship*, Larkin recalls a merry and instructive occasion during the period of his infatuation with Yeats. 'I remember Bruce Montgomery snapping, as I droned for the third or fourth time that evening *When such as I cast out remorse, so great a sweetness flows into the breast ...,* "It's not his job to cast off remorse, but to earn forgiveness." But then Bruce Montgomery had known Charles Williams.' Larkin tells the anecdote to illustrate his early surrender to Yeats's music and also to commend the anti-Romantic, morally sensitive attitude which Montgomery was advocating and which would eventually issue in his conversion to the poetry of Thomas Hardy. Yet it also illustrates that appetite for sweetness flowing into the breast, for the sensation of revelation, which never deserted him. The exchange between Montgomery and himself prefigures the shape of the unsettled quarrel which would be conducted all through the mature poetry, between vision and experience. And if it is that anti-heroic, chastening, humanist voice which is allowed most of the good lines throughout the later poetry, the rebukes it delivers cannot altogether banish the Yeatsian need for a flow of sweetness.

That sweetness flows into the poetry most reliably as a stream of light. In fact, there is something Yeatsian in the way that Larkin, in *High Windows*, places his sun poem immediately opposite and in answer to his moon poem: 'Sad Steps' and 'Solar' face each other on the opened page like the two halves of his poetic personality in dialogue. In 'Sad Steps', the wary intelligence is tempted by a moment of lunar glamour. The renaissance moon of Sir Philip Sidney's sonnet sails close, and the invitation to yield to the 'enormous yes' that love should evoke is potent, even for a man who has just taken a piss:

I part thick curtains, and am startled by
The rapid clouds, the moon's cleanliness.

Four o'clock: wedge-shadowed gardens lie
Under a cavernous, a wind-picked sky.
                        (CP, 169)

His vulnerability to desire and hope are transmitted in the Tennysonian cadence of that last line and a half, but immediately the delved brow tightens – 'There's something laughable about this' – only to be tempted again by a dream of fullness, this time in the symbolist transports of language itself – 'O wolves of memory, immensements!' He finally comes out, of course, with a definite, end-stopped 'No'. He refuses to allow the temptations of melody to chloroform the exactions of his common sense. Truth wins over beauty by a few points, and while the appeal of the poem lies in its unconsoled clarity about the seasons of ageing, our nature still tends to run to fill that symbolist hole in the middle.

However, the large yearnings that are kept firmly in their rational place in 'Sad Steps' are given scope to 'climb and return like angels' in 'Solar'. This is frankly a prayer, a hymn to the sun, releasing a generosity that is in no way attenuated when we look twice and find that what is being praised could be as phallic as it is solar. Where the moon is 'preposterous and separate, / Lozenge of love! Medallion of art!', described in the language of the ironical, emotionally defensive man, the sun is a 'lion face', 'an origin', a 'petalled head of flames', 'unclosing like a hand', all of them phrases of the utmost candid feeling. The poem is unexpected and daring, close to the pulse of primitive poetry, unprotected by any sleight of tone or persona. Here Larkin is bold to stand uncovered in the main of light, far from the hatless one who took off his cycle clips in awkward reverence:

Coined there among
Lonely horizontals
You exist openly.
Our needs hourly
Climb and return like angels.
Unclosing like a hand,
You give for ever.
                        (CP, 159)

These are the words of someone surprised by 'a hunger in himself to be more serious', although there is nothing in the poem which the happy atheist could not accept. Yet in the 'angels' simile and in the generally choral tone of the whole thing, Larkin opens stops that he usually keeps muted and it is precisely these stops which prove vital to the power and purity of his work.

'Deceptions', for example, depends upon a bright, still centre for its essential poetic power. The image of a window rises to take in the facts of grief, to hold them at bay and in focus. The violated girl's mind lies open 'like a drawer of knives' and most of the first stanza registers the dead-still sensitivity of the gleaming blades and the changing moods of the afternoon light. What we used to consider in our Christian Doctrine classes under the heading of 'the mystery of suffering' becomes actual in the combined sensations of absolute repose and trauma, made substantial in images which draw us into raw identification with the girl:

> The sun's occasional print, the brisk brief
> Worry of wheels along the street outside
> Where bridal London bows the other way,
> And light, unanswerable and tall and wide,
> Forbids the scar to heal, and drives
> Shame out of hiding. All the unhurried day
> Your mind lay open like a drawer of knives.
> (CP, 32)

It is this light-filled dilation at the heart of the poem which transposes it from lament to comprehension and prepares the way for the sharp irony of the concluding lines. I have no doubt that Larkin would have repudiated any suggestion that the beauty of the lines I have quoted is meant to soften the pain, as I have no doubt he would also have repudiated the Pedlar's advice to Wordsworth in 'The Ruined Cottage' where, having told of the long sufferings of Margaret, he bids the poet 'be wise and cheerful'. And yet the Pedlar's advice arises from his apprehension of 'an image of tranquillity' which works in much the same way as the Larkin passage:

> those very plumes,
> Those weeds, and the high spear grass on the wall,
> By mist and silent raindrops silvered o'er.

It is the authenticity of this moment of pacification which to some extent guarantees the Pedlar's optimism; in a similar way the blank tenderness at the heart of Larkin's poem takes it beyond irony and bitterness, though all the while keeping it short of facile consolation: 'I would not dare / Console you if I could'.

Since Larkin is a poet as explicit as he is evocative, it is no surprise to find him coining terms that exactly describe the kind of effect I am talking about: 'Here', the first poem in *The Whitsun Weddings*, ends by defining it as a sense of 'unfenced existence' and by supplying the experience that underwrites that spacious abstraction:

> Here silence stands
> Like heat. Here leaves unnoticed thicken,
> Hidden weeds flower, neglected waters quicken,
> Luminously-peopled air ascends;
> And past the poppies bluish neutral distance
> Ends the land suddenly beyond a beach
> Of shapes and shingle. Here is unfenced existence:
> Facing the sun, untalkative, out of reach.
>
> (CP, 136)

It is a conclusion that recalls the conclusion of Joyce's 'The Dead' – and indeed *Dubliners* is a book very close to the spirit of Larkin, whose collected work would fit happily under the title *Englanders*. These concluding lines constitute an epiphany, an escape from the 'scrupulous meanness' of the disillusioned intelligence, and we need only compare 'Here' with 'Show Saturday', another poem that seeks its form by an accumulation of detail, to see how vital to the success of 'Here' is this gesture towards a realm beyond the social and historical. 'Show Saturday' remains encumbered in naturalistic data, and while its conclusion beautifully expresses a nostalgic patriotism which is also an important part of this poet's make-up, the note achieved is less one of plangent vision, more a matter of liturgical wishfulness: 'Let it always be so'.

'If I were called / To construct a religion / I should make use of water' – but he could make use of 'Here' as well; and 'Solar'; and 'High Windows'; and 'The Explosion'; and 'Water', the poem from which the lines are taken. It is true that the jaunty tone of these lines, and the downbeat vocabulary later in the poem involving 'sousing, / A furious devout drench', are indicative of Larkin's unease with the commission he has imagined for himself. But just as 'Solar' and

'Here' yield up occasions where 'unfenced existence' can, without embarrassment to the sceptical man, find space to reveal its pure invitations, so too 'Water' escapes from its man-of-the-world nonchalance into a final stanza which is held like a natural monstrance above the socially defensive idiom of the rest of the poem:

> And I should raise in the east
> A glass of water ·
> Where any-angled light
> Would congregate endlessly.
> (CP, 93)

The minute light makes its presence felt in Larkin's poetry; he could not resist the romantic poet in himself who must respond with pleasure and alacrity, exclaiming, as it were, 'Already with thee!' The effects are various but they are all extraordinary, from the throwaway surprises of 'a street / Of blinding windscreens' or 'the differently-swung stars' or 'that high-builded cloud / Moving at summer's pace', to the soprano delights of this stanza from 'An Arundel Tomb':

> Snow fell, undated. Light
> Each summer thronged the glass. A bright
> Litter of birdcalls strewed the same
> Bone-riddled ground. And up the paths
> The endless altered people came,
> (CP, 110)

– and from that restraint to the manic spasm in this, from 'Livings, II':

> Guarded by brilliance
> I set plate and spoon,
> And after, divining-cards.
> Lit shelved liners
> Grope like mad worlds westward.
> (CP, 188)

Light, so powerfully associated with joyous affirmation, is even made to serve a ruthlessly geriatric vision of things in 'The Old Fools':

> Perhaps being old is having lighted rooms
> Inside your head, and people in them, acting.
> (CP, 196)

And it is refracted even more unexpectedly at the end of 'High Windows' when one kind of brightness, the brightness of belief in liberation and amelioration, falls from the air which immediately fills with a different, infinitely neutral splendour:

> And immediately
>
> Rather than words comes the thought of high windows:
> The sun-comprehending glass,
> And beyond it, the deep blue air, that shows
> Nothing, and is nowhere, and is endless.
>
> (CP, 165)

All these moments spring from the deepest strata of Larkin's poetic self, and they are connected with another kind of mood that pervades his work and which could be called Elysian: I am thinking in particular of poems like 'At Grass', 'MCMXIV', 'How Distant', and most recently, 'The Explosion'. To borrow Geoffrey Hill's borrowing from Coleridge, these are visions of 'the spiritual, Platonic old England', the light in them honeyed by attachment to a dream world that will not be denied because it is at the foundation of the poet's sensibility. It is the light that was on Langland's Malvern, 'in summer season, when soft was the sun', at once local and timeless. In 'The Explosion' the field full of folk has become a coalfield and something Larkin shares with his miners 'breaks ancestrally ... into / Regenerate union'.

> The dead go on before us, they
> Are sitting in God's house in comfort,
> We shall see them face to face –
>
> Plain as lettering in the chapels
> It was said, and for a second
> Wives saw men of the explosion
>
> Larger than in life they managed –
> Gold as on a coin, or walking
> Somehow from the sun towards them,
>
> One showing the eggs unbroken.
> (CP, 175)

If Philip Larkin had ever composed his version of *The Divine Comedy* he would probably have discovered himself not in a dark wood but a railway tunnel half-way on a journey down England.

His inferno proper might have occurred before dawn, as a death-haunted aubade, whence he would emerge into the lighted room inside the head of an old fool, and then his purgatorial ascent would be up through the 'lucent comb' of some hospital building where men in hired boxes would stare out at a wind-tousled sky. We have no doubt about his ability to recount the troubles of such souls who walk the rising ground of 'extinction's alp'. His disillusioned compassion for them has been celebrated and his need to keep numbering their griefs has occasionally drawn forth protests that he narrowed the possibilities of life so much that the whole earth became a hospital. I want to suggest that Larkin also had it in him to write his own version of the *Paradiso*. It might well have amounted to no more than an acknowledgement of the need to imagine 'such attics cleared of me, such absences'; nevertheless, in the poems he has written there is enough reach and longing to show that he did not completely settle for that well-known bargain offer, 'a poetry of lowered sights and patiently diminished expectations'.

From Seamus Heaney, *The Government of the Tongue* (London and Boston, 1988), pp. 15–22.

## NOTES

[Seamus Heaney's essay was initially intended as a tribute to Larkin on his sixtieth birthday. It first appeared in *Larkin at Sixty*, edited by Anthony Thwaite (London, 1982). The essay later came to occupy a significant place in *The Government of the Tongue*, a collection of Heaney's critical prose writings celebrating the special achievements of lyric poetry. Heaney finds something liberating and visionary in Larkin's poetry, which lifts it clear of cynicism and despair. Moments of revelation in Larkin's poetry are closely identified with the pervasive imagery of light in such poems as 'Solar' and 'Deceptions'. Heaney finds much in the breadth and scope of Larkin's poetry to compare with the work of Dante, but he also reveals a modernist dimension that Larkin shares with W. B. Yeats. In drawing attention to Larkin's symbolist tendencies, Heaney points the way to a more positive and appreciative criticism than that which had prevailed since the 1950s. The closing reference to 'a poetry of lowered sights and patiently diminished expectations' is typical of the older critical consensus with which Heaney effectively breaks. The quotation comes from Donald Davie's 'Landscapes of Larkin' in *Thomas Hardy and British Poetry* (London, 1973). In an earlier essay, 'Englands of the Mind', Heaney praises Larkin as 'the poet of rational light, a light that has its own luminous beauty but which has also the effect of exposing clearly the truths which it touches' (*Preoccupations: Selected Prose 1968–1978* [London and Boston, 1980], p. 164). In a review of Larkin's *Collected Poems* titled 'Unresting death', Heaney remarks that 'what will widen and deepen will be the solar and lunar illuminations of the best of his poems' (*Observer*, 9 October 1988). Ed.]

# 2

# Philip Larkin and Symbolism

*ANDREW MOTION*

Larkin has often been regarded as a hopeless and inflexible pessimist. Eric Homberger has called him 'the saddest heart in the post-war supermarket',[1] Geoffrey Thurley has stressed his 'central dread of satisfaction',[2] and Charles Tomlinson has criticised his 'tenderly nursed sense of defeat'.[3] But these are all views that need to be re-examined if the range and resourcefulness of Larkin's poems are to be appreciated. Although he has done a good deal to project the image of himself as 'a Parnassian Ron Glum', he has always denied its complete accuracy. 'The impulse for producing a poem', he has said, 'is never negative; the most negative poem in the world is a very positive thing to have done.'[4] This is particularly evident in bitterly angry or satirical poems like 'Naturally the Foundation will Bear Your Expenses', 'Send No Money', 'Homage to a Government', 'The Card-Players' or 'This Be The Verse': their rage or contempt is always checked by the assuaging energy of their language and the satisfactions of their articulate formal control. But, even when the mitigating function of language is less obvious, Larkin's poems are not as narrowly circumscribed as has often been claimed. By looking at a few of his recurrent themes, it is possible to see that his pessimism is not axiomatic, his attitude to death is in marked contrast to Hardy's, and his hope of deriving comfort from social and natural rituals is resilient. And, by examining his use of symbolist devices, it is clear that his poems describe a number of moments which – qualifiedly but indubitably – manage to transcend the flow of contingent time altogether.

32

What seems to have misled Larkin's critics into regarding him as uniformly depressed is the fact that he clearly has no faith in inherited and reliable absolutes. But, in so far as this means that individuals must discover and develop their own internal resources, his poems have an unmistakably affirmative aspect. It is one that Larkin has pointed out in Hardy's work too, where 'sensitivity to suffering and awareness of the causes of pain' are associated with 'superior spiritual character'.[5] The most obvious cause of this necessary self-reliance is the lack of the most time-honoured absolute of all: religion. As 'Church Going' indicates, Larkin's dilemma is not whether to believe in God but what to put in God's place; he is concerned in the poem, he has said, with 'going to church, not religion. I tried to suggest this by the title – and the union of the important stages of human life – birth, marriage and death – that going to church represents.'[6] It describes, in other words, a strictly secular faith; his speculations about what churches will become when they fall 'completely' rather than partially 'out of use' lead him to a conclusion in which the fear of death and the loss of religious belief are counteracted by an ineradicable faith in human and individual potential:

> A serious house on serious earth it is,
> In whose blent air all our compulsions meet,
> Are recognised, and robed as destinies.
> And that much never can be obsolete,
> Since someone will forever be surprising
> A hunger in himself to be more serious,
> And gravitating with it to this ground,
> Which, he once heard, was proper to grow wise in,
> If only that so many dead lie around.
>
> (CP, 98)

Much the same point is made in a more recent, and apparently more desolate poem, 'The Building' (CP, 191). Like 'Church Going', it is set in a post-Christian era, at least from the speaker's point of view. When he looks down from the hospital, he sees a stubbornly 'locked church'. Religion is closed to him – it can do nothing to bring the world's 'loves' and 'chances' within reach, and cannot provide comfort, as it once did, in the face of death. But, in place of what he has called, in 'Aubade', Christianity's 'vast moth-eaten musical brocade',[7] Larkin hesitantly supplies two consolations. The first is the hospital itself. By admitting that 'its powers' at least have the potential to 'Outbuild cathedrals' and contravene

'The coming dark', he registers the legitimacy of hope at the same time as he rejects the support of the church. The hope, of course, is not that death will be everlastingly withheld from the 'unseen congregations' of patients, but that it will be kept temporarily at bay and that they will have time and suitable circumstances in which to prepare themselves to meet it. The second and similarly qualified consolation is represented by the visitors who come each evening 'With wasteful, weak, propitiatory flowers'. These offerings are as ambiguous as the building itself. On the one hand they are pathetically inadequate props in the 'struggle to transcend / The thought of dying', on the other they are manifestations of a perennial and courageous attempt to do so. Their weakness cannot altogether obliterate the value of the spirit in which they are brought.

In 'Church Going' and 'The Building', as in 'The Explosion', Larkin looks to familiar social and natural rituals for the inspiration that might formerly have come from the church. In other poems he concentrates on the rewards of the natural world more exclusively – but, as 'Cut Grass' or 'Forget What Did' illustrate, they provide an equivalently ambiguous comfort. 'The Trees' is another example:

> The trees are coming into leaf
> Like something almost being said;
> The recent buds relax and spread,
> Their greenness is a kind of grief.
>
> Is it that they are born again
> And we grow old? No, they die too.
> Their yearly trick of looking new
> Is written down in rings of grain.
>
> Yet still the unresting castles thresh
> In fullgrown thickness every May.
> Last year is dead, they seem to say,
> Begin afresh, afresh, afresh.
>
> (*CP*, 166)

'The Trees' denies that nature allows people to believe in their immortality. But, while this denial provokes the same vulnerability as that produced by lack of faith in orthodox religion, there are positive aspects as well. In spite of their steadily increasing age, the trees do at least 'seem' to return unchanged each year, and invite the speaker to follow their example and begin his life 'afresh'. Their towering solidity (they are like 'castles') dwarfs his knowledge of mortality. And this is their consolation: their rejuvenation confirms his human potential, without deceiving him into thinking that it can last for ever. Larkin, here as elsewhere, sees through appearances at the same time as he seizes on them.

That said, he is much less interested in nature for its own sake than for the opportunities it offers to moralise about the human condition. It is this which accounts for what Donald Davie has uncharitably called his 'imperiousness towards the non-human';[8] it is in fact not imperiousness but an admission that the natural world is beautiful, restorative and necessary, yet also vulnerable and transient. 'Going, Going' makes the point forcefully:

> It seems, just now,
> To be happening so very fast;
> Despite all the land left free
> For the first time I feel somehow
> That it isn't going to last,
>
> That before I snuff it, the whole
> Boiling will be bricked in
> Except for the tourist parts –
> First slum of Europe: a role
> It won't be so hard to win,
> With a cast of crooks and tarts.
> (CP, 190)

As poems like 'MCMXIV' and 'Sad Steps' show, the 'celestial recurrences' of the natural cycle are subject to social disruption and personal disaffection, as well as industrial vandalism. But this only confirms their importance as symbols of constancy and hope. Usually their delicacy is emphasised by Larkin's choosing to write about them in fragile lyric forms. In 'Show Saturday', though, their implicit human lessons are treated more expansively. The poem moves towards its climax with an intensely affectionate deliberation, cataloguing the events of the show, transforming precise observation into a long, rapt epiphany: bales 'Like great straw dice', 'blanch leeks like church candles' and 'pure excellences' of scones and eggs and vegetables. They represent an ideal – in themselves and in the style used to describe them – of familiar Englishness:

> Let it stay hidden there like strength, below
> Sale-bills and swindling; something people do,
> Not noticing how time's rolling smithy-smoke

Shadows much greater gestures; something they share
That breaks ancestrally each year into
Regenerate union. Let it always be there.
                                        (CP, 201)

There are, of course, regenerate unions more particularly concerned with people themselves, rather than with things, or the
things 'people do'. On the face of it, social relations are given short
shrift by Larkin – largely because of his view that circumstances
continually drive people back into isolation. While this has the
advantage of encouraging personal autonomy, it also has an unavoidable danger: that the stronghold of the self will become walled
with egoism as it battles to survive. Any commitment to the social
world will be extremely wary, and made less for prospective pleasure than from a fear that staying at home will be unbearable. 'Vers
de Société' is a striking example. The speaker realises that the
people he will meet at the Warlock-Williamses' party are likely
to be 'a crowd of craps', but eventually decides to go as a way of
escaping himself:

    The time is shorter now for company,
    And sitting by a lamp more often brings
    Not peace, but other things.
    Beyond the light stand failure and remorse
    Whispering Dear Warlock-Williams: Why, of course –
                                        (CP, 182)

This conflict between the demands of society and its probable disappointments acquires a special poignancy in the more intimate
context of his love poems. 'Faith Healing' movingly summarises
their common preoccupation:

              In everyone there sleeps
    A sense of life lived according to love.
    To some it means the difference they could make
    By loving others, but across most it sweeps
    As all they might have done had they been loved.
                                        (CP, 126)

Apparently Larkin's 'everyone' is bound to be disappointed: all
people are either unloving or unloved. And their distress is
intensified by the clarity with which they envisage how love 'ought

to be'. In 'Love Songs in Age', typically, it is the 'bright incipience' which promises 'to solve, and satisfy, / And set unchangeably in order' (*CP*, 113). It is the triumphant justification for existence, and its most potent reward. But, precisely because its possible benefits are so great, the opportunities for realising them are small. Sex is often disruptive and miserably disillusioning ('Deceptions', 'Dry-Point'); the fascination of individuals wears thin ('Places, Loved Ones'); and the self is either sickeningly unworthy ('If, My Darling') or unluckily inept ('Wild Oats', 'Annus Mirabilis').

None of Larkin's poems registers the achievement of complete calm success in love, and even those that come closest are heavily qualified. 'Broadcast', for instance, for all its loving attentiveness, leaves its speaker in the dark, 'desperate', and unable to discover the addressee's distinct individuality. 'Wedding Wind', too, in spite of its excitement and fulfilment, offsets its 'happiness' with a barrage of incredulous questions and an admission that the speaker is 'sad' because other people and animals cannot share her contentment. The same kind of ambivalence exists in another of Larkin's poems which seems to break his general rule of disappointment, 'An Arundel Tomb'. Throughout, Larkin carefully weighs losses against profits, without denying the power and fact of affection. On one hand love is merely a theoretical possibility; on the other it does, literally, have the last word. More important, because neither half of the balance is allowed to dominate, he is able to create an effect of still – but not stony – composure. It is an equipoise that suggests the only love acceptable to him is one that knows how much threatens its existence. He realises that the effigies 'lie in stone' – that their faithfulness is a deception – and also admits that for them to be shown holding hands at all is nothing more than 'A sculptor's sweet commissioned grace'.[9] But while the tomb may represent an 'attitude', a 'lie', it has become a kind of truth by virtue of having survived. Larkin contemplates its durable witness of faith and love, 'hoping it might be so' in his own and all lives:

> The stone fidelity
> They hardly meant has come to be
> Their final blazon, and to prove
> Our almost-instinct almost true:
> What will survive of us is love.
>                 (*CP*, 111)

Love, in theory at least, offers the ideal solution to Larkin's isolation in a world without reliably comforting absolutes. In the place of religion and romantic theories of childhood's or nature's beneficence, he cherishes the sanctity of personal relationships. But, far from being the trusted salvation that earlier twentieth-century writers – particularly the Bloomsbury Group – sometimes imagined, Larkin persistently explores the gap between what he expects of love and what it provides.

Comforts that are not readily given by love can sometimes be discovered in a less glamorous form of social commitment: work. Occasionally Larkin's critics have identified the daily grind as a major cause of his discontent – largely because of 'Toads':

> Why should I let the toad *work*
>    Squat on my life?
> Can't I use my wit as a pitchfork
>    And drive the brute off?
>                                         (CP, 89)

Characteristically, though, the poem takes the form of a debate between two sides of his personality – with the rebellious, freebooting, anti-authoritarian aspect having the first say. By the end of the poem his more orthodox and self-critical instincts have asserted themselves:

> For something sufficiently toad-like
>    Squats in me, too;
> Its hunkers are heavy as hard luck,
>    And cold as snow,
>
> And will never allow me to blarney
>    My way to getting
> The fame and the girl and the money
>    All at one sitting.
>
> I don't say, one bodies the other
>    One's spiritual truth;
> But I do say it's hard to lose either,
>    When you have both.
>                                         (CP, 89–90)

After the first eight lucid stanzas, the last one seems disarmingly compacted. In fact it is a statement of what should by now be obvious: that working and not working complement one another. The compression itself forms a crucial part of the poem's meaning.

It conveys a sense of being trapped in an argument, and of a deliberate, difficult effort at self-persuasion. At this relatively early stage
in Larkin's career ('Toads' was first published in 1955), his internal
debate is intensely active, with each point fiercely contested.

Much more recently, in 'Posterity' (*CP*, 170), Larkin has reintro-
duced these terms of argument. Although he is primarily concerned
with the psychological and poetic results of disappointment in the
poem, he investigates them in the context of work – and to appreciate this is to rescue 'Posterity' from the misunderstanding it has suffered. At first glance, it seems entirely scornful of academic life and
methods as they are represented by its anti-hero Jake Balokowsky.
Bruce Martin has said that it attacks 'the shallowness and intellectual hypocrisy of literary criticism',[10] David Timms has called it a
'slashingly satirical portrait',[11] and Clive James, in his discussion of
'Livings', has sneeringly said it is 'full of stuff that Balokowsky is
bound to get wrong'.[12] But for all Balokowsky's caricatured absurdities – his jeans and sneakers, his abusive hip diction and his interest in Protest Theatre – it is the poem's point to draw certain
parallels between his predicament and Larkin's own. They are both,
in Balokowsky's reductively crude phrase, 'old-type *natural* fouled-
up guys' – Larkin by his own admission in a large number of other
poems, and Balokowsky as a result of 'Some slight impatience with
his destiny'. Their disappointments, fears and sadnesses are not
caused by 'kicks or something happening', but by leading a familiar
and ordinary existence. Moreover, they both experience a similar
tension between romantic longings and pragmatic needs. Where
Larkin is habitually torn between revolt and orthodoxy, Balokowsky
once entertained the thought of teaching 'school in Tel Aviv', before
'Myra' and the need for money drew him to his safe, tenured job
and 'an air-conditioned cell at Kennedy'.

The more obvious sequel to 'Toads', 'Toads Revisited', resolves
its arguments by playing down these tensions. The poem is convinced that freedom from work would bring – as isolation did in
'Vers de Société' – 'Not peace, but other things':

> give me my in-tray,
> My loaf-haired secretary,
> My shall-I-keep-the-call-in-Sir:
> What else can I answer,
>
> When the lights come on at four
> At the end of another year?

Give me your arm, old toad;
Help me down Cemetery Road.
(CP, 148)

For all its unavoidable tedium, work helps to combat the thought of impending death, and the main reason for this is its very dailiness – the fact that its repetitive structures allow Larkin to feel palpably involved with life. It is not so much a routine as a ritual and, like all rituals, supportive. Work may be less glamorous than the ceremonies surrounding birth in 'Born Yesterday', or marriage in 'The Whitsun Weddings', or even social communion in 'Show Saturday', but it shares their essential qualities. Hence Larkin's irritation with 'romantic reviewers' who accuse his poems of depicting a 'uniquely dreary life': 'I'd like to know how ... [they] spend their time. Do they kill a lot of dragons for instance?'[13]

But, while rituals offer some comfort in the face of death, they cannot – obviously – prevent its approach. 'Realisation of it rages out / In furnace-fear', Larkin says in 'Aubade', 'when we are caught without / People or drink' – or work, he might have added. From an unusually early age, death has been the rivetingly imagined fact that has forced him to limit his expectations of life. The note struck by the pretentious quatrain in *The North Ship* – 'This is the first thing / I have understood: / Time is the echo of an axe / Within a wood' (CP, 295) – has been repeated throughout his mature work, insistently and with gradually increasing clarity. In 'Aubade' itself – one of his most recently published poems – he is unprecedentedly straightforward:

I work all day, and get half-drunk at night.
Waking at four to soundless dark, I stare.
In time the curtain-edges will grow light.
Till then I see what's really always there:
Unresting death, a whole day nearer now,
Making all thought impossible but how
And where and when I shall myself die.[14]
(CP, 208)

This kind of plainness testifies to a remarkable lack of self-deception. In other contexts, being less deceived has its own rewards – but death, in Larkin's view, is an utterly comfortless blank. The frequency and forcefulness with which he envisages its approach go a long way towards explaining why he is so often regarded as an unrelievedly pessimistic poet. The evidence of 'Going', 'Nothing To Be Said', 'The Building' and 'The Old Fools' makes it hard to think otherwise. They all confirm the categoric statement at the close of 'Dockery and Son':

> Life is first boredom, then fear.
> Whether or not we use it, it goes,
> And leaves what something hidden from us chose,
> And age, and then the only end of age.
> (CP, 153)

There is an obvious affinity between this attitude and one commonly adopted by Hardy. Both poets – not to mention other kindred spirits like Edward Thomas and A. E. Housman – are obsessed with the destructive passage of time, and similarly tend to divide past, present and future into distinct and discrete units. But, while Larkin sees them as being mutually exclusive, they are not mutually oblivious. The present in which his personae live and speak is continually embarrassed or thwarted by the past – which is brimming with missed opportunities – and is also mocked or intimidated by the future – which for all its promise is overshadowed by the memory of past disappointments. Their here-and-now is somewhere they long dreamed of, and will look back on with mingled sadness and nostalgia. Or, as 'Triple Time' puts it: the 'traditionally soured' present was once 'the future furthest childhood saw', and will be the past – 'a valley cropped by fat neglected chances / That we insensately forbore to fleece'. It is a theme he handles most grandly and philosophically at the end of 'Reference Back':

> Truly, though our element is time,
> We are not suited to the long perspectives
> Open at each instant of our lives.
> They link us to our losses: worse,
> They show us what we have as it once was,
> Blindingly undiminished, just as though
> By acting differently we could have kept it so.
> (CP, 106)

Although Larkin admits he cannot alter time's intransigence, let alone escape the fact of mortality, his poems are very far from being records of passive suffering. His response is certainly not Yeats's

heroic struggle to rise above time, but neither is it Hardy's shoul-
der-shrugging acceptance of fate. And only in 'Wants' ('Beneath it
all, desire of oblivion runs' [CP, 42]) does he express anything like
a romantic death wish. Normally, as in 'Aubade', he recoils in
horror from the prospect of dying. His poems, in other words, have
a profoundly moral character, which expresses itself in a need to
control and manipulate life, rather than submit to a predetermined
pattern of unsuccess – hence his emphasis on the necessity of
choice. The power to choose is repeatedly highlighted as the most
fulfilling of all human capabilities. As his poems explore the gulf
between deception and clearsightedness, illusion and reality, solitude and sociability, they constantly discuss the need to decide on
one or other of them: that is, not simply to notice the difference,
but to make an active choice about which to adopt. The two parts
of his poetic personality are constantly in negotiation with one
another, animated by his conviction that – to borrow a phrase from
'Mr Bleaney' – 'how we live measures our own nature' (CP, 102).
In 'The Old Fools', for instance (CP, 196), one of the first and most
appalling signs of death's advance is 'the power / Of choosing
gone', and in 'The Building'(CP, 191) the patients are pitied for –
among other things – being 'at that vague age that claims / The end
of choice'. Choosing, like everything else, is vulnerable to death,
but Larkin's preoccupation with the thought of its loss is a measure
of his commitment to life. He is much too conscious of possible deception to believe in the unshakeable rightness of any decision he
might make, but he is similarly convinced that courting this danger
is preferable to living a life determined by 'something hidden from
us'. At worst the power of choosing is responsible for a life of com-
promise which, for all its frustrations, is still life. At best, it permits
self-knowledge and fulfilment – as the young men of 'How Distant'
discover. Larkin's celebration of their ability to enjoy the present,
and start a new life, is one in which the word 'decisions' plays an
important part:

> This is being young,
> Assumption of the startled century
>
> Like new store clothes,
> The huge decisions printed out by feet
> Inventing where they tread,
> The random windows conjuring a street.
>
> (CP, 162)

In 'How Distant' Larkin gives a rare glimpse of uncompromised achievement – though here as elsewhere it exists for people other than himself. This is both a source of irritation and a spur to imaginative release: the knowledge that life-enhancing opportunities are 'for others undiminished somewhere' prevents his poems from lapsing into the security of settled melancholy. And, even when fulfilment is less evident than in 'How Distant', he persistently offsets his knowledge of human limitations with his appreciation of human potential. It is a frail consolation, and yet by remorselessly delineating threats to faith, love and happiness he discovers these things in their most resilient form. But to deduce from this that he merely reckons it is better to live suffering losses than not to live at all is to draw too simple a conclusion. While it is true to say that he clings to life, no matter how unsatisfactory it might be, there is also a sense in which he views trials and tribulations as rewarding in themselves. This is not because he thinks – in the spirit of self-mortification – that suffering is intrinsically beneficial, but because like Hardy he believes that only by fully comprehending the fact and extent of suffering does any 'Catching of happiness' become possible. Appropriately, it is a point most clearly made in his own words on Hardy. He admits that Hardy's poetry shares his concern with 'time and the passing of time, love and the fading of love', but also affirms that it is 'a continual imaginative celebration of what is both the truest and the most important element in life, most important in the sense of most necessary to spiritual development'.[15]

It would be wrong to say that Larkin's emphasis on the potential and resilience of the human spirit cancelled out his pessimism. The point and value of rescuing the affirmative aspects of his work from neglect is not to make him seem a covertly optimistic poet but to expose the typical structure of his poems as a debate between hope and hopelessness, between fulfilment and disappointment. It is this argument that Larkin's use of symbolist techniques helps to dramatise; for all his cultivation of down-to-earth diction and familiar themes, he has always acknowledged the limitations of a purely neutral tone:

> Very little that catches the imagination can get clearance from either the intelligence or the moral sense. And equally, properly truthful or dispassionate themes enlist only the wannest support from the imagination. The poet is perpetually in that common human condition of trying to feel a thing because he believes it, or believe a thing because he feels it.[16]

It is what Larkin refers to here as 'the imagination' that frequently relies on symbolist strategies for its effects, although – presumably because unadulterated symbolism would be anathema to him – he has tended to deny this. Interestingly, a few of his earliest reviewers commented on it. In The *Times Literary Supplement*, for instance, *The Less Deceived* was said to have a 'sombrely tender vein reminiscent of Baudelaire, as in the poem "If, My Darling". The Baudelairean question "Vivrons-nous jamais?" haunts some of the finest poems in the book.'[17] John Wain made a similar judgement in a letter to the *London Magazine* in 1957 about 'Church Going': 'in terms of ancestry, the central figure is descended from late nineteenth century poetry (Laforgue, Corbière), the intermediary being Mr Eliot's Prufrock'.[18] (Several years later, in *The Society of the Poem* [1971], Jonathan Raban was also to point out resemblances between Larkin's depressed, bicycle-clipped figure and Eliot's world-weary speaker. One might also add that Eliot's premature obsession with old age resembles Larkin's.) More recently, with a few shining exceptions, critics have tended to ignore or botch this aspect of Larkin's work, interpreting it, if at all, simply as allegory or metaphor. But Larkin has in fact stated clearly, if self-deprecatingly, that symbolism was important to him at least as a young man. Referring to his early writing, he has said that 'the real world was all right providing you made it pretty clear that it was a symbol';[19] and in one of his earliest published poems, 'Femmes Damnées' (written in 1943), the symbolist element is clearly apparent – though Larkin himself has disparagingly said 'The piece is evidence that I once read at least one "foreign poem" though I can't remember how far, if at all, my verses are based on the original'.[20] After describing one tousled, weeping woman, Rosemary, the poem turns to a second and ends:

> Stretched out before her, Rachel curls and curves,
> Eyelids and lips apart, her glances filled
> With satisfied ferocity; she smiles,
> As beasts smile on the prey they have just killed.
>
> The marble clock has stopped. The curtained sun
> Burns on: the room grows hot. There, it appears,
> A vase of flowers has spilt, and soaked away.
> The only sound heard is the sound of tears.[21]

It is in fact Baudelaire's 'Femmes Damnées' ('A la pâle clarté des lampes languissantes') that Larkin's poem echoes. Baudelaire's was originally intended for *Les Fleurs du Mal* but was removed on the insistence of the censor in 1857 and has subsequently been printed separately. Both poems describe two sensuously tragic lesbians (Baudelaire's are called Delphine and Hippolyte) and contain marked similarities of phrasing. The first stanza above, for instance, is based on the fourth of Baudelaire's:

> Étendue à ses pieds, calme et pleine de joie,
> Delphine la couvait avec des yeux ardents,
> Comme un animal fort qui surveille une proie,
> Après l'avoir d'abord marquée avec les dents.

Pointing out the resemblances between these two poems demolishes the popular belief that Larkin has never read or liked 'foreign poetry'. His three mature collections, of course, were all written after he had moderated his youthful interest in the symbolists, but it nevertheless asserts itself repeatedly and to considerable effect. Very occasionally, he has hinted at it: speaking on the radio in 1972, he admitted: 'What I should like to do is to write *different* kinds of poems, that might be by different people. Someone once said that the great thing is not to be different from other people, but to be different from yourself.'[22] He in fact manages this feat of transformation more often than his commentators are prepared to concede. Ten years earlier, for instance, he had said about his poem 'Absences': 'I fancy it sounds like a different, better poet than myself. The last line sounds like a slightly-unconvincing translation from a French Symbolist. I wish I could write like this more often.'[23]

> Rain patters on a sea that tilts and sighs.
> Fast-running floors, collapsing into hollows,
> Tower suddenly, spray-haired. Contrariwise,
> A wave drops like a wall: another follows,
> Wilting and scrambling, tirelessly at play
> Where there are no ships and no shallows.
>
> Above the sea, the yet more shoreless day,
> Riddled by wind, trails lit-up galleries:
> They shift to giant ribbing, sift away.
>
> Such attics cleared of me! Such absences!
>                    (*CP*, 49)

The energy of the descriptive language here anticipates a later poem – the second part of 'Livings' (CP, 187), which similarly begins from a naturalistic context and then makes excited leaps between ideas. In the first stanza of 'Absences' the sea's roughness turns waves from fluids to solids – from floors to hollows to towers to hair to a wall – as it mimes the processes of change and purgation experienced by the speaker. In the second stanza a similar transformation occurs 'Above the sea': the day 'trails' ships into the distance so that their natures are altered too. The final, isolated, triumphant line (Larkin later aimed for the same kind of exhilaration in 'The Card-Players') is a joyous assertion of the freedom this represents – not just from the potential distractions of human beings on their ships but from the stereotyped constraints imposed by a strictly empirical view of the world. The line also, appropriately, includes the poem's most radical imaginative jump – from sea to attics and from attics to absence itself – as well as raising to a climax the way in which the poem's language colludes with the theme of transformation. Its two phrases are a variation on a similar structure ('Such attics cleared of me' is recalled but contracted by 'Such absences'), just as the rhyme words, alliterations and echoes ('Riddled'/'ribbing', 'shift'/'sift') in previous lines all enact in linguistic terms the changes and alterations celebrated by the speaker.

The symbolist devices of 'Absences' allow Larkin to be unlike himself because they disrupt the normal relationships between concepts: by liberating him from the familiar, circumscribed world, they allow him to experience and convey a sense of transcendence. But this is not to say that disturbances of this sort always guarantee a positive and indubitable release. In 'Next, Please', for instance, the symbolist conclusion confirms the death-obsessed bleakness of the first five stanzas:

> Only one ship is seeking us, a black-
> Sailed unfamiliar, towing at her back
> A huge and birdless silence. In her wake
> No waters breed or break.
>
> (CP, 52)

These lines perfectly illustrate Yeats's contention that symbols intensify a poem's emotional charge. Although a metaphor of ships and sailing is developed throughout the poem, it is only in the last quatrain that the tone of rational argument and the structure of logical connections ('Always ... Yet ... But ...') is exchanged for the more bizarre concentrations of symbolism proper (ships towing silence). The effect is movingly to confirm the fact and dread of death. There is, though, a sense in which the lines contain a saving grace, for all their denying any chance of actual salvation. They remove the speaker to a position outside familiar and familiarly threatening time because they release him from the world of ordinary events. As they do so, their expression of fear and awe is mitigated by a sense of the marvellous. The lines communicate an imaginative excitement which is at odds with the meaning they contain.

These compensatory effects are limited and provisional, but palpable. And, such as they are, they depend for much of their strength on being part of a dialogue: the rewards of their symbolist intensity are highlighted by the relative restraint of the first five stanzas. This point is confirmed by Larkin's most purely symbolist poem, 'Dry-Point' (see 'Two Portraits of Sex'), where the lack of variety in tone and language emphasises the speaker's preoccupation with being trapped. As he flickers from symbol to symbol, grappling with his horror of sexual disappointment, he finds only confirmation of losses, and proof that fulfilment is unobtainable:

> What ashen hills! what salted, shrunken lakes!
> How leaden the ring looks,
> Birmingham magic all discredited,
>
> And how remote that bare and sunscrubbed room,
> Intensely far, that padlocked cube of light
> We neither define nor prove,
> Where you, we dream, obtain no right of entry.
>
> (CP 37)

There is no interaction here with straightforward, rational, logical progressions of images (and the obscurity of 'Birmingham magic' does not help: it refers to the fact that a particularly cheap and tawdry kind of wedding ring was produced in Birmingham). The result is a degree of uncertainty about the poem's direction, which confirms the speaker's isolation from the 'bare and sunscrubbed room' which is his goal. He is cut off from it not simply by the *tristesse* following sex but by an inability to 'define' and 'prove' the exact nature of his wants. His symbolist vagueness, in other words, is the cause of his predicament, as well as the means by which he expresses it.

Where 'Absences', say, or 'Coming', or even 'Next, Please' in its muted fashion, rise from observed and cramping familiars to a world of imaginative freedom, 'Dry-Point' never escapes its own thwarting imprecisions. It is a revealing but untypical poem, and in the two collections he has published after the one in which it appears – *The Less Deceived* – he never again experimented so radically. In fact, had Larkin stopped writing after *The Whitsun Weddings*, it would have seemed that he had renounced symbolism altogether. Virtually all the poems in this second mature book are Hardyesque reflections, like 'Love Songs in Age', or extended metaphors, like 'Ambulances', or satires of self and society, like 'A Study of Reading Habits'. They are, of course, none the worse for being so – but it is an interesting point, in view of Larkin's supposed lack of development as a writer. *The Whitsun Weddings* is, to put it another way, the book that conforms most exactly to the attitudes and styles associated with the Movement. The Movement was first given popular definition almost exactly as Larkin finished *The Less Deceived*, and this seems to have hardened and accelerated his development towards an unmistakably English ideal. It is clear from the first part of this chapter that the most important and character-forming tensions in *The Whitsun Weddings* are between an undeceived pessimism and a wishful-thinking optimism – but these are seldom reflected in the crossing of two distinct styles and languages, as they are in *The Less Deceived* and *High Windows*.

There are, though, two poems in *The Whitsun Weddings* which show that Larkin did not abandon symbolism altogether during this period, but rather began a process of adaptation that is continued with greater urgency in *High Windows*. One of them is the title poem. Its grand finale is preceded by seven and a half stanzas of spacious, studied realism; it is a switch from one mode to another which recalls 'Absences' and 'Next, Please', but is more sudden and marked, and less obviously introduced by sympathetic metaphors:

> We slowed again,
> And as the tightened brakes took hold, there swelled
> A sense of falling, like an arrow-shower
> Sent out of sight, somewhere becoming rain.
>
> (CP, 116)

Here something potentially threatening is turned into something indispensable and nourishing. Arrows of conflict become – perhaps via an association with Blake's arrows of desire – Cupid's arrows, and during the process of transformation Larkin overcomes his sense of himself as an outsider. He is released from the empirically observed world, and its attendant disappointments, into one of transcendent imaginative fulfilment.

Much the same is true of 'Water', which demonstrates in miniature the same tactics as 'The Whitsun Weddings'. Its expositional opening ('If I were called in / To construct a religion / I should make use of water') introduces a metaphor which is gradually developed and intensified until the final stanza:

> And I should raise in the east
> A glass of water
> Where any-angled light
> Would congregate endlessly.
>         (CP, 93)

The mundane glass of water becomes more than simply a sign and object of worship. It is transformed into an imaginative apprehension of endlessness, in which all knowledge of time and its constraints, and of self and its shortcomings, is set aside.

In *High Windows* the two sides of Larkin's literary personality are more sharply distinguished. The book contains more purely symbolist moments than *The Whitsun Weddings* ('Solar', for instance, or 'Money'), and more freely imaginative narratives ('Livings', 'Dublinesque' and 'The Explosion'), but these things are offset by a more remorseless factuality, a greater crudity of language (in 'The Card-Players', for example), and an often blatantly simple pessimism ('Man hands on misery to man. / It deepens like a coastal shelf'; CP, 180). And as was the case in 'Next, Please' Larkin's exploitation of symbolist techniques does not always guarantee him absolute freedom from time and its ravages. At the end of 'Money', for instance, a gloomily rationalising tone of voice is abandoned only to confirm despair:

> I listen to money singing. It's like looking down
>     From long french windows at a provincial town,
> The slums, the canal, the churches ornate and mad
>     In the evening sun. It is intensely sad.
>             (CP, 198)

The visual freedom here, and the sense of being raised above immediate circumstances, cannot deny the force of the poem's final sentence.
But, while it fails to liberate him from sadness altogether, 'Money'
does draw attention to a recurrent and crucial feature of Larkin's
symbolist innovations. They do not simply offer a potential consolation by representing a departure from the realistic mode which is associated with disappointment. They are nearly all, in one way or
another, actually concerned with ideas of removal from the apparently inevitable frustrations that accompany rational discourse.
Speech, at least notionally, is set aside in favour of sight – of 'looking
down'. 'Solar' provides a more enduring release by the same means:

> The eye sees you
> Simplified by distance
> Into an origin,
> Your petalled head of flames
> Continuously exploding.
> Heat is the echo of your
> Gold.
>                    (CP, 159)

Here, as elsewhere, Larkin adopts the dislocations, illogicalities and
imaginative excitement of symbolism to redeem himself from distressing daily circumstances. But his commitment to the real world
is too great for him to achieve this kind of escape easily or often.
Usually he creates an impression of release only to introduce a re-
minder of responsibilities as well. An earlier poem, 'Here', demonstrates that the very notion of distance is often regarded with
ambivalence, whatever the style in which it is described. The advantages of remoteness are obvious: it means avoiding the shortcomings of others, if not of the self. It is for this reason, perhaps,
that Larkin has always emphasised the isolation of the various
places where he has lived. He has created a kind of private mythology, which in the case of Hull and Holderness has turned an ad-
mittedly cut-off district into a remote pastoral paradise:

> Here silence stands
> Like heat. Here leaves unnoticed thicken,
> Hidden weeds flower, neglected waters quicken,
> Luminously-peopled air ascends;
> And past the poppies bluish neutral distance
> Ends the land suddenly beyond a beach

> Of shapes and shingle. Here is unfenced existence:
> Facing the sun, untalkative, out of reach.
>
> (CP, 136–7)

The few people allowed into this personal Eden are reduced merely to 'shapes' – they are not enough to distract him from his silent self-forgetting. But the poem's final phrase – 'out of reach' – has an arresting ambiguity: the place is both beyond the reach of disturbances and also beyond his reach. It is both 'Here' and nowhere, and attainable only in imagination, not in fact. While this emphasises its privacy, it also hints at a disadvantage: the evocation of distance allows freedom from self, people and time, but it simultaneously denies the theoretical and sometimes necessary support of company. It also, in its neutral vacancy, prefigures the inevitable emptiness of death.

Precisely this tension recurs in the poem of Larkin's which most successfully employs symbolist techniques, 'High Windows'. For its first four verses, he creates a persona who is angrily disappointed that promises made to him as a young man have not been fulfilled. But as he speculates about the new generation's chances of happiness he realises that he might once have been similarly envied. The cycle of time brings round hope and frustration ceaselessly, and no one – to extricate a phrase buried in the image of 'an outdated combine harvester' – gets their oats. As so often in his other poems, the wasted opportunities of the past and the exclusions of the future coalesce to tyrannise the present. But here they provoke a conclusion that contains some hope of reprieve:

> Rather than words comes the thought of high windows:
> The sun-comprehending glass,
> And beyond it, the deep blue air, that shows
> Nothing, and is nowhere, and is endless.
>
> (CP, 165)

The most obvious reward of this 'thought' is that it removes him from the context of actual human fallibility. It is an exalted imaginative alternative – in secular terms – to the false 'paradise' of sexual freedom and godless independence promised on earth. But clearly there are drawbacks. As the speaker imagines himself staring out through the divisive 'sun-comprehending glass' (it recalls Shelley's 'dome of many-coloured glass' between life and death) he cannot entirely suppress the effect of the two negatives 'Nothing' and 'nowhere'. For all their freedom from specific circumstances, they imply extinction. Like the 'unfenced existence' of 'Here', the 'deep blue air' of 'High Windows' reminds him of his commitment to the world. It does so, moreover, by a shift from grumbling, ironical, colloquial speech to symbolist intensity which both illustrates Larkin's mastery of poetic tones and – as in 'Money' and 'Solar' – undermines the notion of the poem as a verbal device altogether. The final lines are offered 'Rather than words'. Obviously they are words – how else could the poem exist? – but it is a crucial part of their function to convey an inexpressible element in the thought they contain.

For all their variety, the methods that Larkin adopts in his pursuit of happiness have at least one thing in common. They suggest – and often actually state – that his ideal is at best elusive and at worst illusory. The only thing he can hope for is a temporary reprieve from a pervasive sense of his own failure, and the ubiquitous evidence of other people's absurdity or self-deception. But, while it is often snubbed, his hope is resolute, and in a very large number of poems it leads him to create a dialogue between opposing attitudes: sociability and singleness, work and idleness, resolution and despair. Invariably, the thwarting, negative side of the argument emerges as the strongest – but this does not mean that Larkin is incapable of finding consolations and satisfactions in existence.

The same life-enhancing struggle between opposites is evident in the style and language of his work. His original admiration for the heroic, aspiring, self-dramatising characteristics of Yeats was not completely dispelled as his sympathy for the humbler manner of the English line developed: it was restrained and made to perform a crucial role in the creation of his mature style. Even in the poems that adopt primarily Hardyesque neutral tones, there are frequent flashes of rhetoric which recall Yeats's grander manner. The result is a number of poems that emerge as 'rhetorically persuasive Yeatsian affirmations, [and] do not disregard the difficulties but hold them magnificently at bay from some superior inch of imaginative height'.[24] Saying so involves contradicting several of Larkin's own resonant self-analyses, as well as several of his commentators' judgements of his unflinching pessimism. Revealingly, though, he opened *The Less Deceived* with a poem, 'Lines on a Young Lady's Photograph Album', which expressly states the losses of a narrowly literal attitude to experience. Photography, the poem says, depends for its charm and successes on depicting 'real' people in a 'real' place, and on being 'in every sense empirically true'. But it is exactly for these reasons that Larkin will not accord it the status of 'art' – which, he implies, depends on allowing the imagination free and potentially transfiguring play. It is a characteristically ambivalent poem – a showpiece of the Movement, but discreetly hinting at the Movement's limitations. His three mature collections have developed attitudes and styles of greater imaginative daring: in their prolonged debates with despair, they testify to wide sympathies, contain passages of frequently transcendent beauty, and demonstrate a poetic inclusiveness which is of immense consequence for his literary heirs.

From Andrew Motion, *Philip Larkin* (London and New York, 1982), pp. 59–83.

## NOTES

[Like Seamus Heaney, Andrew Motion takes issue with the idea that Larkin's poetry is parochial in its outlook and unadventurous in its style. His concern is not to present Larkin as an unacknowledged optimist but to show how his poems typically embrace both dejection and fulfilment. He finds in the poems a continual debate between disappointed pragmatism and romantic idealism. The dislocations and illogicalities of symbolism permit the poems to break momentarily with rational, empirical discourse and experience a world of transcendent imaginative fulfilment. It is these moments of transcendent beauty that Motion finds most 'affirmative' in Larkin's work. He claims that, contrary to his own account of poetic influence, Larkin never completely dispelled the impact of the poetry of W. B. Yeats, and that a modernist, symbolist influence persisted throughout his career. Ed.]

1. Eric Homberger, *The Art of the Real* (London, 1977), p. 74.

2. Geoffrey Thurley, *The Ironic Harvest* (London, 1974), p. 145.

3. Charles Tomlinson, 'The Middlebrow Muse', *Essays in Criticism*, 7: 2(1957), 214.

4. 'A Conversation with Philip Larkin', *Tracks*, 1 (1967), 8.

5. Philip Larkin, 'Wanted: Good Hardy Critic', *Critical Quarterly*, 8: 2 (1966), 178.

6. Ian Hamilton, 'Four Conversations: Philip Larkin', *London Magazine*, 4: 8 (1964), 73.

7. *Times Literary Supplement*, 23 December 1977, p. 1491.

8. Donald Davie, 'Remembering the Movement', in Barry Alpert (ed.), *The Poet in the Imaginary Museum* (Manchester, 1977), p. 75.

9. The clasped hands are actually a nineteenth-century addition.

10. Bruce K. Martin, *Philip Larkin* (Boston, 1978), p. 90.

11. David Timms, *Philip Larkin* (Edinburgh, 1973), p. 64.

12. Clive James, *At the Pillars of Hercules* (London, 1979), p. 54.

13. Hamilton, 'Four Conversations', p. 73.

14. First printed in the *Times Literary Supplement*, 23 December 1977, p. 1491.

15. Larkin, 'Wanted: Good Hardy Critic', p. 178.

16. 'Context: Philip Larkin', *London Magazine*, 1: 11 (1962), 32.

17. Review of *The Less Deceived, Times Literary Supplement*, 16 December 1955, p. 762.

18. John Wain, letter to the *London Magazine* (March 1957), 56.

19. 'A Conversation with Philip Larkin', p. 7.

20. Philip Larkin, 'Femmes Damnées', Sycamore Broadsheet 27 (Oxford, 1978).

21. Ibid. Reprinted in harkin's *Collected Poems*, p. 270.

22. Quoted in Timms, *Philip Larkin*, p. 121.

23. 'Philip Larkin', in Paul Engle and Joseph Langland (eds), *Poet's Choice* (New York, 1962), p. 202.

24. Edna Longley, 'Larkin, Edward Thomas and the Tradition', *Phoenix* (Philip Larkin Issue), 11–12 (1973–74), 87.

# 3

# Philip Larkin: After Symbolism

*BARBARA EVERETT*

When Philip Larkin's *The Less Deceived* first appeared in 1955 the *Times Educational Supplement* called it a 'triumph of clarity after the formless mystifications of the last twenty years'. Now, after two decades of steadily increasing success, Larkin has come to be thought of by many as not only the best English poet but one of the best in Europe. By an odd reversal, however, his most recent volume, *High Windows* (1974), seems to have struck a number of reviewers as – for all its excellence – a triumph of obscurity. Over the last few years, charges of obscurity have cropped up with a frequency that is odd if one recalls how short a time it is since Larkin's almost painfully courteous lucidity and conscientious narrowing-down of range first laid him open to attack for effects quite other than that: for being 'naïf' or 'faux-naïf' or 'genteel' or 'suburban' or 'parochial' or 'provincial' or downright Philistine – for heading a general selling-out of modernistic culture. Moreover Larkin himself has provoked such attacks: his rather rare pieces of literary-critical journalism have often been sceptical about modernism, and the Introduction to a collection of jazz reviews which Larkin published in 1970 went so far as to allege that the 'obscurantism' of modern art has sacrificed a vital relationship with its audience to a mere sterile involvement with its own working-materials. In such a context, it is interesting to watch Richard Murphy contemplating *High Windows* in the *New York Review of Books* (May, 1975) and sagging at the sight of a bewildering triptych called 'Livings', which Clive James has deciphered in a penetrating essay: it juxtaposes three separate lives in far-off periods and places, each full of its own comforting certainties that seem faintly threatened in mysterious ways, the implication being that they are on the verge of catastrophe.

'Bewildering', 'deciphered', 'juxtaposes', 'seem', 'mysterious', 'implication' – these are new (but also familiar) words in the criticism of a poetry that has always seemed to many to have the virtue of not requiring 'penetration'. The 'decipherment' to which Murphy alludes took place in Clive James's *Encounter* review of *High Windows* (June, 1974); and it is equally striking that this highly appreciative account of Larkin's verse refers to the second part of 'Livings' – as also to another poem in this volume, 'Sympathy in White Major' – as being distractingly *obscure*: 'While wanting to be just the reverse, Larkin can on occasion be a difficult poet.' Difficulty is in itself, like obscurity, a difficult subject, but Clive James's remark helps to throw some light on it by the way it begins with what Larkin 'wants'. An effect of poetic failure is not at all general in Larkin's work: his idiosyncrasy is the flawless success of the art with which he records the life *manqué*. So unvarying is this efficiency that he has even been accused of unambitiousness: of doing what clearly comes too easily. Clive James is therefore to some extent deriving, from critical pronouncements or from the *persona* of the poet 'behind' the poems, someone who is capable of 'wanting' anything, other than what the poems are capable of showing him getting. 'Wanting' and 'getting', like the whole concept of poetic *intention*, are inread criteria: not necessarily untrue or unhelpful in reading poetry, but more relative to the reader than to the poet. And the usual partner of 'intention' is 'difficulty' or 'obscurity', which really means our inability to see the poet communicating what we see him as wanting to say.

The problem with all these terms is that they overstress the side of poetry concerned with the communication of statements ('Is that clear?') and understress the side which is a more private, less communicative perpetuation of experience, deriving as much from a universe of *things* as from a language of concepts. They do this unavoidably, because they are philosophical terms abstracted from discourse, and discourse is fully public as poetry is not; to debate about poetry at all is partly to falsify what often takes its strength from inarticulated intelligence; and it is from these necessary falsifications that there proceed the endless and equally necessary infightings of criticism. *High Windows* is both 'clearer' *and* 'more obscure' than *The Less Deceived*; just as Larkin's new style of ferocious lucidity tends often now to the four-letter word, a linguistic prop which one may, as one wishes, find 'easy' *or* 'difficult', emerging as it does from the writer whom Alvarez once called (not wholly without reason) the Poet of Gentility:

> *My wife and I have asked a crowd of craps*
> *To come and waste their time and ours: perhaps*
> *You'd care to join us?* In a pig's arse, friend ...
> (*CP*, 181)

This is the opening of 'Vers de Société', one of the best poems in *High Windows*. Its subject is the terms on which the isolated individual may become socially available; and it displays most aspects of the style in which the later Larkin is available to the reader. 'Livings' and 'Sympathy in White Major' do not differ strikingly from it as poems. If, therefore, they can be found *obscure*, this is not from a lack of plainness of language or from the use of esoteric concepts. It is rather from some failure, for this or that given reader, in the *availability* of the poem, some break-down in specific relationship with the reader, such as Larkin himself has spoken of as characteristic of modernism. With the new Larkin, a reader may see what the words 'say', but not what they 'mean' or 'amount to': ('a bewildering triptych ... it juxtaposes ... each full of its own ... the implication being ...'). John Bayley has praised Larkin – in a *Times Literary Supplement* review expanded in his *Uses of Division* (1976) – above all for the creation of a new, totally sympathetic poetic personality or 'self' which constitutes a relationship with the reader approximating even to 'the intimacy ... of the lounge bar'. What Larkin's most recent volume shows, perhaps, is some degree of retraction or withdrawal of that poetic personality; or, to put the matter more precisely, *High Windows* shows more explicitly a side of Larkin's work present from the beginning – a poetic impersonality. That impersonality cannot, I think, be properly considered except in relation to the 'modernism' which Larkin himself has often and sharply criticised, with the sharpness (perhaps) which a person may reserve for the concerns which most tempt or involve him. It is, in fact, the obscurities of *High Windows* – though they are also its lucidities – which throw light on an aspect of Larkin's verse that has surely always been there. His poems appear to have profited from a kind of heroic struggle *not* to be modernistic, not to be mere derivative footnotes to a Symbolism as much disapproved of as admired; they have wished to be, not merely after, but well after Eliot.

This general impression can be made specific by considering for a moment one of the two poems which Clive James found very obscure. 'Sympathy in White Major' (*CP*, 168) is a linguistically fairly simple, almost monosyllabic poem, whose three stanzas describe a man (the poet, or 'I') who pours himself out a large drink and hears as from a toastmaster his social virtues celebrated in warm clichés. The style is mostly commonplace, the situation being downrightly imagined: the drink fills a stanza, elaborately detailed, and the clichés of praise load every rift with ore. If the poem strikes a reader as obscure, the reason must lie not in the area of paraphrasable meaning but in 'how to take it' – the absence of a sense of why the man and the drink and the fantasies of praise frankly matter at all. The answer to this does not lie in paraphrasable content, as we might expect it to, given some current descriptions of Larkin's poetry, but in the ordonnance of the whole. Rather than offering a strong logic of statements whose syntax follows what we like to think of as normal colloquial usage, the poem works by an interaction (or 'juxtaposition') of striking images. It misses out rational connections between these. Primarily, it refuses to allocate statements, so that all speeches in what is nominally a social situation in fact dissolve into one solitary monologue. It also leaves unexplained connections between the drink, for instance, and the italicised laudations, like '*He devoted his life to others*'; between the apparently sober statements of the second stanza, 'It didn't work for them or me', and the complacent or unbothered éclat of the last, '*A decent chap, a real good sort.*' We never properly know whether the drink is because the praise did not work, or the praise is because the drink did not work, or whether both work or do not work. On the other hand, 'proper knowledge' is not what the poem is about. It exists as a fuddled and yet marvellously clear (clear as ice and gin and tonic are clear, clear as whiteness is blank) tangle of intoxications and illusions; it is a poem about the conditions of a 'sparkling' success in art or life in general, and about the fantasising but commonplace vanities or emptinesses which may be latently present in such success.

If 'Sympathy in White Major' is as readable or available as it is, this is partly because it uses pointers and directions that start us off without difficulty in the right direction. Those who find the poem obscure have happened to miss, or happen to be unable to use, the pointers given. In part this is a matter of what one likes to call 'purely aesthetic' dispositions: the exquisite tonal artistry lavished on a gin and tonic, the 'music' of clichés of praise. But these ridiculous felicities of technique are not self-supporting – they relate backwards to an origin. 'Sympathy in White Major' could actually be called a learned poem, even an esoteric one, precisely in the way in which we expect a modernistic poem to be. And by what can hardly be considered coincidence, the learning in question happens to be something in the nature of a 'history of Symbolism'. It would be radically untrue to say that anything in this poem absolutely depends on a knowledge of this or that fact outside it; all of it except perhaps the title can clearly be understood by any ordinary person with common sense, some intelligence about loneliness and vanity and fantasy-making, and no knowledge whatever of Symbolist poetry. Nonetheless, it remains a fact that this lucid and comical and inarticulate poem reminds one in flashes, as one reads, of a remarkably wide area of aesthetic history – an area that can be evoked by half a line of verse but that takes a disproportionate amount of discourse to sketch in. It can be said that though Larkin's poem does not appear to need or benefit from extraneous information, nonetheless there *is* extraneous information which can lead a reader to find it even cleverer and funnier (or possibly sadder) than at first strikes one; and which in some sense consolidates both its almost imagistic procedure and its argument concerning Vanity in both art and moral life.

This context of information begins where Larkin begins, with the title – the carefully 'gauche', spoofing or horseplaying, spuriously-cultural, abstractly inartistic if synaesthetic half-sentence, 'Sympathy in White Major'. 'Symphonie en blanc majeure', or 'Symphony in White Major' (which Larkin's title parodies with conscious discord) is the title of a poem written in about 1850 by the French Parnassian poet Théophile Gautier: a series of extremely fine, chillily erotic quatrains sensuously detailing the whiteness of a female swan. Some fifteen years earlier Gautier had prefaced his 'shocking' novel of bisexuality, *Mademoiselle de Maupin*, with a defiant statement of Art for Art's Sake, declaring war on the useful and the ugly – on bourgeois civilisation, in short; thus, it was probably with some conscious reference to Gautier's Art-for-Art's-Sakism that a decade after the poem, in the 1860s, a French art critic borrowed from Gautier's title the phrase 'symphonie en blanc' to describe the effect of the work of a different artist, a painting that was on exhibition in Paris. That painting was a study of a young woman in a white dress, Whistler's *White Girl*; and Whistler, who fairly certainly knew Gautier's poem anyway, and who was to become the first conscious exponent of Art for Art's Sake in England, as well as serving as a kind of medium for – and reciprocal influence on – French Symbolism, liked the critic's use of the phrase so much that he promptly rechristened his picture 'Symphony in White No. 1' and went on to do three more paintings on the same theme and with the same titling. The second of these, 'Symphony in White No. 2', shows an exquisite young woman in white framed against a mirror into which she is not quite looking. This now famous image had enormous contemporary success: Swinburne, for instance, wrote a poem based on it, called 'Before the Mirror', in which a beautiful young woman contemplates her image – 'But one thing knows the flower; the flower is fair' – and wonders which is the real person, and which the ghost, as between 'the white sister' and herself.

This chain of Anglo-American-French images appears to enter Larkin's poem with the title 'Sympathy in White Major': the lines which follow are a sympathetic 'symphony in white' as aesthetically clever as Gautier's own; its speaker is framed against an image of himself, as 'the whitest man I know', like Whistler's subject; and hesitates between illusions as Swinburne's beauty does. But Larkin's speaker is not merely 'before the mirror' of self-contemplation; he is actually (if perhaps ironically) toasting himself there. The gesture of this drunken and yet abstaining 'private pledge', which is Larkin's phrase for it, takes us further into Symbolism. For, though not a Symbolist himself, Gautier's purity of aims and extreme technical skill earned him the respect of poetic contemporaries and successors who were: it was to him that Baudelaire dedicated *Les Fleurs du Mal*, and later Mallarmé in his turn – the finest, and most obscure, of the Symbolist poets – wrote 'funeral poems' for both Gautier and Baudelaire. One of Baudelaire's best and best-known prose-poems ironically but seriously exhorts us to 'Get drunk! ... With wine, with poetry or with virtue as you please. But get drunk!' Baudelaire's classic *topos* must have been in Mallarmé's mind (he re-casts many Baudelairean themes) when in 1893 he composed the lines called 'Salut' (Greeting) which Larkin's 'Sympathy in White Major' seems closely related to. This 'Salut', which Mallarmé afterwards used as Preface to his published *Poésies*, was first delivered with champagne-glass in hand, in precisely the gesture which Larkin recalls – 'I lift the lot in private pledge'. For Mallarmé, in many ways the most reticent of men, was asked to act as toastmaster to a banquet given by the review, *La Plume*: and on that occasion first read his brief, oblique and playfully obscure poem. In it, the bubble-filled glass of champagne becomes a symbol of that great Symbolist Nothingness of things which poetry both represents and redeems. The poem opens: 'Rien, cette écume, vierge vers / A ne désigner la coupe' (Nothing, this foam, virgin verse / Defining only the cup); and as the poet speaks the lines, calling the poem into being as he goes, the rhythm assumes the pitch and toss of intoxication, and the whole becomes a small craft rocking on a sea of wine towards arrival or wreck – whatever end awaits the drunk, the sailor and the poet alike: 'Solitude, récif, étoile / A n'importe ce qui valut / Le blanc souci de notre étoile' (Solitude, reef, star / Whatever merited / The white care of our sail).

Mallarmé's 'Salut' is not one of his best poems, but it illustrates well enough an art that one might think of as possible in late-nineteenth-century France but *not* in the England of the late nineteen-seventies. Larkin's poem is by contrast obdurately modern, of the last twenty years, and intensely English, even Little-English: as 'English' in its clichés as other poems in this volume are 'modern' in their obscenities. All the same, 'Sympathy in White Major', with all its appealingly artless, gruff and simple manner, its near-monosyllabic rhythms and its absence of 'images', is in its way as brilliant and as learned a fragment of translation as one is likely to find: a fragment, rather, of that art of Imitation which the Augustans deployed, a form of translation which fully recognises that changes of times and styles make literalism inappropriate. Larkin's first stanza is a remarkably clever game, an exact conversion of Mallarmé's now deeply dated 'champagne and Poesy' conceit into a precise modern and English equivalent which simultaneously records, as a scholar would, its sources of information. For Larkin's cinema-screen-advertisement-large, lights-in-Piccadilly-Circus-high, icily-musically 'chiming' glass of gin-and-tonic that 'voids' (*void* being the key Symbolist concept for the cosmic Nothingness to be confronted and embodied and so – in theory – overcome by Art)

– this fantasia derisively picks up the lingo of a whole tradition; and then makes something new out of it.

It is Larkin's *use* of the symbols of this tradition in his first stanza for purposes of his own that at once arouses some scepticism at the proud claim of the second stanza, that as artist the speaker is morally blameless to the point of sainthood, in his withdrawal from the common human condition of *use* of others: 'Other people wore like clothes / The human beings in their days ...'. This scepticism is already in fact aesthetically implanted, like a form of self-knowledge, in the graces of the first stanza, where we see the vast greedy drink 'void'

> In foaming gulps until it smothers
> Everything else ...
> (CP, 168)

An art which turns aside from what it conceives of, harshly or cheerfully, as the gross Philistine materialism and spiritual emptiness of its own social civilisation, will sooner or later lay itself open to certain moral and intellectual charges. It will become self-obsessed, cold, empty of matter – a ghost staring into a mirror. These dangers or vulnerabilities have probably always been even clearer to those who have at various times pursued purism in the arts (or in morals) than to their adversaries. Gautier's original poem, for instance, ends with a cool ironic turn, 'Cette implacable blancheur' (This ruthless whiteness) which Larkin's closing 'White is not my favourite colour' possibly echoes in fact as well as in effect. There is a critique in all Mallarmé's symbols of reflective imprisonment, of which the best-known is the swan trapped in ice; and there is similarly a force of moral irony in the use of the figure of Narcissus in the work of the last true French Symbolist, Valéry. But such awareness is peripheral in true Symbolism. It moves to the forefront only in a work of late Symbolism or even 'post-Symbolism', Eliot's *Four Quartets*: poems which continually wrestle to justify morally the aesthetic purism which their author inherits, distrusts and loves, just as his early Ode half celebrates and half detests its titular hero, 'Saint Narcissus' – the virtuous starer in the mirror. As critic, too, Eliot made an especial point of objecting to the Narcissism or Vanity latent in the approach of those poets, Mallarmé and Valéry, whom he loved, was indebted to, and in so many ways resembled.[1] In a manner that is almost a brilliant postscript to Eliot, Larkin brings Saint Narcissus into the 1970s. The style is balder, more simply self-mickeying, more seriously involved with commonplace and cliché morality: '*He devoted his life to others* ... It didn't work for them or me'; '*Here's to the whitest man I know* / – Though white is not my favourite colour'. An elegy on Symbolism is delivered in an age of TV commercial; and in its style.

In a *London Magazine* interview published in 1964, Larkin was asked by Ian Hamilton whether he ever read French poetry, and answered: '*Foreign* poetry? *No!*'[2] Larkin's writings often suggest a man of scrupulous honesty, even to the point of some literalness. This exchange therefore opens up some interesting possibilities. Literature is a medium that can seem wonderfully simple in effect, but to produce that effect involves endless complexities. Perhaps the poet simply felt that a joke is a joke, and that one is not on oath in public interviews. Or perhaps he had not read much French verse at that stage, or much contemporary French verse, or had ceased to read it, or to remember it, or had sometimes read it in such excellent translations as C. F. MacIntyre's of Symbolist poetry – without which, a non-bilingualist can hardly feel sure he is really reading this very difficult verse; or perhaps the poet's obvious modesty, like that of scrupulous scholars who say that they have not read something, but only 'looked at it', made him deny reading much foreign poetry. The statement would tie in with the hatred of cultural pretentiousness that Larkin shows elsewhere: a dislike of an abstract and unreal talk of 'poetry' or 'literature' or 'culture' at large which in fact destroys or renders sterile this book, this poem, this line. 'Foreign poetry', *No*; but yes (perhaps), to an image or two experienced once intensely enough to make it survive for a good many years and then re-emerge with enough life in it for another man's poem.

It is hard, at any rate, to manage without conjecturing such survivals. For it is not only 'Sympathy in White Major' which suggests a poet knowledgeably interested in French verse – as in Symbolist art in general. In Larkin's first successful volume, *The Less Deceived* (which on coming out in 1955 was saluted by the *TES* reviewer as a blow dealt to modernism) the poem called 'Arrivals, Departures' reads like a beautiful imitation, in the same technical sense, of Baudelaire's prose-poem 'Le Port'. Larkin's wonderfully English 'Toads', in that same volume, have a strong resemblance to the Chimaeras carried on the shoulders of men in

Baudelaire's prose-poem 'Chacun sa Chimère'. And the title of another in that collection, Larkin's 'Poetry of Departures', refers to a whole phase of French Symbolist verse with the kind of ironic casualness that is liable in Larkin's case to be the detritus of more knowledge than he cares to display. (As in Eliot's case also, any accidental discovery by a reader of the poet's 'sources' usually reveals not less but much more learning than superficially appears). *The Whitsun Weddings* is not a 'French' volume – Larkin seems there to be intent on developing the easy, colloquial and if one likes traditionally 'English' persona that strengthens his mature poetry. But in *High Windows*, published nearly a decade later again (1974), what are conceivably early and original tastes and interests re-assert themselves; for it shows a consistent but perhaps more boldly individual use of French Symbolist poetry, a use that makes new poems, rather than merely 'alluding' or imitating.

Thus, the title-poem, 'High Windows', meditates on the human pursuit of happiness in a style that at first displays an abysmal, rock-bottom four-letter-word 'modernity', the tone of the present day: but this colloquial brutality quietly modulates towards the refined and extreme contradictory intensity of the end –

> And beyond it, the deep blue air, that shows
> Nothing, and is nowhere, and is endless.
> (*CP*, 165)

The radiant colour and the 'nothingness' are too Mallarméan to be only coincidentally similar. '*L'azur*' (the blue) is Mallarmé's most consistent and philosophical symbol, delineating both the necessity and the absence of the ideal, an ideal which we imprint on the void sky by the intensity of our longing; his poetry is full of '*De l'éternel azur la sereine ironie*' (the calm irony of the endless blue). The poem by Mallarmé in which this image becomes most definitive is '*Les Fenêtres*' (the Windows), which compares the state of the poet, sickened by existence and enduring the perpetual life-giving suffering of an always despairing and then re-purified idealism, to that of an old man dying in a dreary hospital, his face wistfully pressed to the windows, longing for the blue sky outside. Larkin's 'thought of high windows' is close enough to Mallarmé's poem to be worth contrasting with it: as it is, in addition, with an earlier treatment of the topic perhaps larger, tougher and more classic than Mallarmé's, and one to which the later French poet must in his turn have been indebted. Mallarmé's 'Les Fenêtres' is presumably dependent on two superb prose-poems by Baudelaire, one of them the very well-known lines with the English title 'Any Where Out of the World', and beginning '*Cette vie est un hôpital où chaque malade est possédé du désir de changer de lit*' (This life is a hospital in which every patient is consumed with the desire to change his bed), and the other similarly titled 'Les Fenêtres' and opening, '*Celui qui regarde du dehors à travers une fenêtre ouverte, ne voit jamais autant de choses que celui qui regarde une fenêtre fermée*' (The man who looks in from outside through an open window never sees as much as the man who looks at a window that is closed).

Most poets have been highly literate, resourceful scholars of language. There is more than one way of being the kind of 'Little-Englander' or even 'suburbanite' that Larkin has sometimes been accused of being (the language-teacher Mallarmé lived an obdurately 'suburban' and domestic existence). Such accusations can in fact never be very sensible when directed at a poet so evidently intelligent and knowledgeable, so aesthetically original and verbally adept. The familiarity with poets like Baudelaire and Mallarmé which his work seems to reveal – though not to display – is not, therefore, primarily interesting: it is only what could be expected. What may be more worth notice is the specific and critical use which Larkin seems to make of Symbolist imagery, or of kinds of thought and feeling which come close to its idealisms. '*High* Windows' is not the same as '*The* Windows', in Baudelaire or Mallarmé, and '*Sympathy* in White Major' is obviously derisive in a way in which Gautier's 'Symphony' is not. In both cases, Larkin is evidently humanising and moralising. His 'Sympathy' (which is, as it happens, another Baudelairean and Mallarméan concept – the later French poet ends one poem by cursing himself for possessing so much of that fluid, irritating and aesthetic quality) – is, however, probably the most direct and ordinary moral and emotional equivalent of aesthetic sensibility, 'tea and sympathy' being what one might call the English translation of French 'champagne and poesy'.

Similarly, to make the windows 'High' gives them a certain metaphysical or even ecclesiastical status that distances them romantically but unsatisfactorily from the real human condition. Symbolism is being used negatively, in a post – or even anti-Symbolist fashion. But it has been rightly said that all negatives in poetry, once stated, become a special kind of poetic positive. Larkin's Symbolist imagery is a disrelation with the idealising originals more than a relationship with them; but the context is one in which disrelations are relations, too. In the poem immediately facing 'High Windows', called 'Forget What Did' (and Larkin's poems do seem to be printed so that they relate to each other in ways like these) the poet describes a diary which had stopped short because the writer wanted to forget, not to record 'Such words, such actions / As bleakened waking'; but the peculiar effect of this remarkable poem is to resurrect and sustain those unendurable half-memories, the uncited words and actions, just as its end devotes the diary's still blank pages to hypothetical 'Celestial recurrences, / The day the flowers come, / And when the birds go'. Larkin often seems to write like this – as a man experiencing and surviving the exact end of something vital, 'out on the end of an event': as one 'stopping the diary ... a blank starting'. And this transitional effect can also be described in a purely literary or technical way. It could be said that Larkin's position as a writer is difficult to chart exactly because of what appears to be a highly ambiguous relationship with an important tradition of aesthetic values. He makes use, and very consistent use, of that species of literary idealism which Symbolism implies, *only* in order to record its unavailability. Thus, 'Sympathy in White Major' is not a '*Symphony* in White Major' – its title implies parody; having translated the original aesthetic intensity into a moral quality, it then finds in this transposed aestheticism only a kind of naïveté, a species of weakness: 'White is not my favourite colour'. Similarly, 'High Windows' is 'Les Fenêtres' Englished and brought up to date: but that entails the violent random flatness with which the new poem modishly opens, with a savage but hardly explicit irony –

> When I see a couple of kids
> And guess he's fucking her and she's
> Taking pills or wearing a diaphragm,
> I know this is paradise ...
>
> (CP, 165)

The conscious baldness of the writing, leaving rhythmic effects naked, makes the repeated dactyls stand out, as though 'fucking her' and 'diaphragm' were each a gross ironic half-rhyme with 'paradise'; the three words jangle together, in the void of their blank unstated relationship, with a disharmony like a verbal headache. This sexy disharmony is broadened by the parallel with the equally pathetic hopeful illusions of the past, the hope felt by some two generations back that a priestless theologyless freedom might descend on to children grown blissfully into 'free bloody birds'. It is perhaps the memory of birds driving themselves against closed windows which provides the logic which closes the poem: in the Symbolist image of blue-containing windows which finally embodies and resolves all its impossibilities.

Any attempt to describe 'High Windows' would have to account for not merely what it says but the tension and extremity of its style: that violent flatness of its opening which modulates into the exaltation of the close. It would also have to point out that this loftiness of the close is altered by its context into something peculiarly hypothetical, unavailable. Symbolism remains a resource like those 'Observed / Celestial recurrences' which might one day fill with images of flowers and birds the remaining pages of a diary left blank years ago: but never precisely with propriety, or within reason. It offers a dead language, like the discretions of Latin, for illuminating human illusions without contempt or condemnation, and in a form more luminous than satire or parody. For some of the poems in *High Windows* achieve this tacit or ironic or contradictory symbolism with extraordinary finesse and depth. Few poems could be more unpretentious, more obdurately turned away from the coerciveness of Symbolism, than the mild and sociological 'Friday Night in the Royal Station Hotel'. It evokes the hushed cosy unnerving meaninglessness that tends to descend at late evening in a hotel, the sense of waiting for something to happen or the feeling that something just has; and it creates this sensation of inhabited void by describing sequences of human gestures first divested of import and then located in interior bric-a-brac: 'Light spreads darkly downwards ...', 'Empty chairs / ... face each other, coloured differently', there is 'loneliness of knives and glass', someone reads 'an unsold evening paper', departure is through 'shoeless corridors'. The image of the Grand Hotel is very 'Thirties, and the writing here has much of Auden's conceitful wit – but Larkin's poem is more concentratedly suggestive, its furniture *broods* more intently. Mallarmé wrote a number of poems, all of them among his most interesting and obscure, featuring late-nineteenth-century household interiors: in them, mana emanates from a fluttering net curtain, a swollen vase or a massive sideboard. Larkin, by comparison (so his poem makes us feel) writes from a place and time from which to recreate such presences would be mere heartless obscurantist antiquarianism, and where furniture is only datable junk: where 'Home' itself becomes the 'Royal Station Hotel', the place where 'Hours pass'. Therefore his poetic objects – the empty chairs, the corridors, the ash-trays – which could hardly be perceived with more intensity if they *were* symbols, have a complex burden to bear: that of not even being capable of symbolising the absence which they happen to remind one of. For Symbolism necessitates and is arrogant; the humbler literature which follows it inherits only the randomness an ebbing symbolism leaves behind, like 'letters of exile' ... '(If home existed)'.

It can often be hard to explain why poems as wilfully modest as Larkin's are, are also as good as they are – as peculiarly potent. There can be few other major poets who have been as often and as reasonably called 'minor' as Larkin has. The power of a poem like 'Friday Night ...' tends to be locked up in the self-denying ordinances of Larkin's special non-symbolic symbols. The laws of this after-symbolism are maintained also, or so it appears, in most of the poet's utterances on aesthetics outside his actual poems. A characteristic moment occurs, for instance, in the *London Magazine* interview from which I have already quoted: where Ian Hamilton refers, very justly, to the poet's consistent habit of turning and shaping his poems by giving them a sharp self-undercutting close, and Larkin sharply undercuts any merit that might be supposed to derive from any such habit by answering ruminatively

> It's a very interesting question and I hadn't realised I did that sort of thing. I suppose I always try to write the truth and I wouldn't want to write a poem which suggested I was different from what I am ... I think that one of the great criticisms of poets of the past is that they said one thing and did another, a false relation between art and life. I always try to avoid this ...

Larkin seems to be positing here a modern ethic of poetic sincerity which is – like his '*Foreign* poetry? *No!*' – not without its own inward complexities. The problem is nicely voiced by the peculiar and even comical lucidity of the prose style used. The poet's presumably quite unironical 'I hadn't realised I did that sort of thing' has an echo of the way in which (for instance) the all-too-understanding Wittgenstein would tell intellectual opponents that he didn't understand them. Larkin's mind frequently reveals itself in both poems and critical statements as capable of considerable intellectual complexity – 'Sympathy in White Major' is not precisely the diary of a simple man. And the simplicity of the conversational style recorded in this interview makes the impression of being related to a courteous *simplesse*, its nearest parallel or indeed even source being that *imbécile-de-génie* manner with which William Empson has always used the playful infantilism of the 1920s to communicate his most difficult ideas.

If such considerations underlie Larkin's simple sentences, then it may be allowed that his criterion of 'sincerity' is not in itself a simple one, either: a 'true relation' of art and life is not an identity of the two. It is sometimes assumed, and Larkin himself occasionally writes as if he were assuming, that the two are in his work identical, and that 'sincerity' and 'truth' are one; that Larkin is a 'simple', in fact a 'clear' poet. But this is the precise assumption that can lead to finding the poems obscure: which is to say, incomprehensible because withdrawn from simple statement in a way that the given reader had not counted on. There is, in short, a continual complexity in Larkin's verse which his treatment of Symbolist images in the poems I have mentioned serves to represent, and which is not summarised with entire justice by terms like 'saying one thing and doing (or not doing) another': for Larkin's poems do not *say one thing*, whether or not he does the same thing in life. In the very funny and characteristically modest introduction Larkin added to the later (1964) edition of his early novel *Jill*, he tells how when he and his friend Kingsley Amis were undergraduates together at Oxford in the early years of the War, the Labour Club magazine, then edited by Amis, accepted one of Larkin's poems for publication, 'but a second, much less ambiguously ambiguous, was denounced by the Committee as "morbid and unhealthy"'. A fair way of describing Larkin's after-Symbolist developments would be to say that he is getting much less ambiguously ambiguous.

From *Essays in Criticism*, 30 (1980), 227–42.

## NOTES

[Barbara Everett's essay offers a highly persuasive account of Larkin's affinities with French poets such as Théophile Gautier and Stéphane Mallarmé. In demonstrating the extent to which Larkin's poetry engages with symbolism and with modernism generally, the essay is undoubtedly one of the most influential revisionary statements in Larkin criticism. Everett's brilliant analysis of 'Sympathy in White Major' claims that Larkin not only employs the techniques of symbolism but simultaneously parodies them. Similarly, her reading of 'High Windows' suggests that Larkin adopts familiar symbols, only to acknowledge their dubious value in the later twentieth century. In this respect, Larkin might be identified not simply as an *anti-modernist* but more accurately as as a *post-symbolist* or *post-modernist* writer. 'Philip Larkin: After Symbolism' concentrates on the striking innovations in *High Windows* but shows conclusively that Larkin had a knowledgeable interest in the poetry of Charles Baudelaire as far back as *The Less Deceived* (1955). The essay first appeared in *Essays in Criticism* in 1980, but was subsequently reprinted in Everett's *Poets in their Time* (London, 1986), pp. 230–44. Ed.]

1. For further evidence on this point, see 'Eliot's *Four Quartets* and French Symbolism', *English*, 29 (1980), 1–37 and 'Eliot's Marianne: *The Waste Land* and its Poetry of Europe', *Review of English Studies*, 31 (1980), 41–53.

2. Ian Hamilton, 'Four Conversations: Philip Larkin', *London Magazine*, 4: 8 (1964), 73.

# 4

# Philip Larkin: The Metonymic Muse

1930s writing was, characteristically, antimodernist, realistic, readerly and metonymic.[1] In the 1940s the pendulum of literary fashion swung back again – not fully, but to a perceptible degree – towards the pole we have designated as modernist, symbolist, writerly and metaphoric. Sooner or later the leading writers of the 1930s became disillusioned with politics, lost faith in Soviet Russia, took up religion, emigrated to America and fell silent. Christianity, in a very uncompromising, antihumanist, theologically 'high' form, became a force in literature (the later Eliot, the Charles Williams–C. S. Lewis circle, the 'Catholic novel' of Greene and Waugh). Bourgeois writers no longer felt obliged to identify with the proletariat. Bohemian, patrician, cosmopolitan attitudes and life-styles became once more acceptable in the literary world. To say that the English novel resumed experimentalism would be an overstatement; but 'fine writing' certainly returned and an interest in rendering the refinements of individual sensibility rather than collective experience. There was a revival of Henry James, and many people saw Charles Morgan as his modern successor. Fantasy, such as Upward and Isherwood had felt obliged to purge from their work, was luxuriated in by Mervyn Peake. There was great excitement at an apparent revival of verse drama, principally in the work of T. S. Eliot and Christopher Fry. Perhaps the movement of the pendulum was most evident in the field of poetry. The reputations of Eliot and Yeats triumphantly survived the attacks launched against them in

71

the 1930s, and the most enthusiastically acclaimed younger poet was Dylan Thomas, a 'metaphoric' writer if ever there was one.

In the middle of the 1950s, a new generation of writers began to exert an opposite pressure on the pendulum. They were sometimes referred to as 'The Movement' (mainly in the context of poetry) and sometimes, more journalistically, as the 'Angry Young Men' (mainly in the context of fiction and drama). Some of the key figures in these partially overlapping groups were: Kingsley Amis, Philip Larkin, John Wain, D. J. Enright, Thom Gunn, Donald Davie, Alan Sillitoe, John Osborne, Arnold Wesker. Others who shared the same general aims and assumptions as these writers, or contributed to the formation of a distinctively 1950s *écriture*, were William Cooper, C. P. Snow and his wife Pamela Hansford Johnson, Colin McInnes, Angus Wilson, John Braine, Stan Barstow, Thomas Hinde, Keith Waterhouse, David Storey and, in precept if not in practice, Iris Murdoch.[2] The 1950s writers were suspicious of, and often positively hostile to the modernist movement and certainly opposed to any further efforts at 'experimental' writing. Dylan Thomas epitomised everything they detested: verbal obscurity, metaphysical pretentiousness, self-indulgent romanticism, compulsive metaphorising were his alleged faults. They themselves aimed to communicate clearly and honestly their perceptions of the world as it was. They were empiricists, influenced by logical positivism and 'ordinary language' philosophy. The writer of the previous generation they most respected was probably George Orwell.[3] Technically, the novelists were content to use, with only slight modifications, the conventions of 1930s and Edwardian realism. Their originality was largely a matter of tone and attitude and subject matter, reflecting changes in English culture and society brought about by the convulsion of the Second World War – roughly speaking, the supersession of a bourgeois-dominated class-society by a more meritocratic and opportunistic social system. The poets dealt with ordinary prosaic experience in dry, disciplined, slightly depressive verse. In short, they were antimodernist, readerly and realistic, and belong on the metonymic side of our bi-polar scheme.

The most representative writers of this generation were Kingsley Amis and Philip Larkin (significantly they were close friends at Oxford). I have written elsewhere of Amis's work and its relation to modernist writing,[4] so I shall confine myself here to Philip Larkin. That he is an antimodernist scarcely needs demonstration. To find his own poetic voice he had to shake off the influence of

Yeats that pervades his first volume of poems, *The North Ship* (1945); and he has made no secret of his distaste for the poetics of T. S. Eliot which underpins so much verse in the modernist tradition. 'I ... have no belief in "tradition" or a common myth-kitty, or casual allusions in poems to other poems or poets', he has written; and, 'separating the man who suffers from the man who creates is all right – we separate the petrol from the engine – but the dependence of the second on the first is complete.'[5] Like Orwell, Larkin believes that the task of the writer is to communicate as accurately as he can in words experience which is initially non-verbal: poetry is 'born of the tension between what [the poet] non-verbally feels and what can be got over in common word-usage to someone who hasn't had his experience or education or travel-grant.'[6] Like most writers in the antimodernist, or realist or readerly tradition, Larkin is, in aesthetic matters, an antiformalist: 'Form holds little interest for me. Content is everything.'[7]

It would be easy enough to demonstrate abstractly that the last-quoted assertion is an impossibly self-contradictory one for a poet to make. A more interesting line of enquiry, however, is to try and define the kind of form Larkin's work actually has, in spite of his somewhat disingenuous denials. (He has claimed, characteristically, that the omission of the main verb in 'MCMXIV', which so powerfully and poignantly creates the sense of an historical moment, poised between peace and war, arrested and held for an inspection that is solemn with afterknowledge, was an 'accident'[8] – as if there could be such a thing in a good poem.) My suggestion is that we can best accomplish this task of defining the formal character of Larkin's verse by regarding him as a 'metonymic' poet.

Poetry, especially lyric poetry, is an inherently metaphoric mode, and to displace it towards the metonymic pole is (whether Larkin likes it or not) an 'experimental' literary gesture. Such poetry makes its impact by appearing daringly, even shockingly unpoetic, particularly when the accepted poetic mode is elaborately metaphoric. This was true of the early Wordsworth, and it was certainly true of Philip Larkin in his post-*North Ship* verse: nothing could have been more different from the poetry of Dylan Thomas and the other ageing members of the 'New Apocalypse'. Larkin, indeed, has many affinities with Wordsworth (in spite of having had a 'forgotten boredom' of a childhood)[9] and seems to share Wordsworth's 'spontaneous overflow' theory of poetic creation, which T. S. Eliot thought he had disposed of in 'Tradition and the Individual Talent'.

'One should ... write poetry only when one wants to and has to', Larkin has remarked; and, 'writing isn't an act of will'.[10] His poetic style is characterised by colloquialism, 'low' diction and conscious cliché:

> Coming up England by a different line
> For once, early in the cold new year,
> We stopped, and, watching men with number-plates
> Sprint down the platform to familiar gates,
> 'Why, Coventry!' I exclaimed. 'I was born here.'
> ('I Remember, I Remember', *CP*, 81)

>                                         I lie
> Where Mr Bleaney lay, and stub my fags
> On the same saucer-souvenir, and try
>
> Stuffing my ears with cotton-wool, to drown
> The jabbering set he egged her on to buy.
> I know his habits – what time he came down,
> His preference for sauce to gravy, why
>
> He kept on plugging at the four aways –
> ('Mr Bleaney', *CP*, 102)

> When I see a couple of kids
> And guess he's fucking her and she's
> Taking pills or wearing a diaphragm,
> I know this is paradise
>
> Everyone old has dreamed of all their lives –
> ('High Windows', *CP*, 165)

With Wordsworth, Larkin might claim that his 'principal object ... was to choose incidents and situations from common life, and to relate or describe them, throughout, as far as was possible in a selection of language really used by men ... tracing in them truly, though not ostentatiously, the primary laws of our nature',[11] though it is from common urban-industrial life that he usually chooses them – shops, trains, hospitals, inner-city streets and parks. The gaudy mass-produced glamour of chain store lingerie –

> Lemon, sapphire, moss-green, rose
> Bri-Nylon Baby-Dolls and Shorties

provides the occasion for a tentative, uncondescending meditation on the mystery of sexual allure:

How separate and unearthly love is,
Or women are, or what they do,
Or in our young unreal wishes
Seem to be: synthetic, new,
And natureless in ecstasies.
('The Large Cool Store', CP, 135)

The topic of death is handled in contexts where modern urban folk
face it, the ambulance and the hospital:

All know they are going to die.
Not yet, perhaps not here, but in the end,
And somewhere like this. That is what it means,
This clean-sliced cliff; a struggle to transcend
The thought of dying, for unless its powers
Outbuild cathedrals nothing contravenes
The coming dark, though crowds each evening try

With wasteful, weak, propitiatory flowers.
('The Building', CP, 192)

Larkin is a declared realist. 'Lines on a Young Lady's Photograph
Album', strategically placed at the beginning of his first important
collection, *The Less Deceived* (1955), is his 'Musée des Beaux Arts',
taking not Flemish painting but snapshots as the exemplary art
form:

But o, photography! as no art is,
Faithful and disappointing! that records
Dull days as dull, and hold-it smiles as frauds,
And will not censor blemishes
Like washing-lines, and Hall's-Distemper boards,

But shows the cat as disinclined, and shades
A chin as doubled when it is, what grace
Your candour thus confers upon her face!
How overwhelmingly persuades
That this is a real girl in a real place,
In every sense empirically true!
(CP, 71–2)

Like a realistic novelist, Larkin relies heavily on synecdochic detail
to evoke scene, character, culture and subculture. In 'At Grass', the
past glories of race horses are evoked thus:

Silks at the start: against the sky
Numbers and parasols: outside,
Squadrons of empty cars, and heat,
And littered grass: then the long cry
Hanging unhushed till it subside
To stop-press columns on the street.
                    (CP, 29)

In Hull

   domes and statues, spires and cranes cluster
Beside grain-scattered streets, barge-crowded water,
And residents from raw estates, brought down
The dead straight miles by stealing flat-faced trolleys,
Push through plate-glass swing doors to their desires –
Cheap suits, red kitchen-ware, sharp shoes, iced lollies,
Electric mixers, toasters, washers, driers –
                    ('Here', CP, 136)

After the Agricultural Show

The car park has thinned. They're loading jumps on a truck.
Back now to private addresses, gates and lamps
In high stone one-street villages, empty at dusk,
And side roads of small towns (sports finals stuck
In front doors, allotments reaching down to the railway);
                    ('Show Saturday', CP, 200)

To call Larkin a metonymic poet does not imply that he uses no metaphors – of course he does. Some of his poems are based on extended analogies – 'Next, Please', 'No Road' and 'Toads', for instance. But such poems become more rare in his later collections. All three just mentioned are in *The Less Deceived*, and 'Toads Revisited' in *The Whitsun Weddings* (1964) makes a fairly perfunctory use of the original metaphor. Many of his poems have no metaphors at all – for example, 'Myxomatosis', 'Poetry of Departures', 'Days', 'As Bad as a Mile', 'Afternoons'. And in what are perhaps his finest and most characteristic poems, the metaphors are foregrounded against a predominantly metonymic background, which is in turn foregrounded against the background of the (metaphoric) poetic tradition. 'The Whitsun Weddings' is a classic example of this technique.

That Whitsun, I was late getting away:
   Not till about
One-twenty on the sunlit Saturday
Did my three-quarters-empty train pull out,
All windows down, all cushions hot, all sense
Of being in a hurry gone. We ran
Behind the backs of houses, crossed a street
Of blinding windscreens, smelt the fish-dock; thence
The river's level drifting breadth began,
Where sky and Lincolnshire and water meet.
                   (CP, 114)

This opening stanza has a characteristically casual, colloquial tone, and the near-redundant specificity ('One-twenty', 'three-quarters-empty') of a personal anecdote, a 'true story' (compare Wordsworth's 'I've measured it from side to side, / 'Tis three feet long, and two feet wide'). The scenery is evoked by metonymic and synecdochic detail ('drifting breadth', 'blinding windscreens', etc.) as are the wedding parties that the poet observes at the stations on the way to London, seeing off bridal couples on their honeymoons:

The fathers with broad belts under their suits
And seamy foreheads; mothers loud and fat;
An uncle shouting smut; and then the perms,
The nylon gloves and jewellery-substitutes,
The lemons, mauves, and olive-ochres that

Marked off the girls unreally from the rest.
                   (CP, 115)

Apart from the unobtrusive 'seamy', there are no metaphors here: appearance, clothing, behaviour, are observed with the eye of a novelist or documentary writer and allowed to stand, untransformed by metaphor, as indices of a certain recognisable way of life. There *is* a simile in this stanza, but it is drawn from the context (railway stations) in a way that is characteristic of realistic writers using the metonymic mode:

As if out on the end of an event
   Waving goodbye
To something that survived it.
                   (CP, 115)

As the poem goes on, Larkin unobtrusively raises the pitch of rhetorical and emotional intensity – and this corresponds to the approach of the train to its destination: the journey provides the poem with its basic structure, a sequence of spatio-temporal contiguities (as in 'Here'). Some bolder figures of speech are introduced – 'a happy funeral', 'a religious wedding'; and in the penultimate stanza a striking simile which still contrives to be 'unpoetic', by collapsing the conventional pastoral distinction between nasty town and nice country:

> I thought of London spread out in the sun,
> Its postal districts packed like squares of wheat...
> (CP, 116)

It is in the last stanza that the poem suddenly, powerfully, 'takes off',[12] transcends the merely empirical, almost sociological observation of its earlier stanzas and affirms the poet's sense of sharing, vicariously, in the onward surge of life as represented by the newly wedded couples collected together in the train ('this frail travelling coincidence') and the unpredictable but fertile possibilities the future holds for them.

> We slowed again,
> And as the tightened brakes took hold, there swelled
> A sense of falling, like an arrow-shower
> Sent out of sight, somewhere becoming rain.
> (CP, 116)

This metaphor, with its mythical, magical and archaic resonances, is powerful partly because it is so different from anything else in the poem (except for 'religious wounding', and that has a tone of humorous overstatement quite absent from the last stanza).

Something similar happens in Larkin's most famous poem, 'Church Going', where the last stanza has a dignity and grandeur of diction:

> A serious house on serious earth it is,
> In whose blent air all our compulsions meet,
> Are recognised, and robed as destinies.
> (CP, 98)

which comes as a thrilling surprise after the downbeat, slightly ironic tone of the preceding stanzas, a tone established in the first stanza:

> Hatless, I take off
> My cycle-clips in awkward reverence...
> (CP, 97)

That line-and-a-half must be the most often quoted fragment of Larkin's poetry, and the way in which the homely 'cycle-clips' damps down the metaphysical overtones of 'reverence' and guarantees the trustworthy ordinariness of the poetic persona is indeed typical of Larkin. But if his poetry were limited to merely avoiding the pitfalls of poetic pretentiousness and insincerity it would not interest us for very long. Again and again he surprises us, especially in the closing lines of his poems, by his ability to transcend – or turn ironically upon – the severe restraints he seems to have placed upon authentic expression of feeling in poetry. Sometimes, as in 'The Whitsun Weddings' and 'Church Going', this is accomplished by allowing a current of metaphorical language to flow into the poem, with the effect of a river bursting through a dam. But quite as often it is done by a subtle complication of metre, line-endings and syntax. For example, the amazing conclusion to 'Mr Bleaney':

> But if he stood and watched the frigid wind
> Tousling the clouds, lay on the fusty bed
> Telling himself that this was home, and grinned,
> And shivered, without shaking off the dread
>
> That how we live measures our own nature,
> And at his age having no more to show
> Than one hired box should make him pretty sure
> He warranted no better, I don't know.
> (CP, 102–3)

Syntactically this long periodic sentence is in marked contrast to the rest of the poem, and marks a reversal in its drift: a shift from satiric spleen vented upon the external world – a Bleaney-world to which the poetic persona feels superior – to a sudden collapse of his own morale, a chilling awareness that this environment may correspond to his own inner 'nature'. This fear is expressed obliquely by a speculative attribution of the speaker's feelings to

Mr Bleaney. The diction is plain and simple (if more dignified than in the preceding stanzas) but the syntax, subordinate clauses burgeoning and negatives accumulating bewilderingly, is extremely complex and creates a sense of helplessness and entrapment. The main clause so long delayed – 'I don't know' – when it finally comes, seems to spread back dismally through the whole poem, through the whole life of the unhappy man who utters it.

Many of Larkin's most characteristic poems end, like 'Mr Bleaney', with a kind of eclipse of meaning, speculation fading out in the face of the void. At the end of 'Essential Beauty', the girl in the cigarette ad becomes a Belle Dame Sans Merci for the 'dying smokers' who

> sense
> Walking towards them through some dappled park
> As if on water that unfocused she
> No match lit up, nor drag ever brought near,
> Who now stands newly clear,
> Smiling, and recognising, and going dark.
> (CP, 144–5)

> [We] spend all our life on imprecisions,
> That when we start to die
> Have no idea why.
> ('Ignorance', CP, 107)

Death is, we can all agree, a 'nonverbal' reality, because, as Wittgenstein said, it is not an experience *in* life; and it is in dealing with death, a topic that haunts him, that Larkin achieves the paradoxical feat of expressing in words something that is beyond words:

> Life is slow dying ...

> And saying so to some
> Means nothing; others it leaves
> Nothing to be said.
> ('Nothing To Be Said',
> CP, 138)

The same theme, I take it, forms the conclusion to the title poem of Larkin's most recent collection, *High Windows*. The poet compares his generation's envy of the sexual freedom of the young in today's Permissive Society to the putative envy of older people of his own apparent freedom, in his youth, from superstitious religious fears.

And immediately
Rather than words comes the thought of high windows:
The sun-comprehending glass,
And beyond it, the deep blue air, that shows
Nothing, and is nowhere, and is endless.

(CP, 165)

From Dale Salwak (ed.), *Philip Larkin: The Man and His Work* (London, 1989), pp. 118–28.


## NOTES

[David Lodge's essay is one of the few structuralist readings of Larkin's poetry to have appeared in the past two decades. It was first published in Lodge's *The Modes of Modern Writing: Metaphor, Metonymy and the Typology of Modern Literature* (London and New York, 1977). Following the example of the Czech structuralist Roman Jakobson, Lodge distinguishes between *metaphor*, which involves the *substitution* of elements from *different* contexts ('ships ploughed the sea') and *metonymy*, which involves the *combination* of elements within the *same* context ('keels crossed the deep'). He argues further that metaphor is a strong characteristic of Romantic poetry, while metonymy is more typically associated with the realist novel. Lodge notes the scarcity of metaphor in Larkin's poetry and identifies the work of the Movement writers generally as realist and metonymic. 'At Grass', for instance, employs metonymic detail to evoke a race-day scene: 'Silks at the start: against the sky / Numbers and parasols'. Lodge also regards Larkin's poetry as essentially anti-modernist, but he agrees with the preceding three critics that there are certain moments (generated by the sudden appearance of metaphor) when the poetry transcends its own constraints. Ed.]


1. See David Lodge, *The Modes of Modern Writing: Metaphor, Metonymy and the Typology of Modern Literature* (London and New York, 1977) for a detailed explanation of these terms.

2. See Iris Murdoch's essay, 'Against Dryness', *Encounter*, 16 (1961), 16–20.

3. In his introduction to the first Movement anthology, *New Lines* (1956), Robert Conquest names Orwell as a major influence on these poets. Orwell's influence is even more evident in the fiction and criticism of the 1950s writers, especially that of John Wain.

4. David Lodge, 'The Modern, the Contemporary and the Importance of Being Amis', in *Language of Fiction* (London, 1966), pp. 243–67.

5. Quoted in David Timms, *Philip Larkin* (Edinburgh, 1973), pp. 60, 109.

6. Ibid., p. 21.

7. Ibid., p. 62.

8. Ibid., p. 112.

9. Philip Larkin, 'Coming', in *The Less Deceived* (London, 1955), p. 17.

10. Quoted in Timms, *Philip Larkin*, p. 61.

11. William Wordsworth, 'Preface' to *Lyrical Ballads* (1800). Thomas Hutchinson (ed.), *Wordsworth: Poetical Works* (Oxford, 1973), p. 734.

12. 'Larkin instructed Anthony Thwaite, then a radio producer, that the poem should be read holding a carefully sustained note until the very end, when it should "lift off the ground"', according to Timms' *Philip Larkin*, p. 120.

# 5

# Reading 'Deceptions' – A Dramatic Conversation

*GRAHAM HOLDERNESS*

**Scene**

*A seminar room in an institution of higher education. Around a circular table sit several teachers of English. Books and papers on the table in front of them. The rest of the room is filled with an audience of teachers and students. Early October; late afternoon.*

**Characters**

CLEANTH, a formalist
RAYMOND, a marxist
KATE, a feminist
COLIN, a poststructuralist
CECIL, a chair

CECIL: Well, ladies and gentlemen, welcome to the first of our staff–student seminars for this new academic year. Thank you all for coming: I know how busy you all are, but I hope your sterling efforts to support this worthy venture will not go unrewarded. We are used to hearing lectures on these occasions, but one must move with the times: and today four of our colleagues have agreed to give brief papers offering contrasting perspectives on [*glances at a paper on the table in front of him*] an interesting poem by Philip Larkin. I'm quite sure we'll have plenty of sparky and controversial ideas to keep us awake and on our toes. Cleanth, perhaps you'd like to kick off, to (as it were) get the ball rolling?

[*sleeps*]

CLEANTH: Thank you, Cecil. Let me first of all read the poem: Philip Larkin's 'Deceptions'. Written in 1950. From his collection *The Less Deceived*.

> 'Of course I was drugged, and so heavily I did not regain my consciousness till the next morning. I was horrified to discover that I had been ruined, and for some days I was inconsolable, and cried like a child to be killed or sent back to my aunt.' Mayhew, *London Labour and the London Poor*

> Even so distant, I can taste the grief,
> Bitter and sharp with stalks, he made you gulp.
> The sun's occasional print, the brisk brief
> Worry of wheels along the street outside
> Where bridal London bows the other way,
> And light, unanswerable and tall and wide,
> Forbids the scar to heal, and drives
> Shame out of hiding. All the unhurried day
> Your mind lay open like a drawer of knives.

> Slums, years, have buried you. I would not dare
> Console you if I could. What can be said,
> Except that suffering is exact, but where
> Desire takes charge, readings will grow erratic?
> For you would hardly care
> That you were less deceived, out on that bed,
> Than he was, stumbling up the breathless stair
> To burst into fulfilment's desolate attic.
>                    (*20 February 1950, CP*, 32)

I'm sure my colleagues will be proposing that this poem should be treated as a statement *about* something – about illusions, about exploitation, about rape, about the act of writing. Of course these things are real experiences, or at least real beliefs, sincerely held. But if we try to explain a poem in terms of ideas and attitudes that lie outside it, we are likely to find the poem itself collapsing into a discussion about philosophy, or politics, or history. Poetry uses language in a different way from other forms of communication – prose, or historical documentation, or ordinary speech – and what criticism should always seek to define is the unique, individual, irreplaceable quality of that poetic language. To do that we need to approach the poem without preconceptions, without prior judgements, without passionate convictions: approach it with an open and ready sensitivity to the particular qualities of its creative language.

So I'd like to start off by proposing that the poem isn't *about* anything at all. But, you will say, of course the poem is about something: it's about a young girl who was drugged and raped in Victorian London, and whose story was recounted in Henry Mayhew's book about the London poor. Her experience is indeed the object of the poem's address: but she herself is explicitly defined as long dead and buried, her existence obliterated by time and historical change – 'Slums, years, have buried you'. There is no possibility of communication or emotional exchange between the poet and his subject: 'I would not dare / Console you if I could'. The woman herself, and her experience, are gone, vanished: they survive only in the bare prose of Mayhew's sociological documentation. What Larkin has done is to take that vanished experience of suffering, which in itself can hardly be regarded as 'real' to us, and to give it a kind of poetic vitality that enables the woman's story to live, and resurrects her as a fully concrete dramatic presence. The poem makes something real – an achieved work of art – out of material that could not possibly, expressed in any other form, engage our emotional responses or our critical attention to anything like the same degree. But we can only appreciate that reality of art by appreciating the poem 'as in itself it really is'.

As in every successful poem (though I will be arguing that this poem is not wholly successful) there are here internal conflicts and tensions between apparently contradictory statements. The poet's acknowledgement that the woman is a mere creature of history, remote from his sympathy and consolation, is challenged by the opposing impulse to enter fully into her dramatic situation: 'Even so distant, I can taste the grief'. The poet imagines he can recreate the sensations of this remote event, and share them as if they were his own sensations: he can 'taste' the 'bitterness' that belonged both to the narcotic used to drug her, and to the shameful and humiliating sexual assault inflicted on her. The sonorous impact of 'gulp' conveys exactly that sensation of swallowing against resistance – the drugged liquid forced down her throat, the 'bitter' acridity of a rapist's semen.

The dramatisation of mood and atmosphere then proceeds by a technique of saturating surrounding physical objects with the significance of her experience: as she lies in the sordid room 'all the unhurried day', 'inconsolable', fleeting glimpses of sunlight 'print' themselves onto her vision, as the rape has 'printed' an indelible mark onto her mind and body; the noise of wheels from the street outside sounds like her own anxiety – 'brisk worry of wheels'. The images of wounding, of light, and the concrete precision of 'your mind lay open / Like a drawer of knives' all work together to convey the sensations of something vulnerable that has been forced open, dragged out into the hard light, left exposed as a self-tormenting consciousness filled with sharp humiliation, unable to close.

The second stanza then immediately proceeds to distance the experience so vividly dramatised and recreated. And yet the poet's retreat into inarticulacy ('What can be said?') is not a withdrawal from any reality of experience, but from the concrete presence of what he has himself created, a vivid realisation of experience in poetic language. The second half of the poem is a denial of the first, a betrayal of the achieved reality of art, a failure of the poetic imag- ination. Everything that was in the first half realised in precise images, is here translated into lifeless abstractions: 'your mind lay open like a drawer of knives' becomes 'suffering'; the imagery of wounding and violation and 'bitterness' is translated, strangely, into the abstraction 'desire'; where previously the poet was concerned to dramatise the exactness of an imagined experience, here he takes refuge in the detached activity of 'reading'. Larkin's attempt to dramatise the man's experience fails by comparison with the achieved realisation of the woman's: and the attempt again to link emotion with physical surroundings – 'breathless stair', 'desolate attic' – seems merely mechanical in comparison.

Ultimately the poem is an imaginative failure, precisely because Larkin was not content to let the poetic drama, the enacted realis- ation of a wholly imaginary experience, speak for itself. The impulse to tamper, to explain, to reflect and philosophise, to inter- vene with some deliberate, willed intention, finally destroys the poem. A poem should not *mean*, but *be*; and what damages this poem is the poet's reluctance to let it 'be', his determination to make it 'mean' something other than itself.

RAYMOND: Well I must say I envy Cleanth's serene detachment from reality. Like Henry James, he has a mind so fine that no idea could ever violate it. Unfortunately for his method, this poem is very much *about* something; it addresses people and situations we should have no difficulty in recognising as 'real'; it is rooted in that 'history' of which we are all (apart from Cleanth) 'mere creatures'; and it cer- tainly contains a deliberate 'intention', which is that of forcing the reader to confront and become aware of unpalatable social realities.

The quotation from Henry Mayhew is there precisely to locate this dramatic situation in a real history, that of the London proletariat in the mid-nineteenth century. The social world Mayhew documented is that of Dickens: a world of extreme contrasts between wealth and poverty; a world of deprivation and undeserved suffering; a world of cruelty and exploitation. Cleanth talks about these social realities as 'vanished', 'buried' in the past. Such detachment is impossible for those of us who believe that poverty and exploitation have not by any means been abolished. It is perhaps because we are aware of these things as continuing realities – still here and now in our own cities, let alone in the impoverished and exploited Third World – that we are more willing to acknowledge their reality in the past.

During the historical period dramatised in the poem, simply to speak or write about the sufferings of the oppressed underclass, even if it was only in the 'bare prose' of a 'sociological documentation', a government report or census survey, was by itself a kind of commitment or intervention, since the ruling class of the time was so determined to deny the existence of poverty and deprivation. But writers like Mayhew and Dickens (and, indeed, Engels in *The Condition of the Working Class in 1844*) made much more of their sociological material than mere documentary record, because they were directly concerned, whether politically or morally, with the actual concrete experience of the people who suffered. Further, even beyond this attitude of sympathetic involvement in the lives of the poor – so unlike Cleanth's pseudo-objectivity – these writers were capable of letting the poor speak for themselves, of recording (albeit in an edited form) the voices of the oppressed. So the *dramatic* and *imaginative* aspects of the poem are not achieved by a systematic denial of historical and social reality: they are on the contrary a necessary dimension of history, when history is understood as a narrative of human exploitation and resistance.

One aspect of the poem that hasn't been mentioned at all is the fact that it is about illusions: the very title, 'Deceptions' draws attention to the centrality of this key idea. There are in the poem two kinds of deception. First there is the relatively simple trick practised on the girl by her assailant – she is 'deceived', like the heroine of a Victorian melodrama, by the unscrupulous cunning of a man; she is drugged into unconsciousness so she doesn't know what's happening to her. The story of her 'ruin' is completed by the corollary of that oblivion, a dreadful *dis*illusionment symbolised by that image of the mind as an open drawer full of knives. But there is also another level of deception, that experienced by the man: and his illusions are in some ways larger and deeper than those inflicted on the girl. The poem explicitly states that she is 'less deceived' than he (the phrase was important enough for Larkin to use it as the title of the volume in which the poem was published), since while she, although the injured party, has illusion thrust upon her, his deception is constitutive of his very experience. This is the point where Larkin takes the poem beyond the simple framework of a conventional melodramatic story of the 'ruined maid' variety: he draws attention to the experience of the man also, and observes that the inevitable disillusionment of his desire is in some ways harder to bear than the injury sustained by the girl. His 'breathless' passion of 'desire' ends in the desolation of an empty experience in a sordid attic. Clearly 'deception' has a much larger and wider significance in the social world dramatised by the poem, than the particular betrayal of trust encountered by an innocent rape victim.

This is the true importance of the poem, which consists in Larkin's recognition that every member of that oppressed Victorian underclass – not merely its most obvious casualties – was a victim of deception, blinded by ideological illusions to the real conditions of their lives. The man who exploits the woman is himself in turn exploited by a more powerful agency. His 'desire' begins as the most basic human need – for love, for recognition, for an end to isolation. But in these conditions of alienation, where men and women cannot know either themselves or one another, can only see and use one another as objects, this 'desire' is deflected, distorted and turned to cruelty and appetitive lust. 'Deception' is thus a general condition, typical of the universal social context dramatised in this stereotypical situation of exploitation.

Cleanth has analysed those images which work to particularise, to realise the girl's wounded consciousness; but there are other images that operate to suggest this general social condition. There is a society outside the limits of that 'desolate attic', an outside world that penetrates the girl's isolation in two forms: as the sounds and traces of the city, imagined as a (virgin) 'bride' turning away from her plight in disgust; and as the irresistible power of daylight, dramatised as in some way like the man who has mastered and violated her – 'unanswerable and tall and wide'. Women will now turn away from her, men will violate her in other ways, by forcing a knowledge of her crime into the open, refusing with their harsh morality to permit any healing of her 'scar'. The cruelty and indifference of Victorian England is wider and deeper than this particular situation, although the particular situation is part of that general social condition. It is in that historical grasp of a general condition that the poem's true value rests.

KATE: We've heard a great deal about the suffering of women: but every word we've heard so far has been spoken by a man. And when we look back at the poem, we find that identical pattern, simply repeated over and over again. The poem is about a woman who has suffered at the hands of a man. But her story is told first of all by a man, Henry Mayhew: that quotation from *London Labour and the London Poor* is not the authentic voice of a working-class woman, but her voice mediated by the language of a middle-class observer – surely she didn't actually say 'I never regained my consciousness'? Her voice, the only authentic testimony to the exact quality of her suffering, is mediated to us first by Mayhew, and then by another male writer, Philip Larkin. By the time it has been further processed through the masculine language of the previous speakers, all trace of genuine femininity has completely disappeared. Clearly the imperative task facing us when we read a poem like this, is that of recovering, by means of a feminist rereading, the female experience that has been so densely encoded into varying registers of masculine discourse.

Raymond has insisted that we shouldn't read the poem independently of our contemporary convictions and ideas. It's all the more surprising to me that he doesn't consider our contemporary view of rape to be an important interpretative context. Yet I am quite sure no woman could read a poem about sexual enforcement without our modern perspective on rape colouring her poetic responses. The essential point is that Larkin in 1950 was apparently able to consider rape as a matter of 'desire': and to use that assumption as the basis for a sympathetic representation of the rapist. We don't any longer regard rape as a 'crime of passion': we view it as a crime of violence, more akin to beating or killing a woman than to an act of sexual love. That distinction introduces a fundamental ideological difference into our reading of this poem.

Larkin's is a masculine view of rape: one which regards the crime as an aberration of natural sexual passion, an excess of desire; one which looks sympathetically on the male perpetrator as a victim, either of his own desires or of woman's provocation. This is the widely held belief that leads judges to excuse rapists and to blame their victims, thus exculpating the guilty and making the innocent suffer over again. Now it is not part of Larkin's treatment to project the guilt onto the woman: on the contrary, his approach to her is sympathetic, consolatory. But it is part of his treatment to excuse the violator, by casting him as equally a victim. Unable to console the woman (for the past is another country, and besides, the wench is dead) the poet prefers to exculpate the man.

Reading the poem from a modern perspective, we have to insist that 'desire' is a mistaken explanation of why men ravish women. Rape is about violence and power. Certainly the suffering of the female victim is acknowledged in the poem, her pain conveyed by an 'exactness' of imagery and detailed description. But then she is betrayed over again by the poet, who introduces the fallacious category of 'desire', and insists that this factor makes any simple judgement of the situation impossible.

Consider that phrase 'where desire takes charge'. No doubt Larkin intended to objectify 'desire' into a universal imperative, a biological urge powerful enough to hold the man as well as the woman in its thrall. But the word 'charge' is part of a vocabulary of masculine authority: it has hierarchical ('in charge') and military associations that place it firmly within the discourse of masculine power. So the 'desire' that takes power here is a construction of the male imagination: woman is its abject victim. What makes an accurate 'reading' of this situation impossible, is not the helplessness of men and women in the throes of desire, but the contradictoriness and instability of masculine authority. But that instability becomes visible only when we reread the poem from a feminist perspective: it was quite invisible to Philip Larkin. The real 'deception' constructed by this poem – and ratified here, again and again, by one male speaker after another – is that attempt to shift the responsibility for this fundamental masculine crime onto some abstract power beyond actual men and women. Such a projection of guilt beyond the living criminal can only serve to blur the real power-relations – and to blur the real structure of moral responsibility – between men and women in this, or any other, society.

COLIN: I agree with certain details of analysis made by each of my colleagues: but I would take issue with them all on one fundamental point. It seems to me that the poem is certainly 'about' something, but like Cleanth I find no need to hypothesise its relation to things outside itself. What the poem is about is language. In other words, it is a critical and self-reflexive interrogation of the medium of its own existence: it is 'about' nothing more or less than itself. That does not mean, however, that the poem is some kind of purely autonomous aesthetic object: being about language, it is also about 'reality' and 'ideology' and 'experience'. But these things are all contained within language, they do not lie outside it. What distinguishes 'literary' language from other forms of linguistic communication is this capacity to inspect itself, to reveal and comment on the mechanisms of its own construction. In this way poetic language can be used to demonstrate how everything we call 'reality' is actually made, constructed in language. We know the world through language: there is nothing beyond texts.

Raymond, predictably, has talked about the poem's title 'Deceptions' as a representation of Victorian ideology – it only surprises me that he resisted the temptation to link the drug in the poem with Marx's phrase about 'the opium of the masses'. But surely the title is an ironic reflection on the poem itself, and on what it is trying to do. The poet is admitting that he is deceiving himself by pretending that he can enter into the experience of a historical character, or indeed into anyone else's experience. Cleanth is quite right to insist that the first part of the poem, which Raymond and Kate both want to see as a *representation* of 'real experience', is in fact purely an imagined, constructed version of reality made by a male poet in 1950, and bearing no relation at all to the world as it may have been known to a Victorian child prostitute. But he is quite wrong to attribute another category of 'reality' to that piece of descriptive writing. It is pure fiction: and if there is any direct address to 'reality', it is to be found in the second half of the poem.

I think the poem is also technically more complex than anyone else has admitted. There are really four separate narratives within its structure. First there is the woman's own story, as she told it herself, and as it can be glimpsed through Mayhew's textualisation of her actual words. So one might say that the phrase 'I ... cried like a child to be killed' probably belonged to her own linguistic register: there we can hear her voice. Then secondly there is Mayhew's narrative, which incorporates the woman's own language into a discourse of Victorian bourgeois-liberal reformism: however sympathetic and charitable his intentions, Mayhew could not help editing and sanitising her language to convert her into the kind of 'case' with which his readers would have no difficulty in sympathising. Thirdly, there is Philip Larkin's attempt to represent the woman's experience: that first part of the poem, which works in the manner of an interior monologue (i.e. this is exactly how the woman felt), but also partly draws attention to the presence of the poet-observer, so that we are never unaware of the extent to which he is putting thoughts into her head – '*I* can taste the grief'; '*your* mind lay open'. It is that combination of references – backwards and outwards towards a character of history, and inwards towards the act of writing itself – that for me makes this poem a self-reflexive fiction. It never pretends to be anything other than a poet in 1950, using a Victorian sociological document to tell a story about Victorian life.

Or rather a series of stories: for now we come to our fourth narrative, that which takes place in the second half of the poem, and which is for me the most important aspect of the whole poem. It is here that the poet recognises that the reality of experience he has been pursuing is simply not there: just as the woman's existence has been obliterated, so the effort to capture a reality beyond language is doomed to failure. The poet has been trying to fix the 'exact' quality of the woman's suffering: but he is of course left with his own linguistic construction. That construction can have no 'objectivity', since it can articulate nothing more than the poet's relationship with language. Suffering itself may be 'exact'; but any attempt to describe, or interpret, or evaluate suffering is a matter of 'reading'. Or rather, as Larkin says, 'readings' in the plural: for once we acknowledge this plurality of the literary text, there are many different ways of interpreting the signs organised by the text, just as there are many different ways of narrating the woman's story, or of interpreting those narratives once they have been composed.

It is precisely because the poem so openly demonstrates its own plurality, and is so insistent in acknowledging that there is nothing beyond language, that it is of interest to us today ...

CECIL: [*waking with a start*] ... and that seems an appropriate moment at which to close. I'm sure you'll all join me in thanking our speakers for their presentations; and I'm sure you'll all agree that they've given us much food for thought. Whether or not we agree with their respective positions, there is something enlightening in each: and I'm sure we can say that we will leave here just a little 'less deceived' than we were when we came in.

*Polite, embarrassed laughter. A few whispered remarks, inaudible. Shuffling of papers. Scraping of chairs. People begin to file out.*

**Blackout**

From *Critical Survey*, 1: 2 (1989), 122–9.

## NOTES

[Graham Holderness presents his essay as a mock seminar-style discussion among critics of different theoretical persuasions. The 'conversation' about 'Deceptions' nevertheless serves a serious purpose in showing how Larkin's poetry is amenable to a variety of critical perspectives. Cleanth, in the conventional mode of 'new criticism' or 'practical criticism', is largely concerned with the extent to which mood, atmosphere and imagery 'enact' a particular experience. Raymond, a Marxist, suggests that the poem's true value lies in its historical grasp of a general social condition, while Kate's feminist approach is concerned with the way in which rape is perceived and interpreted within the poem. Colin argues from a poststructuralist perspective that the poem can only ever be about itself, since the attempt to capture a reality beyond language is doomed to failure. The great value of this essay is that it entertains the possibility of critical pluralism (combining the methods and insights of a variety of theoretical approaches), while at the same time recognising the difficulty of reconciling some fundamentally opposed ideas and assumptions. The Marxist critique attributed to Raymond should be read alongside a rather different Marxist analysis proposed by John Goode in 'A Reading of "Deceptions"' (see *Philip Larkin 1922–1985: A Tribute*, ed. George Hartley [London, 1988], pp. 126–34). Ed.]

# 6

# 'Get Out As Early As You Can': Larkin's Sexual Politics

*STEVE CLARK*

One scarcely thinks of sex in relation to the work of Philip Larkin; or, to qualify a little, only in terms of jaundiced disparagement, a fertile source of negation. The erotic Larkin would appear to be pretty meagre fare, in his own phrase from 'Spring', an 'indigestible sterility' (*CP*, 39). Such an emphasis would seem unlikely to displace the more familiar image of Larkin as wry commentator on the 'lowered sights and patiently diminished expectations' of contemporary Britain.[1] But the fact that the major English poet of the post-war period (and even the recent spate of iconoclastic polemic implicitly concedes this centrality) appears to be an uncompromising advocate of male celibacy should at the very least give pause for thought. The greater availability of biographical material has revealed personal entanglements of some complexity. Nevertheless this does not alter the cumulative impact of his literary self-presentation. His verse immediately conjures up an image of sour and wizened bachelorhood – 'One of those old-type *natural* fouled-up guys', as Jake Balokowsky puts it (*CP*, 170) – and its anti-paternity motif has often been noted. Far from being a minor aberration, this stance is integral to the characteristic persona of his poetry: the excluded onlooker, slightly wistful, yet nevertheless resolute in his self-conserving detachment. This point of vantage is well exemplified in 'Reasons for Attendance', where

94

the narrator is momentarily drawn 'to the lighted glass / To watch the dancers':

> sensing the smoke and sweat,
> The wonderful feel of girls. Why be out here?
> But then, why be in there? Sex, yes, but what
> Is sex?
>
> (CP, 80)

The question seems to be implicitly answered by the rhyme, 'what / Is sex' / 'sweat', but this cannot quite stifle the appreciative 'wonderful feel of girls'. (The phrase is typical of the unobtrusive yet explicit quality of Larkin's sexual vocabulary, with the lascivious suggestiveness of a 'full feel' followed by the further specificity of 'in there'.) The balance is tilted, however, by the 'individual sound' of the trumpet that 'insists I too am individual':

> Therefore I stay outside,
> Believing this; and they maul to and fro,
> Believing that; and both are satisfied,
> If no one has misjudged himself. Or lied.
>
> (CP, 80)

The emphasis on the insight gained through 'staying outside' recurs throughout Larkin's verse (as, indeed, does the uncomfortably equivocal relation between 'satisfied' and 'lied'). This can be linked to what I would venture to call the epistemological Larkin, whose unsparing meditation on ageing, death, 'endless extinction' aspires to a kind of agnostic sainthood, to 'importantly live / Part invalid, part baby, and part saint' ('Waiting for breakfast, while she brushed her hair' [CP, 20]). One cannot fear a thing one cannot know, and his poetry of mortality seeks to produce tangible cognitive equivalents to fill this gap. It stages a continual drama in which awareness of continual erosion ('Life is slow dying' [CP, 138]) is countered by strategies of self-withholding – a refusal to expend, a kind of sustenance through habit, routine, and confinement. 'I *don't* want to take a girl out and spend *circa* 5 pounds when I can toss off in five minutes, free, and have the rest of the evening to myself.'[2]

This aloofness inevitably comes into conflict with the demands of sexuality for a breaking down of the monadic self through contact with another being: 'saying love, but meaning interference' ('He

Hears that his Beloved has become Engaged' [*CP*, 66]; see also 'Marriages' and 'Love'). Even a wedding-day, however, can be enlisted as testimony to our fundamental solitude: 'Church Going' speaks of 'marriage', along with 'birth, / And death', as 'what since is found / Only in separation' (*CP*, 98). Similarly, the disquieting effect of the famous phrase from 'Talking in Bed', the 'unique distance from isolation', comes from the utter lack of enthusiasm with which this intimacy is regarded: it is presented in terms of intrusion, unwanted obligation, a 'distance' from the necessary privacy and preferred autonomy of 'isolation' (*CP*, 129). Larkin responds to this temptation (or threat) through offering a cool, almost laconic, critique of the adequacy of the representations presumed to be the correlative of desire. The characteristic movement of his poetry involves freezing an image, detaching it, contemplating it, in a way that reduces its circumstantial narrative to selective emblems. The erotic Larkin is obsessed not so much with loss as with discrepancy: 'the enormous disparity between his imagination and what actually happened.'[3] Here the Yeatsian heritage is crucial. The standard by which the contingent manifestations of desire prove insufficient is that of the ideal, 'eternal requirings' that are checked and qualified but never wholly rebuffed ('The Dedicated' [*CP*, 10]. I think there is far less 'settling for' in Larkin than Donald Davie and others would have us believe: the vision of 'such order, such destiny' that Katherine Lind experiences at the close of *A Girl in Winter* is achieved only through the arduous purging of delusion – 'Against this knowledge, the heart, the will, and all that made for *protest* could at last sleep'.[4]

So, to summarise. The sexual politics of Larkin's verse can be seen as one of principled and unillusioned abstention. This is most immediately apparent in his meditations on paternity, but perhaps its most interesting developments concern the socially sanctioned image. It is striking how many of his poems start with representations of women in posters, magazines, photographs, and how his own memories take on a similarly estranged quality, a succession of frames rather than a fluid continuum. Sexuality is never the source of personal authenticity in Larkin. His verse displays a sophisticated semiotic conception of passion as constituted by images that have already been consumed and sullied. This helps to explain how what may initially seem a morbid singularity comes to assume a culturally representative status. Whereas Eliot's subjective idealism sought to dissolve the world into a system of private significations, Larkin has no wish to protect some privileged private space away from the public realm: he retains a quasi-Augustan faith in the accessibility of common experience. The price of this social consolation, however, is the reduction of desire to no more than 'Sharp sensual truisms' ('The Dance' [CP, 156]): in Jill, John Kemp experiences a 'horrible embarrassment' that 'shocked him deeply', when he realises 'that what he had imagined to be his most secret feeling was almost cynically common'.[5] In 'Annus Mirabilis', 'Sexual intercourse began / In nineteen sixty-three' in the sense of being identified with a new libertarian and consumerist ethic, which the poem defines in relation to a best-selling paperback ('Chatterley') and record ('the Beatles' first LP'), both of which are seen as contributing to an oppressive homogenisation of desire – 'Everyone felt the same' (CP, 167). As 'Money' puts it, 'I am all you never had of goods and sex. / You could get them still by writing a few cheques' (CP, 198). Dignity and freedom can only be found in simultaneous acknowledgement of the socially constructed nature of desire, and voluntary estrangement from the continued barter and recirculation of 'the exchange of love' ('Ambulances' [CP, 132]).

This aspect, I think, tends to be overlooked because of the undue emphasis on those great sombre orations, 'The Old Fools', 'The Building', and 'Aubade', as the necessary destination of Larkin's verse. It is important to realise that the preoccupation with imminent death only becomes the dominant strain in his late verse, and that a tendency to relatively simplistic polarities is introduced along with it. In this essay, I shall first examine the treatment of paternity in his final collection, High Windows, and elsewhere; second, look at 'Dry-Point' and 'Wild Oats', and relate them to Larkin's early debt to Yeats in The North Ship; and then finally go on to discuss his mature handling of the iconography of desire.

## I

In Larkin's later verse, there is an absence of participation in the sexual problematic. There is a shift from the children that might have been sired to the unedifying spectacle of other people's offspring: instead of the lingering attraction of choosing to 'erect a crop', a raucous contempt for 'putrid / Infancy' ('I am washed upon a rock' [CP, 23]; 'On Being Twenty-six' [CP, 25]). To give a few further comments from Required Writings: 'children are very horrible, aren't they? Selfish, noisy, cruel, vulgar little brutes'; 'it was that verse about becoming as a little child again that caused the first sharp waning of my Christian sympathies'; 'children themselves have been devalued: we know them for the little beasts they are.'[6] This is well demonstrated in the absolute division between young and old set out in 'High Windows':

> When I see a couple of kids
> And guess he's fucking her and she's
> Taking pills or wearing a diaphragm,
> I know this is paradise
>
> Everyone old has dreamed of all their lives –
> Bonds and gestures pushed to one side
> Like an outdated combine harvester,
> And everyone young going down the long slide
>
> To happiness, endlessly ...
>
> (CP, 165)

This is one of Larkin's most famous pieces, and is usually taken as one of his most representative. To point out some typical felicities: the arresting obscenities, or what he called in Anthony Powell the 'vernacular *oratio recta*' (RW, 222); the briskly demotic tone that can simultaneously contain a poignant formal cadence (if the stress is put on 'kids', 'couple' is simply an off-handed way of saying one or two; if on 'couple' itself, the sense shifts to bonded or wedded pair); the metrical nicety, pointed out by Barbara Everett,[7] of the rhythmic linking of 'fucking her', 'diaphragm', and 'paradise'; the sly rhyming (for example, 'she's' and 'paradise'); and the imagery, which can both be curiously abstract and elusive (the 'long slide' of moral decline, sexual penetration, and children's playground), and boldly particular (the forlorn and cumbersome 'combine harvester'). As with much of the later verse, this starts out looking like a poem about sex, and becomes a poem about religion. The 'paradise' without 'Bonds and gestures' takes on an explicitly eschatological dimension in the final epiphany of 'the thought of high windows':

> The sun-comprehending glass,
> And beyond it, the deep blue air, that shows
> Nothing, and is nowhere, and is endless.
>
> (CP, 165)

To be 'sun-comprehending' is also to be uncomprehending in any recognisably human sense; and this state of blankness and absence is valorised as a kind of 'solving emptiness' ('Ambulances' [*CP*, 132]). I think the poem is vulnerable to the charge that it uses a churlish and ungenerous presentation of 'everyone young' to support a regression into an ecstatic nullity. On a basic level the argument simply will not hold: even if the pursuit of happiness through sexuality is squalid and misguided, that doesn't render religious consolation any the less 'outdated'. And compared to 'Church Going', this is poor stuff, so much less humanised in its 'devaluing dichotomies' ('On Being Twenty-six' [*CP*, 25]).

So I would dissent from the tendency to regard the symbolist leanings of Larkin's final volume as necessarily a laudable enlargement of his work. The negative critique, however, holds good; and its impact is further developed in 'This Be The Verse', which might be seen as the retort of the 'kids' to their elders:

> They fuck you up, your mum and dad.
>    They may not mean to, but they do.
> They fill you with the faults they had
>    And add some extra, just for you.
>
> But they were fucked up in their turn
>    By fools in old-style hats and coats,
> Who half the time were soppy-stern
>    And half at one another's throats.
>
> Man hands on misery to man.
>    It deepens like a coastal shelf.
> Get out as early as you can,
>    And don't have any kids yourself.
>           (*CP*, 180)

This is a poem about origins – 'fucked up' takes on the sense of knocked up, fortuitously concocted, a view of conception as mechanical, quantitative, and essentially meaningless continued in 'fill' and 'add' – but also about revenge, about injuries inflicted and compulsively repeated. 'Mum and dad' are subsumed into an anonymous 'they', the family scene, the collective destiny: there's an additional obscenity of molestation implied in the phrasing 'they fuck you up your ... they were fucked up in their ...'. This psychoanalytic slant is taken up in the latent pun on 'faults' and 'thoughts', and the second stanza becomes a comic depiction of parental sexuality, 'soppy-stern' before the children yet in private 'at one another's throats', voraciously, erotically. There's a passing intimation of fully-clothed marital relations, and one should not forget that in *The Interpretation of Dreams*, Freud equates hat with the male genitals and putting on a coat with wearing a contraceptive.[8]

'Man hands on misery to man': the final stanza becomes a specifically masculine homiletic on the nature of paternity, bequeathing, 'handing on'. What is the 'it' that 'deepens like a coastal shelf'? Most obviously 'misery', but the pronoun also seems in opposition to 'man ... to man'; the 'deepening' suggests both a gradual aggregation and a steep downward plunge, out of sight, unknowable, somehow vulval. 'Get out as early as you can': out of what? Out of the womb, of the woman, of the whole cycle of procreation, with its profligate expenditure of self and semen. Behind all these lies the insistent presence of death. On one level this simply reiterates the old truism of the moment of siring being a moment of transference, of the emergence of another being that will, to adapt the lines from 'Afternoons', 'push you to the side of your own life' (*CP*, 121). 'Don't have any kids yourself' because they represent an acknowledgement of loss, displacement, and mortality: 'Unsheath / The life you carry and die' ('At the chiming of light upon sleep' [*CP*, 14]); and will undoubtedly direct the sentiments of the narrator towards you. But there's also a positive force to this iconoclasm, a breaking with the overriding impulse of biological determinism, the necessity to reproduce: Larkin introduces the possibility of a standing back, a 'stuff the species' attitude which repudiates the encroachment of 'coarsened fertility' upon the individual (*CP*, 14). (Compare Hardy's 'I said to Love': 'Man's race shall perish, threatenest thou, / Without thy kindling coupling-vow? ... / We fear not such a threat from thee; / We are too old in apathy!') It may be the case that 'No one can tear your thread out of himself. / No one can tie you down or set you free' ('Oils' [*CP*, 36]), but under scrutiny 'Like a fuse an impulse busily disintegrates / Right back to its roots' ('Sinking like sediment through the day' [*CP*, 27]).

*High Windows* tends to present this disengagement as sustainable in absolute terms: Larkin's earlier verse, however, explores the paradoxes of involvement in desire more subtly and poignantly. *The Whitsun Weddings*, in particular, gives a vivid and somehow appalling evocation of socially constructed and responsible masculinity, perhaps best exemplified in 'Self's the Man':

Oh, no one can deny
That Arnold is less selfish than I.
He married a woman to stop her getting away
Now she's there all day,

And the money he gets for wasting his life on work
She takes as her perk
To pay for the kiddies' clobber and the drier
And the electric fire,

And when he finishes supper
Planning to have a read at the evening paper
It's *Put a screw in this wall* –
He has no time at all,

With the nippers to wheel round the houses
And the hall to paint in his old trousers
And that letter to her mother
Saying *Won't you come for the summer.*

(CP, 117)

Though the typical motifs of 'having no time' and 'wasting his life' are present, the chief recoil appears to be from the passive acceptance of culturally sanctioned duty encapsulated in 'The Life with a Hole in it' by 'that spectacled school teaching sod / (Six kids, and the wife in pod ...)' (CP, 202). Larkin gives a dramatisation of unparalleled eloquence of hostility towards obligation from a masculine view point: 'the quarrel between the necessity & beauty of being united with a woman one loves, & the necessity of not being entangled or bullied or victimised or patronised, or any of the other concomitants of love & marriage'.[9] The Freudian insights into the necessary burden of civilisation, the renunciation of instinctual satisfaction, are acted out in an inglorious suburban context. He praises Ogden Nash's 'let-down rhymes and wait-for-it metrics' as

> perfect stylistic equivalents for the missing chairs and slow burns of which civilised masculine living is compounded: waiting for women, putting up with children, social boredom and humiliation, having to work, the agenbite of inwit ... He is in fact in line with those humorists who make you laugh at things not because they are funny but because laughing at them makes them easier to bear.
>
> (RW, 135)

While there's a complete absence of pity towards Arnold ('He was just out for his own ends'; 'If it was such a mistake / He still did it for his own sake', the voice of the narrator is tinny, bereft of the social identity imposed on Arnold by his mundane routine. ('To the Sea' at least acknowledges the possibility that 'It may be that through habit these do best' [*CP*, 173].) The poem finely balances two equally un-appealing options: a masculine self either wholly identified with the onerous chores of man-about-the-house, or preserved by a peevish astringency towards this collective gender identity.

There is a reversal of power: the pursuer becomes captive. The home, as usual in Larkin, is a female domain: one thinks of Mr Bleaney at those curious lodgings, 'the Bodies', one of a succes-sion of interchangeable tenants at the beck and call of an anonymous and autocratic landlady (*CP*, 102); or Jake Balokowsky, obliged to carry through the drudgery of his research because of the need to support Myra and the kids (*CP*, 170). The state of being homeless is also partly the state of being loveless as the title 'Places, Loved Ones' (*CP*, 99) suggests, but home involves ownership, long-term obliga-tion, an abandonment of all claims to the 'unfenced existence' so hauntingly evoked in 'Here' (*CP*, 137). The relative merits of the two positions are examined in 'Dockery and Son' (the title recalls *Dombey and Son*, the family firm and practical realities of inheri-tance). Journeying back from his old Oxford college, the narrator ex-periences a dynastic epiphany through the vision of 'ranged / Joining and parting lines' presided over by a 'strong / Unhindered moon':

> To have no son, no wife,
> No house or land still seemed quite natural.
> Only a numbness registered the shock
> Of finding out how much had gone of life,
> How widely from the others.
> (*CP*, 152)

To be without a son is immediately equated with the absence of property; the narrator has 'registered' neither birth certificates nor title deeds. There is a defiant appropriation of 'natural' to the state of being unsonned, unlanded. The 'shock' comes in realising the depletion of the quantity of 'life', a usage hovering between time-on-earth, life-span, and physical potency. This second sense is taken up in Dockery's ability to 'take stock' and 'be capable of', and his conviction that

> he should be added to!
> Why did he think adding meant increase?

To me it was dilution.

(*CP*, 153)

Larkin is drawing on a venerable tradition here, dating back to Aristotle, of semen expenditure as permanent loss or 'dilution'. One notices how patrilineal the poem is: the issue of reproduction is discussed in terms of father and son, with the role of wife and mother entirely elided. The poem begins in the wholly masculine environment of a single-sex Oxford college (and behind that, military service, and the landscape of heavy industry, 'fumes / And furnace-glares'; the question why there is no woman in the narrator's life simply does not arise. Instead the final meditation centres on the origin not of sons but of 'innate assumptions':

Suddenly they harden into all we've got
And how we got it;

(*CP*, 153)

The use of 'got' recalls the earlier 'did he get this son / At nineteen, twenty'; a typical combination of the colloquial and the Biblical. There is also a double play on 'harden' as both tumescence (hence transient, and also embarrassing in its 'suddenness') and the setting of a mould, permanent and enclosing. These premises 'warp tight-shut, like doors' (recalling the earlier 'locked' college-room:

looked back on, they rear
Like sand-clouds, thick and close, embodying
For Dockery a son, for me nothing,
Nothing with all a son's harsh patronage.

(*CP*, 153)

The parental terms, 'rear' and 'embodying', are set against the atomistic 'sand-clouds'. The balance at first seems one-sided in Dockery's favour, 'nothing' versus 'son', but this is wrenched back by the 'harsh patronage', a form of subtraction. Yet to what extent does this equation justify the bold sententiousness of the final lines?

Life is first boredom, then fear.
Whether or not we use it, it goes,
And leaves what something hidden from us chose,
And age, and then the only end of age.

(*CP*, 153)

Is this offered as diagnostic insight or as the forlorn bluster of a disappointed narrator? How legitimate is the move to the impersonal when the 'we' who 'use' life refers to Dockery and the narrator, hence an exclusively masculine and partial perspective? And what status have propositions on 'age, and then the only end of age' when their coherence depends on 'what something hidden from us chose'?

'Ignorance', the poem immediately after 'Dockery and Son' in *The Whitsun Weddings*, isolates and concentrates the paradoxes of an empiricist semantics of death (a subject which leaves, as the title of another poem puts it, 'Nothing to be Said'). And these in turn become statements about bodies, sexuality, origin.

> Strange to know nothing, never to be sure
> Of what is true or right or real,
> But forced to qualify *or so I feel*,
> Or, *Well it does seem so*:
> *Someone must know.*
>
> Strange to be ignorant of the way things work:
> Their skill at finding what they need,
> Their sense of shape, and punctual spread of seed,
> And willingness to change;
> Yes, it is strange,
>
> Even to wear such knowledge – for our flesh
> Surrounds us with its own decisions –
> And yet spend all our life on imprecisions,
> That when we start to die
> Have no idea why.
>
> (*CP*, 107)

The tone is deceptively casual, hesitant, self-deprecating: the rhyme, 'decisions' / 'imprecisions', suggests a Prufrockian lineage for the persona. But though the final 'idea why' is plaintively colloquial, it also specifically alludes to the positivist criteria of verification. The 'things' that 'work' include the body's decline and its reproduction, the 'punctual spread of seed' and the imperative of 'change'. The 'willingness' to enter this cycle is set against ignorance as to its ultimate purpose. There's a peculiar detached air to these statements: the first sentence has no governing verb; the second only a deferred 'it is'. (Even if one inserts a 'so' before the final 'that', the literal grammatical meaning is that 'imprecisions have no idea why'.) What does it mean to say that 'our flesh / Surrounds us' when flesh is always someone's flesh, his or hers or yours or mine? Its 'decisions' are to grow old, to wear out, to perpetuate itself: the seemingly prolix diction conceals a sex / death equation in 'spend all our life' and the mordant Jacobean pun on 'start to die'. (The motif is reworked in the title poem of the collection, 'The Whitsun Weddings', where the marriages are perceived by the women as a 'religious wounding' and a 'happy funeral' [*CP*, 115].)

We 'wear such knowledge' rather than possess it; and the awkwardness of this relation points to a more general problem of the status of statements about desire, the body. How can one resist the perennial temptation to lay claim to a linguistic finality, to achieve the proto-immortality of an axiom, that separates off the speaker from the condition referred to? Larkin resorts to disclaimers, statements about ignorance, handled with a scrupulous sense of paradox. The poem compares favourably, I think, with the slightly specious resonances of 'Dockery and Son'; but there nevertheless remains something dowdy about such verse. I now wish to look at two poems in which Larkin tries to offer a more intimate rendition of the processes of desire: first a brief glance at 'Dry-Point', then a more sustained examination of 'Wild Oats'.

## II

'Dry-Point' is a good example of Larkin as symboliste, or perhaps it is more accurate to say abstractionist, at any rate operating in a mode which he is commonly assumed to abhor. Increasing critical emphasis has been laid on the romantic tonalities in Larkin's verse in an attempt to establish its range and flexibility; but this has tended to concentrate on his response to the natural world, the poignant beauty of transience, the occasional intimation of a kind of agnostic faith. The difficult Larkin still meets with general disapproval. This, it must be admitted, is a comparatively minor strain, quite prominent in *The Less Deceived* ('If, my Darling', 'Whatever Happened'), seldom glimpsed in *The Whitsun Weddings*, but regaining strength in *High Windows* ('Sympathy in White Major', 'Solar', 'Livings II'). What I would stress is that this is in accordance with the empiricist leanings of the earlier volume, of being 'forced' to the 'real'. Telling it how it is, the facts of the case, demands a convoluted, opaque idiom when the poem situates itself on the terrain of desire: the 'incessant recital' that 'If, my Darling' tells us must be 'double-yolked with meaning and meaning's rebuttal' (*CP*, 41).

> Endlessly, time-honoured irritant,
> A bubble is restively forming at your tip.
> Burst it as fast as we can –
> It will grow again, until we begin dying.
>
> Silently it inflates, till we're enclosed
> And forced to start the struggle to get out:
> Bestial, intent, real.
> The wet spark comes, the bright blown walls collapse ...
> (*CP*, 36–7)

The poem was originally published as the second of 'Two Portraits of Sex': its companion-piece, 'Oils', is a rather uncomfortable Lawrentian mythicisation (or mystification) of the sexual act ('Sun. Tree. Beginning'). The OED defines 'dry-point' as a 'sharp-pointed needle used for engraving without acid'; so the title indicates a concern with images, creativity, fertility. (Compare 'to observe a life / Dissolving in the acid of their sex' ['Disintegration', *CP*, 266].) But 'dry' also implies arid, infertile (as in 'dry-bob', intercourse without emission): 'bubble', 'wet spark', and the later 'salted shrunken lakes', contrast with the 'many rains and many rivers' in 'Oils'; the 'new delighted lakes' and 'all-generous waters' of 'Wedding Wind' (*CP*, 11); and 'the emblematic sound of water' in 'Negative Indicative' (*CP*, 79). 'Point' is an obvious colloquialism for penis (compare 'tip'); but it is also an emphatic direction and lesson learnt.

What happens? A bubble is blown up, increases in size till it entraps its originator, then bursts: so, on a basic level, this is a narrative of illusion and disenchantment, conducted in a surreally extrapolated erotic imagery. (Compare Freud's analysis of the dream of the 'captive balloon'.[10]) This occurs within indeterminate or rather discrepant temporal denotations: the adverbial time of 'Endlessly' (as in *High Windows*, tediously, predictably) and the more specific regulation of 'fast', 'again', 'until'. These perspectives in turn are set against the biological context of 'grow again, until we begin dying', with verbs of origin, 'start', 'begin', and the abrupt demise of 'Burst'.

The noun 'irritant' itself works on two levels: both as an immediate stimulation (clearer in the French '*irriter*', to excite sexually), and a longer-term inducement, as grit in the pearl-oyster. 'Burst it as fast as we can' can be read as either curt imperative of immediate pleasure ('Burst it', recalling the climactic line of 'Deceptions', 'To burst into fulfilment's desolate attic' [*CP*, 32]) or wistful subjunctive of a deterministic cycle (though we may 'burst it, it will grow again'). In both senses, it prefigures the later appeal for release, 'Get out as early as you can'. Male sexuality becomes a simultaneous expression of aggression and helplessness, summarised by Larkin with magnificent judgemental explicitness: 'Bestial, intent, real'. The 'collapse' of 'the bright blown walls' refers most obviously to the shimmery inflated bubble of the erection, but also has intimations of Jericho: the breakdown of the barrier between self and other becomes a kind of pitiful exposure. It should be noted that the poem ignores any interpersonal contact: it is concerned with a relation to desire that is predefined as uncontrollable and inherently disappointing. It treats the physical fact of the rise and fall of male arousal as the determinant of sexual relations *per se*; the oxymoron of 'wet spark' insists on the intrinsically self-defeating nature of the experience. (Larkin himself summarised the theme of the poem as 'how awful sex is and how we want to get away from it'.[11])

One may well wish Larkin had written more poems in this idiom; but I think it should also serve to highlight the strength of his more characteristic verse, its firm commitment to the public domain. I have chosen 'Wild Oats' as representative of this vein. Like 'Dry-Point', it offers a narrative of disillusion, clinging to an unattainable ideal, with the recurrence of certain key images such as 'spark', 'ring', and 'magic'. Here the sexual relationship possesses a social dimension, but one conducted through the mediation of received images.

> About twenty years ago
> Two girls came in where I worked-
> A bosomy English rose
> And her friend in specs I could talk to.
> Faces in those days sparked
> The whole shooting-match off, and I doubt
> If ever one had like hers:
> But it was the friend I took out.
>
> And in seven years after that
> Wrote over four hundred letters,
> Gave a ten-guinea ring
> I got back in the end, and met

At numerous cathedral cities
Unknown to the clergy. I believe
I met beautiful twice. She was trying
Both times (so I thought) not to laugh.

Parting, after about five
Rehearsals, was an agreement
That I was too selfish, withdrawn,
And easily bored too love.
Well, useful to get that learnt.
In my wallet are still two snaps
Of bosomy rose with fur gloves on.
Unlucky charms, perhaps.

(*CP*, 143)

This seems to be a poem that, in the phrase Ashbery used of Larkin, 'has a bottom to it'.[12] It contains the recollection of specific occurrences, people, times and places; a moral anecdote, wry, precise, and downbeat, aspiring to the proverbial status of the title ('useful to get that learnt'). The oats that are sown, however, could hardly be classified as 'wild'. The poem establishes a running counterpoint between this staple diet and the longed-for, untouchable 'beautiful', the ideal and the plausibly available, 'A bosomy English rose / And her friend in specs'. Both are unnamed, along with the vast majority of women in Larkin's poetry – most notably, perhaps, the victim of 'Deceptions' and the narrator of 'Wedding-Wind'. The only exceptions are Myra in 'Posterity' and the haunting close to 'Dublinesque': 'A voice is heard singing / Of Kitty, or Katy / As if the name meant once / All love, all beauty' (*CP*, 178). In 'Maiden Name', the disparate 'old lists, old programmes, a school prize or two, / Packets of letters' are seen as no longer bound together in a single identity: 'You cannot be / Semantically the same as that young beauty' (*CP*, 101).

Their faces are similarly non-individual, but still (or perhaps therefore) capable of sparking 'The whole shooting-match off'. (Notice 'spark' recurring as a term of desire, igniting the 'match' that in turn would lead to 'shooting' or ejaculation.)

The final line gives a characteristic shift from the contemplation of ideal beauty to 'real action' (the theme of *Jill* in short),[13] and the second stanza recounts the numerically exhausted possibilities of courtship conventions: seven years, four hundred letters, ten-guinea ring. The 'friend' is conspicuously absent as the recipient of these attentions: they exist in their own right, to perform these ceremonies is to enter into negotiation with oneself. This is particularly apparent in the virtually intransitive use of 'met'; and yet the subsequent line retains considerable poignancy. The 'cathedrals' represent the kind of grand setting inaccessible to this kind of courtship; the 'numerous ... cities' open up a prospect of breadth and magnitude; the extent of the itinerary suggests an admirable degree of enthusiasm and stamina from both participants; and finally, to be 'Unknown to the clergy' implies a fuller sexual 'knowing' of each other.

This formal eroticism is taken up at the beginning of the third stanza: 'Parting', disengaging, withdrawing. The gerund is suspended in relation to the final 'agreement' of contractual self-accusation: 'That I was too selfish, withdrawn, / And easily bored to love'. (Given the sheer quantity of romantic gestures recorded in the previous stanzas, the charge of being 'too easily bored' seems particularly unfair.) The poem ends by returning to a contemplation of 'beautiful', as indeed have the preceding two stanzas:

> I doubt
> If ever one had like hers:
> But it was the friend I took out.
>
> I believe
> I met beautiful twice. She was trying
> Both times (so I thought) not to laugh.
>
> In my wallet are still two snaps
> Of bosomy rose with fur gloves on.
> Unlucky charms, perhaps.

Does this loyalty to the ideal involve the foolish sacrifice of possible happiness? Or is this a case-study to prove that 'love must be earned and not idly pursued' (*RW*, 243)? The option of reading the narrator ironically is certainly supported by his cultivated air of diffidence; by the grudging switches between women; and by the muted and rather pathetic triumph he feels in getting the ring back 'in the end'. The 'two snaps' in the 'wallet' (like dirty postcards) are certainly more than slightly seedy; 'bosomy rose with fur gloves on' (and maybe nothing else), and the 'charms' can equally well be read as photos or her breasts. But the status of these hoarded images is no more and no less artificial than that of the memories of the actual courtship, a similar frozen succession of framed tableaux. I think it is wrong to dismiss this as merely parodic, the pathetic gesture of a dessicated and self-deluding persona. The concluding possession of these images as a resource (like currency, stashed away) represents a logical progression, a stripping away of accidents from the ideal. (It should be compared, perhaps, to the effort of the narrator of 'Broadcast' to hold on to the thought of 'your face among all those faces / Beautiful and devout' [*CP*, 140].) I would stress the degree of defiance with which this stance of continued invocation is invested. This is centred, paradoxically enough, in the throwaway 'perhaps', which goes against the whole self-belittling tone of the previous recital. Perhaps, but perhaps not. The possibility arises that for Larkin this effort of idealisation is absolutely intrinsic to desire. This may be compared to Yeats's 'The Lamentation of the Old Pensioner':

> There's not a woman turns her face
> Upon a broken tree,
> And yet the beauties that I loved
> Are in my memory;
> I spit into the face of Time
> That has transfigured me.

Take away the sham bravado, and Larkin's poem becomes a re-statement of Yeats's theme: the preservation of ideal beauty in the context of personal decay. I now wish to go back to *The North Ship*, and trace the relation between the two poets in greater detail.

## III

On first reading, one could hardly be blamed for not detecting genius in *The North Ship*; in fact one could be forgiven for doubting the presence of talent. Larkin's 1966 preface freely acknowledges a 'predominance' of Yeats; and in a later interview he was prepared to dismiss the collection as 'painfully imitative' (*RW*, 29, 42). Critical accounts of his development have tended to follow this lead, and celebrate the displacement of the 'Celtic fever' by the drab, empirical, and prosaic. Enter the Movement. I believe that the continuities between the phases of his writing are greater than commonly acknowledged; and that his first volume establishes the preoccupation with monadic and unreciprocated desire that will dominate the work of his maturity.

Larkin describes himself at the time of composition as 'isolated in Shropshire with a complete Yeats stolen from a local girls' school'; and this juxtaposition gives, I think, the crucial modulation of his precursor's 'particularly potent music' into an education of furtive desire. (What *Jill* described as 'iridescent, tingling feelings that had not any obvious cause, shadowy wishes and more shadowy dreams of fulfilment' [*CP*, 100].) Larkin dissolves the terse clarity of the idiom and transforms it into a vehicle for tentative sexual self-definition: nowhere in Yeats would we get so delicately vulnerable a phrase as 'the deft / Heart grows impotent' ('If grief could burn out') [*CP*, 298]). Its onanistic basis is freely acknowledged, but not, as in the early poems of Dylan Thomas, endorsed without reservation: 'Last night you came / Unbidden, in a dream' is deflated by the quaintly explicit 'we've not met / More times than I can number on one hand' ('Morning has spread again' [*CP*, 281]); a prayer to the 'snow-white unicorn' closes with the ingenuous request that it 'put into my hand its golden horn' ('I see a girl dragged by her wrists' [*CP*, 279]). The dream does not subsume the real, but remains a subordinate interlude:

> I dreamed of an out-thrust arm of land
> Where gulls blew over a wave
> That fell along miles of sand;
> And the wind climbed up the caves
> To tear at a dark-faced garden
> Whose black flowers were dead,
> And broke round a house we slept in,
> A drawn blind and a bed.
> ('I dreamed of an out-thrust arm
> of land', *CP*, 267)

'I was sleeping, and you woke me': the poem traverses its slightly precious erotic landscape to finish by locating itself in a bed, a conversation, a restrained grief. And in this movement there always lies the possibility of disengagement:

> To wake, and hear a cock
> Out of the distance crying,
> To pull the curtains back
> And see the clouds flying –
> How strange it is
> For the heart to be loveless, and as cold as these.
> ('Dawn', *CP*, 284)

In a reversal of the aubade form, the 'heart' remains 'loveless' and cold': but the 'strange' is unevaluative, certainly not pejorative.

Instead of reciprocation or concern, the solitary awakening becomes the condition of a new finality of forensic insight.

> Here, where no love is,
> All that was hopeless
> And kept me from sleeping
>     Is frail and unsure;
> For never so brilliant,
> Neither so silent
> Nor so unearthly, has
>     Earth grown before.
>         ('The horns of the
>             morning', *CP*, 275)

It is the 'hopeless' that becomes 'frail and unsure', and there is a slightly peevish identification between love and being 'kept... from sleeping'. The absence of love is what permits the earth to 'grow', and this reversal is in line with other occurrences of fertility imagery:

> Then the whole heath whistles
> In the leaping wind,
> And shrivelled men stand
> Crowding like thistles
> To one fruitless place;
> Yet still the miracles
> Exhume in each face
> Strong silken seed,
> That to the static
> Gold winter sun throws back
> Endless and cloudless pride.
>         ('Winter', *CP*, 286–7)

What is disconcerting is the triumphant commitment to the 'fruitless place': the sterile landscape of 'wind', 'thistles', and 'shrivelled men'. The 'Strong silken seed' will not reclaim this desert: instead it can only be 'exhumed' from faces. Sex remains in the head rather than in the body (though notice the tactile exactitude of 'silken' for semen); but far from causing frustration, this becomes the justification of an 'Endless and cloudless pride'. (Compare the narrator's boast in 'No Road', that his 'liberty' lies in watching 'a world where no such road will run / from you to me / ... come up like a cold sun' [*CP*, 47].)

There are five poems of direct address to a presumed lover ('Within the dream you said', 'Love we must part now', 'Morning has spread again', 'Is it for now or for always', and 'So through that unripe day'), plus a more characteristic indeterminate 'you' in several more. But there is no sense of apostrophe, invocation, the Petrarchan heritage that Yeats glories in – indeed little sense of any specific object of desire.

The characteristic posture of early Yeats is supplication to a woman reduced to an image: an unending pursuit of the 'glimmering girl' created out of the 'fire ... in my head' ('The Song of Wandering Aengus'). She must always remain an adjunct of the masculine passion – 'For *my* dreams of your image that blossoms a rose in the deeps of *my* heart' ('The Lover tells of the Rose in his Heart'; my emphasis). Even poems like 'He wishes for the Cloths of Heaven' become an indirect technique of control: such an extravagant gesture of self-abasement as 'Tread softly because you tread on my dreams' serves to ratify the authorial power of conferring an idealisation, of fixing and ranking and passing judgement. (And being elevated into the symbolic pantheon is not without its drawbacks: in 'Michael Robartes and the Dancer', for example, woman's status as muse is used to justify not educating her.) The defining feature of Yeats's early poetry is its emphasis on romantic love as a relation to an image rather than to a person. Maud Gonne emerges as an icon with a cluster of heroic attributes; and it is this that permits the elaboration of concentric symbolic patterns around her. Thus a lyric such as 'He wishes his Beloved were Dead' becomes the logical consequence of this attitude: not as a wish to spare her the torment of inevitable decline, but as a recognition that the poet's triumph lies in celebrating a perfection that has been wholly ascribed, and so can exist independently of its object.

The relation to the image, which in Yeats is resonant, confident, and brazen, becomes interrogatory and self-undermining in Larkin:

> And I am sick for want of sleep;
> So sick, that I can half-believe
> The soundless river pouring from the cave
> Is neither strong, nor deep;
> Only an image fancied in conceit.
> I lie and wait for morning, and the birds,
> The first steps going down the unswept street,
> Voices of girls with scarves around their heads.
>     ('The bottle is drunk out by one', *CP*, 277)

This plaintive and excluded eroticism, more early Eliot than Yeats perhaps, does not preclude a declared scepticism towards any 'soundless river' of potent subconscious desire (though the narrator still 'half-believes'). There is an implied movement from morbid self-preoccupation to the life of the street; but the apparently tangible 'girls with scarves around their heads', it should be noted, are equally an 'image fancied in conceit', evoked from their voices rather than seen.

'So through that unripe day' prefigures Larkin's later verse in viewing this distance as a source of comfort and security:

> So through that unripe day you bore your head,
> And the day was plucked and tasted bitter,
> As if still cold among the leaves. Instead,
> It was your severed image that grew sweeter,
> That floated, wing-stiff, focused in the sun
> Along uncertainty and gales of shame
> Blown out before I slept. Now you are one
> I dare not think alive: only a name
> That chimes occasionally, as a belief
> Long since embedded in the static past.
>
> Summer broke and drained. Now we are safe.
> The days lose confidence, and can be faced
> Indoors. This is your last, meticulous hour,
> Cut, gummed; pastime of a provincial winter.
>
> (*CP*, 283)

This may perhaps be read as an expansion of the 'two snaps' of 'Wild Oats': 'leaves' and 'Cut, gummed' suggest the 'pastime' of the photo-album. The poem is not addressed to a woman, but to an image, a 'you' that is 'focused', defined solely through reference to a perceiver/collector, and in common with the vast majority of female figures in Larkin's poetry, unnamed. She nevertheless produces 'uncertainty' in the narrator; and also, it seems fair to infer from 'shame' and 'Blown out' (compare the 'bright blown walls' of 'Dry-Point'), physical arousal. All the possible sexual immediacy of 'embedded', however, is stifled: a more specific erotic reference is momentarily glimpsed, though in negative form, in 'broke and drained' (what? our relation? me? my physical potency?), only to be finally expelled with the sanctimonious pronouncement, 'we are safe'. But what was the threat that had to 'be faced'? I would stress how the edgy nostalgia acquires peculiar mythic reverberations through a discreet series of Medusa references: the 'head' that has been 'severed', now 'cold', floating 'wing-stiff' in mid-air, the retrospect implied by 'name', 'belief', and 'past', and the hint of monstrosity of 'you are one / I dare not think alive'. (Compare Rossetti's 'Aspecta Medusa': 'Let not thine eyes know / Any forbidden thing itself, although / It once should save as well as kill, but be / Its shadow upon life enough for thee'.) Here I think that Freud's 1922 article, 'Medusa's Head' can be relevantly invoked.[14] It may seem excessive to treat the poem as a 'representation of woman as a being who frightens and repels because she is castrated': but at the very least it must be acknowledged that this detached contemplation of the image serves to ward off an unspecified but powerful anxiety. (Simon Petch, for example, describes the poem as 'chillingly defensive'.[15]) And this compensatory domination becomes in Larkin a fundamental structure of desire.

This leads rather neatly into the opening poem of *The Less Deceived*, 'Lines on a Young Lady's Photograph Album':

> At last you yielded up the album, which,
> Once open, sent me distracted. All your ages
> Matt and glossy on the thick black pages!
> Too much confectionery, too rich:
> I choke on such nutritious images.
>                     (*CP*, 71)

Initially this appears to be no more than a rather stilted whimsy. But the stanza, once stripped down, takes on a decidedly Baudelairean air (for more in this vein, see 'Femmes Damnées' [*CP*, 270]).

> At last you yielded up the **** which,
> Once open, sent me distracted. All your
> **** glossy on the thick black ****
> Too much confectionery, too rich:
> I choke on such nutritious images.

There is obviously an implied seduction where 'At last' a yielding occurs that sends the narrator 'distracted': notice how 'once open' becomes an explicit image of sexual availability. But the poem directs its attention not towards the control and domination of a woman who is present, but towards a collection of 'severed images'. The terms that I have omitted are of framing and estrangement – 'album', 'ages', 'matt', 'pages': even 'nutritious' suggests a dietary regime rather than a headlong plunge into desire. The overt voyeurism continues:

My swivel eye hungers from pose to pose ...

To revel in a succession of tableaux, the 'static past'.

> In pig-tails, clutching a reluctant cat;
> Or furred yourself, a sweet girl-graduate;
> Or lifting a heavy-headed rose
> Beneath a trellis, or in a trilby hat.
>
> (CP, 71)

There's a crude pun on pussy floating around, particularly in the context of puberty, maidenhood and innocence: 'furred yourself' set against the traditional emblem of the rose.

> From every side you strike at my control ...

A 'control' which is also the camera focus, and so the means of further images, gratification, as well as an appeal to self-restraint:

> But o photography! as no art is,
> Faithful and disappointing ...
>
> what grace
> Your candour thus confers upon her face!
> How overwhelmingly persuades
> That this is a real girl in a real place,
>
> In every sense empirically true!
>
> (CP, 71-2)

The apostrophe is significantly lower-case, the absence of art and elevation: yet the 'real girl in a real place' is none the less fictive, invoked, an effort of 'persuasion'. And is to be 'empirically true' the same as being emotionally faithful, or its utter antithesis, because acknowledging the distance between past and present?

> you
> Contract my heart by looking out of date.
>
> Yes, true; but in the end, surely, we cry
> Not only at exclusion, but because
> It leaves us free to cry.
>
> (CP, 72)

To 'Contract' is both to reduce and engage; and 'looking out of' seems to suggest the gaze being returned from the past. There's a complex sense of freedom in detachment, 'exclusion' as a privilege: despite the preceding reference to 'misty parks and motors', 'to cry' comes across as a gesture of self-assertion rather than of defeat, and the subsequent 'grief' still contains a possible exuberance, preda-toriness, even relief:

> So I am left
> To mourn (without a chance of consequence)
> You, balanced on a bike against a fence;
> To wonder if you'd spot the theft
> Of this one of you bathing; to condense,
>
> In short, a past that no one now can share,
> No matter whose your future; calm and dry,
> It holds you like a heaven, and you lie
> Unvariably lovely there,
> Smaller and clearer as the years go by.
>
> (CP, 72)

There is a peculiar disjunction between the apparently intransitive 'mourn' and its deferred object 'You' (the first occurrence of the pronoun since the opening line, introducing four rapid usages). This in turn has no unchanging essence but instead becomes equated with a 'past' that we are obliged to interpret and 'condense', and an unspecified future (note the humility in the lack of any prediction, the unfettered choice granted as a kind of benediction). There is no attempt to pass the sequence of images off as a human identity; but conversely there is no attempt to pretend that any individual can be known other than through the mediation of such images. To 'yowl across / The gap from eye to page' becomes the paradigm of inter-personal knowledge: there is always the text of the other to be tran-scribed in a kind of 'theft'.

So this is a poem about the truth of images, perhaps in all human relations, but here particularly associated with knowledge of the 'young lady'. It offers an ocular but unbodily desire (only one passing reference to 'faintly disturbing'); one unwilling to forgo the 'control' and prepared to pay the cost of 'exclusion' in return for being 'free to cry'. The poem succeeds in establishing the relation of the 'swivel eye' to 'nutritious images' as central to the process of desire; 'If, my Darling' conjectures what would happen if the woman 'were once to decide / Not to stop at my eyes, / But to jump, like Alice, with floating skirt into my head' (*CP*, 41). This is presented not as an unassailable urge, but as subject to sceptical analysis, the choice of abstention. ('I find it easier to abstain from women than sustain the trouble of them and the creakings of my own monastic character.'[16]) But one can only choose not to desire, not to desire differently, purely.

The photographic motif is continued in 'Whatever Happened?':

> At once whatever happened starts receding.
> Panting, and back on board, we line the rail
> With trousers ripped, light wallets, and lips bleeding.
>
> Yes, gone, thank God! Remembering each detail
> We toss for half the night, but find next day
> All's kodak-distant. Easily, then (though pale),
>
> 'Perspective brings significance' we say,
> Unhooding our photometers, and, snap!
> What can't be printed can be thrown away.
>
> Later it's just a latitude: the map
> Points out how unavoidable it was:
> 'Such coastal bedding always means mishap.'
>
> Curses? The dark? Struggling? Where's the source
> Of all these yarns now (except in nightmares, of course)?
>                                               (*CP*, 74)

Here we rejoin the 'Dry-Point' idiom, tortuous, opaque, yet here curiously jaunty. The title of the poem itself seems to shift from a direct question to a euphemism ('What can't be printed'). An inquiry into desire can only be answered in words, which are inevitably secondary, self-deluding. Where should we locate ourselves in order to achieve the 'Perspective' that will 'bring significance' to sexual pleasure ('bedding'), an experience that 'At once ... starts receding', ludicrous and perhaps degrading to recall? A dive into oceanic emotions is here imaged as a comic routine of clambering back 'on board', 'With trousers ripped, light wallets, and lips bleeding', the final image unexpectedly disquieting (whose blood?). The sequence of sea-voyage imagery is continued in 'latitude' (or permissiveness), 'map', 'coastal' and 'yarns'. In this context, 'kodak-distant' most obviously evokes a tourist souvenir, but it should also be read as a mechanism constitutive of desire, preserving and making safe. 'Remembering each detail /

We toss for half the night', another of Larkin's audacious obscenities; and more comically 'Unhooding our photometers, and snap!'
The camera is an erotic device; the stability of its images holds at
bay the 'nightmares' of carnal fantasy: 'Curses? The dark?
Struggling? Where's the source ...'.

Here, and elsewhere in *The Less Deceived*, the relation of camera
to image, desire to its object, tends towards the solipsistic: its
equivocations are something to be worked out privately as aspects
of a wholly personal identity. (Though 'Wants' offers an appealing
image of the connection between political and patriarchal authority:
'However the family is photographed under the flagstaff' [*CP*, 42].)
In *The Whitsun Weddings*, it becomes a form of cultural analysis of
consumer longings. The volume begins with 'residents from raw
estates' who

> Push through plate-glass swing doors to their desires –
> Cheap suits, red kitchen-ware, sharp shoes, iced lollies,
> Electric mixers, toasters, washers, driers –
> (*CP*, 136)

and this conjunction of 'driers' and 'desires' reaches a crescendo
in the final poems. The billboards of 'Essential Beauty', with their
'sharply-pictured groves / Of how life should be' (*CP*, 144) are
followed by 'the trite untransferable / Truss-advertisement, truth'
in 'Send no Money' (*CP*, 146); and this concern continues in
'the albums lettered / *Our Wedding*, lying / Near the television'
in 'Afternoons' (*CP*, 121), and the climactic icon of matrimonial
love in 'An Arundel Tomb' (*CP*, 110). 'The Large Cool Store'
is perhaps the finest example of the radical edge to Larkin's political verse (as opposed to the occasional flourishes of romantic
patriotism):

> The large cool store selling cheap clothes
> Set out in simple sizes plainly
> (Knitwear, Summer Casuals, Hose,
> In browns and greys, maroon and navy)
> Conjures the weekday world of those
>
> Who leave at dawn low terraced houses
> Timed for factory, yard and site.
> But past the heaps of shirts and trousers
> Spread the stands of Modes for Night:
> Machine-embroidered, thin as blouses,

Lemon, sapphire, moss-green, rose
Bri-Nylon Baby-Dolls and Shorties
Flounce in clusters. To suppose
They share that world, to think their sort is
Matched by something in it, shows

How separate and unearthly love is,
Or women are, or what they do,
Or in our young unreal wishes
Seem to be: synthetic, new,
And natureless in ecstasies.

(CP, 135)

This is a poem of desire and commodity, or rather, desire as commodity. The first point I would make is the acuity of the verb 'conjures'. The 'large cool store ... Conjures the weekday world'. In one sense it evokes the whole environment of 'those / Who leave at dawn low terraced houses', and their precisely 'Timed' routine. Are these the 'store's' employees or its customers? Is there any distinction to be made? And this leads on to the second sense: that the store 'conjures', magics up through spells, a world of illusion for them all to inhabit, a sorcerer, benign or otherwise. But it's not drab realism versus pathetic fantasy; both worlds are equally constructs, products of incantations, 'Machine-embroidered'. There's a peculiar cartoonic sense of the independent lives of clothes; 'those' are certainly less specified or animated than the 'heaps of shirts and trousers' before whom the 'Modes for Night' are 'spread' enticingly. (Their sexual gender is acquired, determined solely by what they have bought.) The descriptive tone is still dominated by the initial 'plainly'; to be 'thin as blouses' implies meagreness rather than slimness, a sense taken up in the later 'Shorties', anaemic, undernourished. The use of 'rose' as both adjective and verb is a characteristic Yeatsian device (compare 'rose / Bri-Nylon Baby-Dolls', Aphrodite-like from the 'stands' with Yeats's 'The Sorrow of Love'), and 'Shorties / Flounce' can similarly be read as a compound noun, or a subject/verb, with homonyms on pounce and flaunt. Who governs 'To suppose', does 'that world' belong to readers, customers, or garments, or is 'their sort' (fate, kind, social grouping) indistinguishable? To be 'Matched' is to have compatible garments, or sexual partners; both, however, are a nebulous 'something'. Here we have a move from commodity fetishism to a quasi-Platonic realm; or rather the whole process is judged against the standard of a 'separate and unearthly love'.[17] The 'young unreal wishes', handled almost tenderly here, contain longing both for the ideal and also for the actual 'Baby-Dolls' that are none the less fabricated, and so equally 'unreal'. (Compare 'The Whitsun Weddings': 'the perms, / The nylon gloves and jewellery-substitutes, / The lemons, mauves, and olive-ochres that / Marked off the girls unreally from the rest' [CP, 114].) Desire is viewed as 'synthetic' from its very outset: it has no definite object – in the case of women, 'are', 'do' and 'Seem to be' are interchangeable, there is no distinction between reality and appearance. There's a vivid eroticism in 'natureless in ecstasies': free from nature, without essence, but therefore assembled, marketed along with other commodities.

'Sunny Prestatyn' continues this opposition between purchased fantasy and actual world:

> Come To Sunny Prestatyn
> Laughed the girl on the poster,
> Kneeling up on the sand
> In tautened white satin.
> Behind her, a hunk of coast, a
> Hotel with palms
> Seemed to expand from her thighs and
> Spread breast-lifting arms.
>
> (CP, 149)

'The girl on the poster': yet another of Larkin's precise observations on mass-produced ideals, giving a compliant come-on which involves the expenditure of hard cash, in this case beckoning towards what is presumably an illicit amorous weekend. So she laughs: at her clients, at what she is offering, out of general exuberance perhaps. 'Kneeling up' involves a more definite act of submission; 'In tautened white satin', both her swimsuit and her skin, that has become another glossy commodity. 'Tautened'; skimpy, pulled tight over, but also perhaps a term of arousal in the male spectator (subsequently supported by 'expand'). This leads into the positioning 'Behind her' of a 'hunk of coast', a 'hunk' being the slang term for an attractive man as well as an outcrop, and by extension, a sexual reference. The 'palms' can be seen as themselves phallic but the more subtle reference comes with the pun on hands, which seem to come from between her thighs in order to 'Spread breast-lifting arms': to borrow a term from 'Maiden Name', she is by no means 'unfingermarked' (CP, 101). This erotic dimension becomes clearer if the localising references are removed: poster, sand, coast, hotels:

> the girl
> Kneeling up
> In tautened white satin.
> Behind her, a hunk ...
>     palms
>     expand from her thighs and
> Spread breast-lifting arms.

A real girl in a real place, the place of fantasy and potential violence.

> She was slapped up one day in March.
> A couple of weeks, and her face
> Was snaggle-toothed and boss-eyed;
> Huge tits and a fissured crotch
> Were scored well in, and the space
> Between her legs held scrawls
> That set her fairly astride
> A tuberous cock and balls
>
> (CP, 149)

She ceases to exist in an inviolate realm of images, 'slapped up', casually plastered on, given a beating. A tone of shrugging inevitability ('A couple of weeks, and ...'), with an undertow of approval particularly in the use of 'well in', and also with 'fairly', appropriately, justly. The point is, I think, that this is not degraded reality replacing unavailable ideal (the 'unfocused she' of 'Essential Beauty' [CP, 144]) but the translation of one image of desire into another. 'The space / Between her legs held scrawls': an absence, lack, inviting inscription, here by the 'cock and balls'. (The banter of college high-table in 'Livings III' [CP, 188] displays the same impulse to impose 'Names for *pudendum mulieris*' [rhyming with 'fairest'].)

> Autographed *Titch Thomas*, while
> Someone had used a knife
> Or something to stab right through
> The moustached lips of her smile.
> She was too good for this life.
> Very soon, a great transverse tear
> Left only a hand and some blue.
> Now *Fight Cancer* is there.
>
> (CP, 149)

There is an allusion to the colloquialism for penis, John Thomas; Titch may be compensatory or triumphant. Who performs this act, a 'someone'? A child, a youth? Or every man in every penetration, a form of hatred, an assertion of ownership, a desecration of a false ideal? The 'tuberous cock', clumsy, vegetable, comparatively inno-cent, becomes 'a knife / Or something to stab'; and 'right through' has a similar sense of validation as the previous 'well'. 'She was too good for this life': the glimpse of beauty, paradise, escape, or a pre-tentious mockery of 'this life', our life, and therefore deserving of assault. (Note that 'this life', bound by rhyme to 'knife', has becomes synonymous with the blade, the 'cock and balls', the violation.) The 'great transverse tear' recalls the continental dimen-sions of 'fissured' (and the 'coastal shelf' of 'This be the Verse' [*CP*, 180]), but also gives the fleeting possibility of weeping. The 'hand' could be imploring; or the masturbatory clutch of the on-looker, taking satisfaction in 'some blue', sexually explicit material. The poem can be turned inside out: '*Fight Cancer*' can refer to the disease of sexual violence, its hopeless and irreversible encroach-ment; or it can be yet another irrelevant slogan, vacuous induce-ment. What is the appropriate response for the male reader? To feel liberated by the violation of the image (distinct from violence against actual women); satisfied by the desecration as prefiguring violence against them; or appalled by this depiction of his own 'tuberous' sexuality? (This may be compared to the 'corpse-faced undergraduate' whose pin-up collection 'Baited his unused sex like tsetse flies / Till maddened it charged out without disguise / And made the headlines' in 'Under a splendid chestnut tree' [*CP*, 43]; and the magnificent close to 'Love again: wanking at half past three', 'Something to do with violence / A long way back and wrong rewards, / And arrogant eternity' [*CP*, 215]).

It's interesting to look at responses to the poem in gender terms: male critics almost invariably stress the falsity of the ideal rather than the savagery of the treatment meted out to it. To take a couple of examples from usually illuminating commentators. Simon Petch claims 'the violence of the human response expresses an enraged insistence that the image on the poster accords with no reality whatever' and that 'the natural impulse reacts angrily against the imposition of an illusion'.[18] Terry Whalen comments that 'it is, of course, the "less deceived" mentality of the rebellious graffiti which captures Larkin's praise', to the point of the poem being a 'celebra-tion of the act' which is 'relished' for its 'healthy rebellion' and its 'ironic vengeance'.[19] The opposing view is put forward by Janice Rossen (wondering how much complicity the poet shares in the act')[20] and Matt Simpson (arguing that 'the poet, in the act of recording, discovers himself to be too intently voyeuristic, an accomplice').[21] Neither party is prepared to acknowledge that the relation of viewer to poster might represent a more general underlying structure, the possibility that all desire might be subject to this falsity to some extent, And neither can bring themselves to condemn the exhibition of male sexual violence that retaliation against this 'imposition' might involve.

Where Larkin outmanoeuvres his critics is in his awareness of the constructedness of both sides of the equation: the ideal and its violation. 'But I thought wanting unfair: / It and finding out clash', as 'Send no Money' puts it (*CP*, 146), and the strength of his erotic poetry lies not only in its awareness of exclusion from the 'fair', the just and the beautiful, but also in its direct and unsparing address of the comparable inauthenticity of masculine desire. Its emblems undoubtedly verge on cliché but are occasionally no less ferocious for that: the narrator of 'A Study of Reading Habits' fondly recalls

> ripping times in the dark.
> The women I clubbed with sex!
> I broke them up like meringues.
> (*CP*, 131)

'Meringues' serves as an oddly disconcerting *mot juste*: white and brittle on the outside, creamy inside, yielding to the uninhibited pressure of teeth, 'broken up' with a kind of brutal analytic impulse. But to 'club women with sex' has no intrinsic neanderthal authenticity: it remains as culturally derived as the 'girl on the poster': this time from popular Gothic fiction rather than the jargon of holidays in the sun. For Larkin, 'finding out' involves a refusal of illusion so fundamental that it repudiates the whole biological imperative of what 'Wants' calls 'the printed directions of sex' (*CP*, 42) (genetically imprinted, photographically reproduced, listed in a popular erotic manual); and challenges outright any lingering assumption that sex must necessarily be good for us, where we must find our happiness or not at all.

I do not accept that this resolute espousal of 'the patience to expose / Untrue desire' ('Many famous feet have trod' [*CP*, 18]) lays Larkin open to the charge of being irredeemably negative, anti-life, displaying at best 'intelligent rancour, / An integrity of self-hatred' ('Marriages' [CP, 64]). An immediate defence might be offered by stressing the Lawrentian elements of his work, such as the evocations of the 'vast flowering' of the natural world in 'Long roots moor summer' (CP, 96); the sacramental reverence for the rite of consummation in 'Wedding-Wind'; and the lyrical evocation of sexual release at the climax of 'The Whitsun Weddings'. (The influence is repeatedly confirmed in the correspondence [*Letters*, 12, 19, 21, 56, 140] and Rossen suggests its negative impact on Larkin's actual relations with women.[22]) The terse and understated idealism of poems such as 'When first we faced' is itself a rare and precious quality:

> Admitted: and the pain is real.
> But when did love not try to change
> The world back to itself – no cost,
> No past, no people else at all –
> Only what meeting made us feel,
> So new, and gentle sharp, and strange?
> (*CP*, 205)

I would prefer, however, to stress the seriousness with which Larkin addresses the whole question of sexual identity. John Bayley[23] stresses Larkin's awareness that 'femininity was invented in words by men'; and this insight is neatly brought out in 'Breadfruit':

> So absolute
> Maturity falls, when old men sit and dream
> Of naked native girls who bring breadfruit
> Whatever they are.
> (*CP*, 141)

The point being that the final clause applies as much to the 'girls' themselves as to the exotic fruit, 'Whatever they are': both are equally only known through the medium of 'uncorrected visions'. There is an acceptance of a gap between representation and woman ('such a jumble of forms & ideas about them in one's head' [*Letters*, 151]), with a pessimism about knowing beyond the image, and a fierce resentment as to how it has been inculcated. There are poems of sexual fear: 'Next, Please' reverts to an opposition between the life-giving 'figurehead with golden tits' which 'never anchors' and the 'black-sailed unfamiliar' in whose wake 'No waters breed or break' (*CP*, 52); and 'Myxomatosis' transforms the sufferings of a wounded rabbit into the common predicament of the male:

> *What trap is this? Where were its teeth concealed?*
> You seem to ask.
>                     I make a sharp reply.
> Then clean my stick. I'm glad I can't explain
> Just in what jaws you were to suppurate:
>                                             (*CP*, 100)

The 'jaws' are simultaneously of the trap, of death, and of the *vagina dentata*; and 'suppurate' identifies the dying animal with a diseased wound or organ. (One may perhaps recall Rossiter's description of the male as a 'thinking rabbit'.) What should surprise us is not that some element of this imagery is present, but that it should assume so little prominence: there is no possibility of compiling 'daily quotations for a misogynist's calendar' from his verse (*RW*, 261). And where it appears, it will tend to be explicitly ascribed to a masculine perspective: in 'The North Ship', for example, the warning that 'A woman has ten claws' is followed by 'Sang the drunken boatswain' ('Above 80 degrees north' [*CP*, 305]). As Janice Rossen notes, Larkin 'capitalises on the energy which derives from seeing sexual politics solely from the man's point of view'.[24] This holds true for Larkin's use of abstract language: it is acknowledged as interested, for example, in the pronoun shift at the end of 'Reasons for Attendance', 'If no-one has deceived *him*self' (my emphasis). The most emphatic example comes in 'Deceptions'. The poem opens with an epigraph from Mayhew describing the abduction and rape of a young girl: the subsequent evocation of the sensations of her awakening mind is abruptly retracted in the second stanza:

> Slums, years, have buried you. I would not dare
> Console you if I could. What can be said,
> Except that suffering is exact, but where
> Desire takes charge, readings will grow erratic?
> For you would hardly care
> That you were less deceived, out on that bed,
> Than he was, stumbling up the breathless stair
> To burst into fulfilment's desolate attic.
>                                             (*CP*, 32)

Larkin has often been criticised for equating the suffering of the victim with the self-delusion of her assailant.[25] 'Slums, years' have buried him with equal thoroughness, but something in his action is seen as inviting and enticing continued empathy. Here we see the transferred epithets of 'breathless' (because doped) and 'desolate' (because ravished) ascribed to the male perception. Yet to make no claim to speak for the woman other than to state 'suffering is exact' is perhaps a question of moral tact; the specific issue of gender allegiance emerges in the decision not to claim distance from her violator. The lines, 'I would not dare / Console you *if I could*' (my emphasis) are surely a declaration that 'where / Desire takes charge', the masculine perspective is the only one the poet can truly share, however 'erratic' the subsequent 'readings'. To be 'less deceived' involves a refusal of pious disavowal, an open acknowledgement of shameful complicity.

I would like to close by stressing the regenerative aspects of this refusal of illusion, this opting out of the coercive force of contemporary sexual ideology. Larkin's uniquely acute sense of the intrusive and demeaning nature of desire brings about a corresponding upgrading of alternative human bonds. We should not underestimate how often and how movingly, in particular in *The Whitsun Weddings*, he offers direct propositions about human love:

> The glare of that much-mentioned brilliance, love,
>   Broke out, to show
> Its bright incipience sailing above,
> Still promising to solve, and satisfy,
>   And set unchangeably in order.
>               ('Love Songs in Age', *CP*, 113)

> In everyone there sleeps
> A sense of life lived according to love.
> To some it means the difference they could make
> By loving others, but across most it sweeps
> As all they might have done had they been loved.
>               ('Faith Healing', *CP*, 126)

> On me your voice falls as they say love should,
> Like an enormous yes.
>               ('For Sidney Bechet', *CP*, 83)

Is 'love' here opposed to desire or subsuming it or in some other more elusive relation? Is its assent, order, permanence, unavailable, or at least unenduring in the context of mortality? 'Love Songs in Age' ends with 'lamely admitting how / It had not done so then, and could not now' (*CP*, 113); 'Faith Healing' closes with the assertion that 'all time has disproved' (*CP*, 126); and 'For Sidney Bechet' can only sustain its 'appropriate falsehood' for the duration of a single 'note' (*CP*, 83). There's no cancellation of the aspiration, however, but rather a poignant impasse, and this is most fully explored in the closing poem of *The Whitsun Weddings*, the justly celebrated 'An Arundel Tomb'.

> Side by side, their faces blurred,
> The earl and countess lie in stone,
> Their proper habits vaguely shown
> As jointed armour, stiffened pleat,
> And that faint hint of the absurd –
> The little dogs under their feet.
>
> Such plainness of the pre-baroque
> Hardly involves the eye, until
> It meets his left-hand gauntlet, still
> Clasped empty in the other; and
> One sees, with a sharp tender shock,
> His hand withdrawn, holding her hand.
>                                      (*CP*, 110)

It is important to stress the position of the poem as the culmination of the sequence dwelling on emblems of desire (note the quasi-photographic 'blurred' and 'vaguely shown'). Whatever affirmation is here forthcoming must be made in full awareness of the preceding sceptical analysis and the difficulty of finding what 'Talking in Bed' famously described as 'words' that were 'not untrue and not unkind' (*CP*, 129).

The narrator begins by contemplating the 'faithfulness in effigy' of the tomb-carvings of an unnamed medieval couple. Their individual 'identity' has been eroded: they no longer possess feudal or dynastic claims. The 'endless altered people' treat them merely as a source of casual spectacle. All that distinguishes them is their gesture of clasped hands. In a complex and paradoxical development, it is this unconcerned anonymity, their reduction to a single 'attitude' that allows them to be 'transfigured' into a 'final blazon'. The poem celebrates the perfect icon of desire, one sufficiently deracinated to be cast forward in time, to be shared without self-deception or appropriation. The generous, indeed rhapsodic, finale, can only exist in conjunction with an unceasing undertow of scepticism: the truth-claim involved in an 'almost-instinct' that is 'almost true' fluctuates on every reading.

But more is offered than the emotional agnosticism of the freely acknowledged 'untruth'. There is also a fundamental renunciation of the privileged masculine gaze on the representation of the female. The refusal to exempt the 'earl' from a similar arrestedness in 'stone fidelity' places the masculine simultaneously inside and outside the frame. The inevitable condescension of the detached observer ('One sees') experiences a 'sharp tender shock' not only at the embrace but also the empty gauntlet that reaches out to meet the eye. There is both a present intentionality about 'holding her hand' and a kind of voluntary self-exposure: the omission of 'he' as governing subject seems to parallel the removal of the armour. 'What will survive of us is love', and the 'us' reaches out to include narrator (and reader) in its plea for a relinquishing of mastery and possession in a humility of ardour.

## IV

There are those who remain resolutely unconvinced even by the finale to 'An Arundel Tomb'. Andrew Motion, for example, argues that 'behind the tender triumphalism of its ending lies an assumption that no living couple could ever be truly happy and remain permanently in love'; and the recent publication of Larkin's letters has provided plentiful ammunition for denunciations of his 'easy misogynism'.[26] Even here, the disparaging asides to his male friends ('as far as I can see, all women are stupid beings' [*Letters*, 63; see also 104, 119, 150, 165] must be set against the warmth and intimacy of his correspondence with Judy Egerton, Barbara Pym, and Winifred Bradshaw. And it is naïve to assume that the letters somehow represent the truth behind the poetry rather than the assumption of a different set of (equally ironised) epistolary conventions. Statements such as 'my relations with women are governed by a shrinking sensitivity, a morbid sense of sin, a furtive lechery & a deplorable flirtatiousness' clearly possess a strong element of comic, if self-defensive, hyperbole (*Letters*, 157). His predilection for pornography ('WATCHING SCHOOL GIRLS SUCK EACH OTHER OFF WHILE YOU WHIP THEM' [*Letters*, 596]) is perhaps more difficult to accept, although one might argue that his acute sense of the

intrusiveness of erotic representations was derived from his familiarity with this area. The letters may, as Lisa Jardine claims, serve
to 'alert us to a cultural frame within which Larkin writes, one
which takes racism and sexism for granted as crucially a part of the
British national heritage'. This might, however, not be the least of
their value, in so far as his work continues to elicit the hermeneutic
quality which she elsewhere defines as 'strenuous denial'.[27]

It is undeniably tempting simply to endorse Martin Amis's description of 'the reaction against Larkin' as 'unprecedently hypo-
critical, tendentious, and smug'.[28] Nevertheless, Jardine's argument
raises a crucial question which may be applied not only to Larkin
but to all the other writers in this volume. To varying degrees, they
may be seen as participating in and perpetuating a history of injustice. If this is the case, why continue to study their texts?

Larkin's collection of pornography may well take its place
alongside Shakespeare's second-best bed, Pope's escapade at a
brothel, and Eliot's traumatic first marriage-night, as part of a
larger cultural narrative which is itself intrinsically misogynist. It
would be foolish to deny that these figures bring with them cultural prestige and a cumulative momentum of imposition. But the
formalist question of the capacity of the text to generate meanings
remains to be answered. Why do these poems retain their power to
compel attention?

Sexist language requires an intention: to remain dominant if not
to insult, whether this is placed at the level of individual agency or
cultural formation. So if linguistics has concentrated on individual
terms, the sentences in which they function, and the positions from
which they are delivered, how do texts differ? Through the simple
fact of temporal deracination, they cannot work in the same way.
They are better thought of as something made rather than spoken:
the hermeneutic relation is between reader and text, the language
having undergone a process of distanciation. A text cannot be sexist
in the way a direct enunciation can: certain institutional usages may
be made of it, but in itself it escapes the specificity of context in
which the authority of masculine speech resides. Either this is exter-
nally acquired or internally produced. The difference between the
sexist statement and the misogynist text is one of formal coherence
and disengagement from empirical rationale.

Misogynist texts are commonly regarded by feminist criticism as
a particularly blatant and brutal form of support for a repressive
hierarchy. It seems to me premature and unsatisfactory to treat

them simply as instruments of consolation, reassurance, or cultural reinforcement. One can perhaps endorse stereotypes, feel familiarity, recognition, and approval towards them. But this is not necessarily to value them. They are boring for male readers too. These poems seem more designed to promote rather than alleviate anxiety, to disrupt and disorientate rather than to naturalise and justify. Their attraction lies not in the way they assert control but in the way they threaten it. The complexity of the mechanisms of ascription and reattribution in these texts should not be underestimated. Put crudely, power in these texts lies at least as much with what is denounced as with who denounces.

The question that still remains is whether threat, disruption, subversion merely results in an ever-firmer reinscription. And it remains to be shown why the repetition of crisis should not be as tedious as the repetition of stereotype.

In one tradition of feminist reading, what is disturbing is not the representation but the structure which it exemplifies. The question of value is oddly inverted. Pragmatically speaking, the worst images are the best because exemplifying the violence of the underlying structures most clearly (as sadistic pornography is frequently held to exemplify the field as a whole).

Yet even the pornographic imagination remains an imagination; and the effectiveness of any given hermeneutic stance must be assessed in terms of its productivity. Here I would insist on the priority of close textual analyses over the totalising ambitions of all too many theoretical models. The actual practice of interpretation reveals a precarious, intermittent and paradoxical authority in these texts, at least as much concerned to disown and disavow as to impose and dominate.

It is difficult to find a vocabulary that does not resort to a euphemistic aestheticism: vividness, force, impact. This is a non-cathartic aesthetic. It arouses rather than purges, and the emotions with which it deals may themselves rightly provoke suspicion. Yet if feminist criticism does not seek fairness, balance, progressiveness, but instead seizes upon that which it would deny, male criticism must also have a legitimate interest in these texts.

There is no comfortable position to adopt with regard to them. The misogynist text is something which one undergoes, resists, protests against. It makes demands.

On a simple empirical level, its language is dense, provocative, opaque. It is not subject to abrupt demystification because the act of scepticism itself bears testimony to the paradoxical productivity of these texts. They must be acknowledged to possess the meaning-generating and world-disclosing capacity traditionally ascribed to the poetic. They can perhaps no longer be 'believed in as the most reliable', but they are not simply 'therefore the fittest for renunciation' (Eliot, 'Dry Salvages'). In renouncing, we create. Doubt, scepticism, and repudiation need not be regarded as antithetical to the male reading, but may be incorporated within it as a necessary stimulus. It is in this interplay of power and loss, complicity and disengagement, that the fascination of these texts lies. It is in this sense that I would justify Larkin's verse, along with all the other 'sordid images' that I have studied in the course of writing this book. If, in the wake of feminism, literary texts must be acknowledged to be misogynistic, the converse, I would contend, is also the case: misogynistic texts must be respected as literary: the great tradition.

From S. H. Clark, *Sordid Images: The Poetry of Masculine Desire* (London and New York, 1994), pp. 220–57

## NOTES

[Steve Clark's essay first appeared in *Philip Larkin 1922–1985: A Tribute*, ed. George Hartley (London, 1988), pp. 237–71. It was revised after the publication of Andrew Motion's biography of Larkin and reprinted as a chapter in *Sordid Images: The Poetry of Masculine Desire* (1994). In this book, Clark presents a highly original account of 'the idiom of misogyny in English poetry', including chapters on Shakespeare and T. S. Eliot. Although he draws on recent debates on gender and psychoanalysis to explore the complex and contradictory nature of Larkin's sexual politics, Clark parts company with many feminist critics in his evaluation of misogynist texts. What he values in these texts is 'the marginalised and customarily repressed elements of male erotic discourse that they express' (p. 27). In the essay that follows, he stresses the seriousness with which Larkin's work addresses problems of sexual identity and sexual desire, and he shows how the imagery of the poems conceals a deeply suppressed eroticism. Larkin's poems insist on the preservation of male autonomy, but their 'opting out' of contemporary sexual ideology has a positive purpose in revealing the extent to which attitudes and assumptions about sex are socially constructed and conditioned. In demystifying sex, the poems expose many of the myths and stereotypes associated with it. Ed.]

1. Donald Davie, 'Landscapes of Larkin', in *Thomas Hardy and British Poetry* (London, 1973), p. 62.

2. Andrew Motion, *Philip Larkin: A Writer's Life* (London, 1993), p. 62.

3. Philip Larkin, *Jill* (London, 1946; 1964), p. 170.

4. Philip Larkin, *A Girl in Winter* (London, 1975), p. 248.

5. Larkin, *Jill*, p. 109. Compare this with Larkin's own '*scorching embar-rassment*' at a failed seduction in *Selected Letters of Philip Larkin 1940–1985*, ed. Anthony Thwaite (London, 1992), p. 105.

6. Philip Larkin, *Required Writing: Miscellaneous Pieces 1955–82* (London, 1983), pp. 48, 111, 191. Further references will be abbreviated as *RW* and included in the text.

7. Barbara Everett, 'Philip Larkin: After Symbolism', *Essays in Criticism*, 30 (1980), 227–42. [Reprinted in this volume – see pp. 55–70. Ed.]

8. Sigmund Freud, *The Standard Edition of the Complete Psychological Works of Sigmund Freud* (24 vols), translated by James Strachey (London, 1953–74), Vol. 4, p. 186; Vol. 5, pp. 360–2.

9. Anthony Thwaite (ed.), *Selected Letters of Philip Larkin 1940–1985* (London and Boston, 1992), p. 151. Further references will be abbreviated as *Letters* and included in the text.

10. Freud, *Complete Psychological Works*, Vol. 5, 364–6.

11. John Haffenden, *Viewpoints: Poets in Conversation* (London, 1981), p. 85.

12. John Ashbery, 'Profile', *Times*, 23 August 1984, p. 8a.

13. Larkin, *Jill*, p. 158.

14. Freud, *Complete Psychological Works*, Vol. 5, pp. 105–6.

15. Simon Petch, *The Art of Philip Larkin* (Sydney, 1981), pp. 24–5.

16. Motion, *Philip Larkin: A Writer's Life*, p. 186.

17. James Booth, *Philip Larkin: Writer* (Hemel Hempstead, 1992), p. 125.

18. Petch, *The Art of Philip Larkin*, p. 77.

19. Terry Whalen, *Philip Larkin and English Poetry* (London, 1986; 1990), p. 44.

20. Janice Rossen, *Philip Larkin: His Life's Work* (Hemel Hempstead, 1989), p. 74.

21. Matt Simpson, '"Never such innocence" – a reading of Larkin's "Sunny Prestatyn"', *Critical Survey*, 1: 2 (1989), 178.

22. Rossen, *His Life's Work*, p. 67.

23. John Bayley, 'Too Good For This World', in George Hartley (ed.), *Philip Larkin 1922–1985: A Tribute* (London, 1988), p. 200.

24. Rossen, *Philip Larkin: His Life's Work*, p. 70.

25. Graham Holderness, 'Reading "Deceptions" – a dramatic conversation', *Critical Survey*, 1: 2 (1989), 122–9; Rossen, *Philip Larkin: His Life's Work*, pp. 88–90; Booth, *Philip Larkin: Writer*, pp. 111, 127.

26. Motion, *A Writer's Life*, p. 275; Lisa Jardine, 'Saxon Violence', *Guardian*, 8 December 1992, Section 2, p. 4.

27. Jardine, 'Saxon Violence'.

28. Martin Amis, 'A Poetic Injustice', *Guardian Weekend*, 21 August 1993, p. 6.

# 7

# Difficulties with Girls

*JANICE ROSSEN*

Larkin's fury against women is not so much a declared state of siege against them personally as it is an internal battle raging within himself. In a world characterised largely by deprivation, women come to stand for the fact that:

> Life is an immobile, locked,
> Three-handed struggle between
> Your wants, the world's for you, and (worse)
> The unbeatable slow machine
> That brings what you'll get.
>
> (*CP*, 202)

People – and life in general – seem to have disappointed Larkin enormously. Still, deprivation often takes a uniquely feminine cast for him. Larkin is constantly encountering difficulties in his relations with girls – experiencing the pain of 'Love again: wanking at ten past three', the inability to work out why things should be so impossible (being unable to 'say why it never worked for me'), and the frustration of trying to accommodate his own needs (*CP*, 215). As he once wrote to Sutton in a moment of sheer exasperation, 'Fuck all women! I am quite fed up with the whole business: sooner be half full of beer. SEX is designed for people who like overcoming obstacles. I don't like overcoming obstacles.'[1] Larkin's views of women are clearly part of his larger struggle with life in terms of encountering its 'having-to', and feeling continually forced into enduring that which he dislikes (*CP*, 202). As another letter to Sutton about his own relations with women states: 'Unselfishness is forced upon one at every turn, *I* find, and its [sic] only by cunning and sleight of hand that one gets anything for oneself at all.'[2]

The difficulties which Larkin lays bare exist in a complicated tangle of cause and effect; it is difficult to know whom to blame. It may be difficult even to gauge what women are really like; as an early letter to Sutton states, written while Larkin was still up at Oxford: 'I am of the opinion that I shall never know anything about the woman I marry, *really*. What do I know of you? Nothing at all. Preserve me from interesting personalities.'[3] This remark dates from an early period in Larkin's life, before he had had time to revise his views, but to some extent it typifies the dilemma of his generation of men, who were educated apart from the 'girls' who came to seem mysterious and inaccessible. It assumes that women are 'other' and distanced. Further, compared with the excitement felt by Larkin's generation of undergraduates at Oxford when avidly reading D. H. Lawrence's novels, life beyond the University – when they actually met and courted women – may well have seemed awkward. For anyone whose ideas or expectations of women were modelled, even remotely, on Ursula and Gudrun Brangwen or Lady Chatterley, real life encounters are likely to have been a far cry from fiction. Lawrence's heroines may be *femmes fatales*, even dangerously so, or emotionally problematic (like Miriam from *Sons and Lovers*, with whom Paul Morel experiences his own difficulties); but they are usually highly charged sensually and available sexually to men. (Ironically, of course, Lawrence's ideal was not promiscuity, but fidelity to one woman; Birkin of *Women in Love* formulates this philosophy.) Still, as Larkin insists in his poetry, to enjoy this kind of intense and sexual relationship might have been difficult for his generation; not only were the right kind of women hard to find, but to carry off a seduction – always supposing one could square it with one's conscience – called for a certain *savoir faire*. 'Annus Mirabilis' hints at both these difficulties, and connects the problem directly with Lawrence. Once the prophetic message of *Lady Chatterley* was widely recognised, the poet implies, sex became possible; in addition, this is a private joke, since Larkin and his fellow undergraduates had been reading Lawrence with admiration long before the 'ban' was removed:

> Sexual intercourse began
> In nineteen sixty-three
> (Which was rather late for me) –

> Between the end of the *Chatterley* ban
> And the Beatles' first LP.
> (*CP*, 167)

As the poem suggests, attaining a sense of freedom which enables one to indulge uninhibitedly in sexual intercourse requires not only a change in the social system; the difficulties here are internal as well as external to the poet, which creates a complicated situation. As Larkin wrote to Sutton some years after going down from Oxford (and in self-mockery): 'I don't know about women and marriage. One thing I do think is that if we had known as many women as we have read books by DHL [sic] we should have a clearer idea of the situation.'[4]

Though he did consider deeply Lawrence's and Freud's discussions about unresolved sexual conflicts as they relate to one's earliest years, Larkin seems to have declined (at least in the context of his letters to Sutton) to press the issue further in order to gain insight into the problem. He records revulsion at such a possibility, but also relative unwillingness to explore its implications: 'No, if I consider my state of permanent non-attachment, my perpetual suspension, my sexual indifferences, I should put it down to Mother – complex if I were honest, I suppose. How irritating! And nasty, too!'[5] He seems to have taken no comfort from the fact that unresolved feelings about one's parents are a universally experienced affliction – except, of course, in later satiric versions of this theme such as 'This Be The Verse', where he parodies Freudian insistence on the importance of childhood in the pronouncement: 'They fuck you up, your mum and dad. / They may not mean to, but they do' (*CP, 180*). However, this latter poem also seems to avoid both introspection and insight at the same time as it complains about his present misery.

The poem 'Love Again' comes closer to formulating a reason for his inability to avoid the pain of love, by deeming it impossible to 'say why it never worked for me' and asking 'but why put it into words?' – and yet suggesting a reason nonetheless: 'Something to do with violence / A long way back, and wrong rewards' (*CP, 215*). Larkin's poetry on this subject often halts in a middle ground where he points tentatively in the direction of his suffering, but does not fully explore its implications. 'Love Again' suggests a strong desire to avoid finding the source of his misery – always supposing that source were possible to find – by resisting the task of putting it 'into words'. Even so, the more cogent source of that 'usual pain' is his feeling of being victimised by the outside world, which disregards him completely and mocks his desire (CP, 215). While the poet's rival has enjoyed the woman sexually for the evening, the poet, alone in his bed, is treated as negligible: 'And me supposed to be ignorant, / Or find it funny, or not to care' (CP, 215). The frustration is all the more ironic because the woman in question is seen as devouring; the rival man may enjoy her sexually, but he becomes 'drowned in that lash-wide stare' (CP, 215). The bitterness of being mocked by another's success pains the poet as much as being denied pleasure (of a dubious sort) himself. Love is clearly an illness, a sickness 'like dysentery', and unable to confer pleasure (CP, 215).

Larkin's general sense of frustration and alienation from the outside world is evident in a cartoon entitled 'Portrait of the Author and Family, 1939', which he drew during his late adolescent years.[6] It pictures the artist's family: his father, mother and sister are facing one another and talking about various subjects; all of these figures are talking at once, and disregarding each other's conversation, yet they are still loosely connected in that they face each other while engaged in other occupations. The father is reading a newspaper, the mother is knitting, and the sister is standing facing them, gesturing with one hand. What is most striking about the cartoon is that the figure of the young artist is sitting completely outside the circle, scribbling at a desk with one hand while looking up; his face is turned toward the viewer, suffused with dark emotion, while a huge wordless exclamation point hovers over his head. This sense of enormous, inexpressible emotion characterises much of his writing, and it also informs many of his views on women and family life. The difference which is often articulated in the poetry between selfishness and selflessness seems to derive from a deep conviction that one can never do anything other than react to other people. He is so much distressed by the pressure of others' expectations that he cannot act on his own impulses, and feels compelled to be polite to others rather than pursue his own desires. Thus the love-letters which the poet writes instead of writing a novel in 'At thirty-one, when some are rich' become something whose value and significance he cannot gauge except in the context of frustration:

> Why write, them, then? Are they in fact
> Just compromise,

Amiable residue when each denies
The other's want? Or are they not so nice,
Stand-ins in each case simply for an act?
Mushrooms of virtue? or, toadstools of vice?
(*CP, 70*)

Women primarily represent time 'wasted', as in this poem, or stolen
and appropriated entirely, as in 'Self's the Man', where 'the money he
gets for wasting his life on work / She takes as her perk' (*CP, 117*).
The fear of becoming entirely subsumed by a woman leads to a corresponding insistence on the absolute *necessity* of selfishness in order
to survive, or to sustain the barest existence.

Despite the evident anguish which much of Larkin's writing on
the subject betrays, his view of relations between men and women
can be quite funny, as when he enthusiastically admires men who
play the adroit seducer: 'Costals is something of a dream figure', he
says of the hero in a Montherlant novel, 'what every man would
like to be if he had the courage (he adds up how long women keep
him waiting, and drops them when the total reaches five hours).'[7]
The corresponding view of women which this attitude suggests is
one which Larkin isolates as a dichotomy of 'men this, women
that', and it defines a firmly articulated division in his own work
(*RW, 261*). To call Larkin a misogynist would be an overstatement
– to call him a misanthropist might be closer to the mark. Yet
women tend to play a role in his writing which finds him not far
from misogyny; at the least, he capitalises on the energy which
derives from seeing sexual politics solely from the man's point of
view, and from projecting much of his frustration onto women,
thus locating the source of his anger there. This view, because it is
based on universal human conflicts, reflects a dilemma with which
his readers (even, I think, his female readers) can readily identify –
and which accounts in part for the appeal of his work. In addition,
this largely negative and hostile view of women is countered by the
lyrical, tender side of his poetry which sees women as inspirational
and pure, as in poems such as 'Maiden Name', 'I see a girl dragged
by the wrists', 'Latest Face' and 'Broadcast'.

In the scheme which Larkin adopts in most of his poetry, though,
men are generally seen as victimised while women are powerful
and able to hurt or control them. The habitual sense of self-
consciousness which men feel in relation to women can be ex-
cruciating; to escape from man-hunting harpies requires all one's

wits and energies. Larkin's male characters remain convinced that no woman, attractive or unattractive, would look twice at them without the light of matrimony in her eye, and they see themselves doomed, to their chagrin, to relationships only with women in the latter category. Along with the heroes of some of his favourite comic novelists such as Kingsley Amis and Peter de Vries, Larkin's own bachelor characters usually assume that beautiful women will pay absolutely no attention to them. Should one be so fortunate as to meet a 'bosomy English rose', as does the speaker in 'Wild Oats', one may be certain that the beauty will be 'trying' for her part, 'not to laugh' (*CP, 143*). Moreover, the only available women are either ugly (and therefore undesirable) or, ironically, devalued by their accessibility. As Larkin formulates this view in the terms of Montherlant's novels, 'Marriage is absolutely contrary to nature, both because man cannot help desiring many women and because women in any case become undesirable at twenty-six' (*RW, 260*).

This situation poses a dilemma for the middle-aged bachelor, both personally and morally. Larkin addresses the problem in his poetry in a variety of complaints against life, his own powerlessness, and women themselves as the probable cause of his suffering; and he does so directly and forthrightly. In a sense, what Larkin does is to adopt the freedom of the sexual revolution in talking about sex openly – even brashly – all the while proclaiming that he can't enjoy its fruits in actual fact. As the poems 'Annus Mirabilis' and 'High Windows' suggest, he feels caught between two generations. This grievance is compounded by the fact that he feels personally affronted by women; and in consequence his poetry approaches the problem entirely from the man's view-point as a victim of the system, and from the related perspective where women are seen as entirely responsible for his deprivation. He reworks this unresolved conflict repeatedly, insisting that the relationship between men and women is antagonistic and that sex consists of 'obstacles' to be overcome.[8] As Jean Hartley recalls of Larkin, 'he'd say things like "Oh I wish you could get sex and pay for it monthly like you do the laundry, because it's all so difficult"'.[9]

One aspect of the inaccessibility of desirable women – and its frustrating effect on men – is in their artistic representation. Four of Larkin's poems, 'Lines on a Young Lady's Photograph Album', 'Sunny Prestatyn', 'Essential Beauty', and 'Wild Oats', depict idealised and beautiful women who are enshrined in fiction or in photographs. Their removal from the realm of present reality stresses their unavailability and thus subtly raises their value. At the same time, when these women appear in advertisements, men are invited by the photographer and others who create these glamorous images to appropriate and possess these women in fantasy, and create for themselves an unsatisfying illusion. Ironically of course the inaccessibility of the beloved can also define romance, in another context. The poem 'Latest Face' acknowledges the fleeting nature of romantic attraction and enshrines it in that moment. For fear of upsetting the balance, the poet would choose to leave it that way: 'Precious vagrant, recognise / My look, and do not turn again' (*CP*, 53). Romantic distance is in some ways the most desirable relationship one can have with a woman.

Another possible result of distance is simply that of envy. The girl pictured in 'Lines on a Young Lady's Photograph Album' stirs his jealousy; she is present with the poet when he views the photographs of her, yet in some ways remains inaccessible. Though rivalries are theoretically long past, he dislikes the competition which appears in the photographs in the form of the 'chaps' who 'loll / At ease about your earlier days' (*CP*, 71). In an almost Proustian moment of possessiveness, he becomes jealous about the times in the past when he was not present. The girl, or the 'real' girl as she existed in the past, remains inaccessible to him. In addition to arousing his jealousy of potential rivals, the photographs reflect the futility of his desire to possess her. When he contemplates the surreptitious theft of one of the pictures, he still can only grasp the image of her, not the woman herself. What staggers him is a sense of exclusion from her life: the photographs comprise 'a past that no one now can share' (*CP*, 72).

The distance from the young woman is all the more painful because she is seen to be a 'real girl in a real place' through the convincing medium of the camera (*CP*, 71). This problem of remoteness is compounded in regard to idealised women who appear on posters in the service of advertising, and who seem actively to solicit men's admiration, which they demand without giving anything substantive in return. The women in 'Essential Beauty' and 'Sunny Prestatyn' represent an exalted, infinitely distanced version of femininity. Using their sexual powers for a specific purpose, they seem to promise themselves through the medium of the product they represent; 'Essential Beauty' depicts a girl in a cigarette advertisement, while 'Sunny Prestatyn' depicts a girl who advertises a beach resort. These are at once 'real' girls, because photography reproduces them faithfully, and yet unreal – because they are artfully glamorised and because they exist only in a photograph. Thus photography becomes a kind of metaphor for not being able to communicate with or touch a woman. Further, the women are seductive in that they attempt to sell something through the suggestion of selling themselves. The potential effect these women have on the men who behold them is, therefore, frustration: the women fail to deliver on their promises, and never appear in the flesh. Moreover, the girl in the cigarette advertisement in 'Essential Beauty' is a decadent, beautiful harbinger of death:

> ... dying smokers sense
> Walking towards them through some dappled park
> As if on water that unfocused she
> No match lit up, nor drag ever brought near,
> Who now stands newly clear,
> Smiling, and recognising, and going dark.
> (*CP*, 144–5)

The girl is thus cast as a *femme fatale*; death overtakes those who smoke in an effort to conjure her into reality, and she accepts complicity in this relationship by 'recognising' their adoration.

This description suggests a complex situation, where the smokers and the girl in the advertisement both perpetuate an unfulfilled, unfulfilling relationship. She requires adoration from them, and is seductive but does not deliver on her promises (offering a cigarette is a poor substitute for sex) and the men are unable to break from her. Women thus induce a kind of illness of dependency – in fact, the successor to the 'Sunny Prestatyn' poster is one which urges its viewers to '*Fight Cancer*' (*CP*, 149). This implies that men must struggle to free themselves from a relationship which they feel unable to renounce, although they see it as unhealthy. The pathology exists on both sides, of course – the men refuse, figuratively and literally, to give up smoking, and thus to some extent invite death in the presence of the *femme fatale*.

The girl on the poster in 'Sunny Prestatyn' is portrayed by those who made the poster as figuratively prostituting herself, as she identifies herself with the holiday beach resort. From the male point of view, she provocatively invites him to take his pleasure: '*Come to Sunny Prestatyn* / Laughed the girl on the poster, / Kneeling up on the sand / In tautened white satin' (*CP*, 149). The invitation is a calculated sexual advance. The woman merges with the place itself, seeming to sustain it and take pleasure in it; coast and hotel seem to 'expand from her thighs and / Spread breast-lifting arms' (*CP*, 149).

Interpretations of this poem tend to be problematic, as the poster's subsequent defacing is described in such brutal language; in light of its crudity and intensity, one wonders how much complicity the poet shares in the act. Terry Whalen sees the poster as exhibiting a 'source of imaginative decadence, and also as a stimulus to common grief and disappointment'.[10] In this context, the advertisement seems to promise an impossible ideal as something attainable, and thus, on purely moral grounds it deserves to be ruined. Whalen sees the defacing of the poster as a protest against this shoddy kind of commercialism, a means of 'attacking such fraudulence' and restoring 'life lived according to the dominant imaginative hungers of the familiar contemporary world'. This view in the end seems to applaud the 'graffiti [which] oddly signify a critical capacity in the common man'.[11]

Yet the poet discerns a primitive sexual urge at work here as well, and enthusiastic participation in the ritual perhaps suggests less a critical capacity on the part of '*Titch Thomas*' than it does menacing lust, and the indulging of a sexual fantasy expressed in the form of sadistic violence (*CP*, 149). The defacing of the poster may attack only the poster, and not the girl herself, but it also seeks to punish and humiliate her image in pointedly sexual terms. The poet goes on to describe in detail the various assaults made on the figure, from the mutilation of her face and exaggeration of her sexuality ('Huge tits and a fissured crotch / Were scored well in') to the 'tuberous cock and balls' which she is set 'astride', and which seem to constitute dangerous weapons which will hurt her (*CP*, 149). This catalogue of violent acts evokes the anger felt by the defacers, who figuratively rape the icon – and the scene is recounted in not especially satirical terms. The attacks are sadistic, in asserting power over the woman, and grotesque – at the least, they are intended to satisfy an urge for revenge. He seems to justify violence against women by suggesting that access to the woman is something men have been unfairly deprived of; therefore, she is fair game. The viewers of the intended icon assault and deface it partly as a means of revenge for deprivation (holidays, like women, cost money) and partly as a means of taking up the covert sexual invitation. The corporate masculine response to the photographic image of the woman is violent in part because she is unattainable in the flesh, and the men resent her attempts to use sex as power. If she appears to mock them, their only defence is to use fantasies of rape and disfigurement as a weapon against her, in order to destroy her beauty and thus negate the source of their envy.

The detached observer offers this reason for the attack: 'She was too good for this life' (CP, 149). This points a moral of a certain sort – the beautiful woman is 'too good' in the sense that such idealisation as the poster employs removes her from being attainable, or from being held responsible for her invitation (CP, 149). The poet somehow puts the burden back on her, implying that she tempts men out of her own vanity and that she also comprises the source of their deprivation. As a siren, she drives men to commit bizarre and brutal acts in response; as a prostitute, according to this logic, she deserved the punishment anyway. Still, even if this conclusion were reasonable, it nonetheless seems a harsh judgement; the lust which drives men to deface a poster can also lead one to rape an actual woman, as the poem 'Deceptions' suggests. Thus a large part of Larkin's depiction of women has directly to do with violence against them, and he seems to speak powerfully both for a corporate group of men and *from* a deep subconscious level.

To show the effect the inaccessibility of a glamorous woman has on him, Larkin evokes the image of an icon photograph again in a different context in 'Wild Oats'. In another instance of strict dichotomy, he splits the image of women into the unattainable beauty and the accessible but less attractive woman, and defines male sexual desire in this light:

> About twenty years ago
> Two girls came in where I worked –
> A bosomy English rose
> And her friend in specs I could talk to.
> Faces in those days sparked
> The whole shooting-match off, and I doubt
> If ever one had like hers:
> But it was the friend I took out,
>
> (CP, 143)

The 'shooting-match' is a sexual and violent image which covertly hints at the man's intentions towards the two women, and he regards their appearance even in this ordinary context as almost a deliberate provocation. They seem to present him with a choice –

though since he assumes that his attainment of anything he desires will be frustrated, he knows that he must of necessity forgo pleasure ('But it was the friend I took out' [*CP*, 143]).

The women themselves embody two versions of femininity, both seductive in different ways. The 'rose' is attractive to him not only because she is beautiful, but because she is exaggeratedly feminine. She is 'bosomy', possessed of a beautiful face, and is later pictured wearing 'fur gloves', which suggests a sensual, voluptuous side to her nature (*CP*, 143). In addition, she is exalted beyond his reach, such dazzling attraction combined with inaccessibility comprises the stuff of romance. The poet's half-hearted pursuit of the 'friend in specs' is counterpointed throughout by his real desire for the 'bosomy rose' (*CP*, 143). The 'friend in specs' tries to capture the man through the use of feminine wiles other than beauty, most notably that of sexual accessibility: the couple meet 'At numerous cathedral cities / Unknown to the clergy' (*CP*, 143). She also shows herself able and determined to keep him; she is skilled at forestalling a break, as parting entails 'about five / Rehearsals' (*CP*, 143). Nonetheless, the image of the bosomy rose overshadows the friend completely, making a relationship with her impossible for the poet. Thus the women work together to deprive him of pleasure. The end of the poem finds him having consistently worshipped an idealised image: 'In my wallet are still two snaps / Of bosomy rose with fur gloves on. / Unlucky charms, perhaps' (*CP*, 143). Hence the photographs which capture the ideal of beauty possess a kind of arcane power. The glamorous woman is unattainable in person, and yet the would-be lover remains captivated by her image. Beautiful women in Larkin's poems all tend to be 'too good for this life', as 'Sunny Prestatyn' phrases it, and remain exalted in another sphere (*CP*, 149). This is all of a piece with his picture of male sexual fantasy, which regards women primarily in a remote, even ethereal way: as the poet in 'The Large Cool Store' observes, the 'Modes For Night' which belong to women show 'How separate and unearthly love is, / Or women are, or what they do, / Or in our young unreal wishes / Seem to be' (*CP*, 135).

The dichotomy of 'men this, women that' extends also to a fine distinction between beautiful and not beautiful women, and to accessible and inaccessible women (*RW*, 261). The problem for Larkin's bachelors is how to get what they want, or, how to obtain women who fit both the first and third categories. This division between different types of women appears most notably in 'Letter to a Friend about Girls', where the poet regrets his comparatively unsuccessful attempt to seduce attractive women, concluding: 'all the while / I've met a different gauge of girl from yours' (CP, 122). This distinction between kinds of women also includes the related issues of class consciousness, and of constructing some means of coping with rejection and deprivation. [ ... ]

In a way which perhaps even equals the passion of Montherlant, Larkin argues forcefully about the difficulty of being a man. For one thing, he points out that the problem of sexual frustration is all the more irritating because the poet did not choose it. Sexuality and its greed are thrust upon him; they are part of the limitation of being human which he did not want. In 'Ignorance', the poet chafes under a sense of being imprisoned in his body:

> Strange to be ignorant of the way things work:
> Their skill at finding what they need,
> Their sense of shape, and punctual spread of seed,
> And willingness to change ...
>
> (CP, 107)

Here the Darwinian process of selection is shown to be a random, external force which he cannot control. Such 'knowledge' is intrinsic to being alive: 'for our flesh / Surrounds us with its own decisions' (CP, 107). He is saying that one has been placed in this situation with no recourse to anything outside the system; and sexual desire is something he would rather not have to manage. In its very nature sexual desire is recurrent and for that reason never ultimately satisfying. Even willed renunciation appears unavailing in 'Dry-Point', which describes the poet's struggle against the recurrence of desire, yet which also posits inevitable anti-climax even in achieving one's desire: 'But what sad scapes we cannot turn from then: / What ashen hills! what salted, shrunken lakes!' (CP, 36–7).

Just as John Kemp's sexual misadventures in *Jill* are doomed to disaster, so, seemingly, are the endeavours of all of Larkin's other protagonists, who argue endlessly with themselves and with others about the necessity of renouncing sex. What often results from Larkin's avowed pessimism about love is a statement of two opposing view-points, one which asserts that women are best given up, and the other which suggests either that the poet pursue something else instead or that he make light of his difficulties lest he seem a fool. The basic opposition which Larkin creates is between the individual self (often allied with art, as in 'Reasons for Attendance') and marriage and domestic life.

His bachelor characters encounter what they perceive as unfair disapproval, and resent being accused of selfishness because they have not married. 'Self's the Man' in particular mounts a tortuous self-defence against this charge:

> To compare his life and mine
> Makes me feel a swine:
> Oh, no one can deny
> That Arnold is less selfish than I.
>
> But wait, not so fast:
> Is there such a contrast?
> He was out for his own ends
> Not just pleasing his friends;
> (CP, 117)

Larkin's protagonists protest against the frustration which they experience, caught between desire and social convention. In denouncing marriage, the poet creates a satirical portrait of a husband surrounded by wife and children (and potentially by a mother-in-law, further evidence of the horrible ties that bind familes together). In the speaker's view, Arnold has become the property of his family, and even the pursuit of sexual fulfilment becomes reversed; Arnold is virtually emasculated, as it is the shrill wife who symbolically demands performance of duties from the husband:

> And when he finishes supper
> Planning to have a read at the evening paper
> It's *Put a screw in this wall* –
> He has no time at all...
> (CP, 117)

The cumbersome domestic duties which the bachelor envisions smothering a married person are heaped on Arnold with relish: the hapless husband appears dutifully engaged 'With the nippers to wheel round the houses / And the hall to paint in his old trousers' and so on (CP, 117).

The tactic here is to be literal about what marriage could do. From the poet's point of view, Arnold wanted sex and was thus forced into marriage – and the result is all too predictable: 'He married a woman to stop her getting away / Now she's there all day' (*CP*, 117). Marriage is thus seen entirely in the context of sexual drives, and it offers only another variation on the perennial theme of frustration. In keeping with the general emphasis on dichotomy, there seems to be no reasonable middle ground. The woman either '[gets] away' or is 'there all day' (*CP*, 117).

The main force of the satire, however, works against the speaker himself. What annoys him is his feeling of inferiority to Arnold as husband and father. To prove himself in the right, he must therefore overstate the problems attendant on Arnold's marriage, having internalised a burden of guilt which leaves him furious at everyone. Significantly, he does not try to argue against marriage on the grounds that it excludes other things; the poet does *not* defend himself by saying that he requires solitude for creating art, or that the individual identity which he possesses apart from marriage is more important. The question centres on his innate character and abilities, or on 'what [he] can stand / Without them sending a van – / Or I suppose I can' (*CP*, 118). In effect, the poet seems so determined to convince himself and others that he should avoid such entrapment that he pleads imminent death as an excuse for not marrying. This is reason enough to desist, yet at the same time is an overly extravagant defence. In addition, the qualification in the final phrase undercuts the argument, which betrays uncharacteristic uncertainty, whereas up to this point the poet has seemed aggressive and assured. The fact that he appears to hedge at the last minute suggests another side to the question without actually deflating the entire argument. It deflates his pomposity, but not his passionately expressed beliefs. While 'Self's the Man' dramatises the difficulties involved in working out satisfactory sexual relations for a man, it also seeks to make plain the sheer horror of marriage (a dread which is in some ways understandable). And though it may be a satirical pose, this villifies women and casts them as foreign and other.

Although he feels lucky not to be Arnold, Larkin's speaker is also aware of the loss entailed in not being a husband or father; 'Dockery and Son' speaks poignantly of the realisation of possessing 'no son, no wife, / No house or land' (*CP*, 152). 'The View', a poem written on the occasion of Larkin's fiftieth birthday, finds the poet thinking again in negatives: he is 'Unchilded and unwifed', seeing with awful clarity the 'drear' remainder of life (*CP*, 195).

Thus although 'Self's the Man' emphasises the intrusion of wife and children into one's life, there is another side to it as well; their absence can seem a loss. The final conclusion to be drawn, then, is that the entire system is exasperating. Larkin's bachelor characters generally alternate between blaming themselves for their own inadequacy in the matter – in effect, for not being able to get what they want (being a Montherlant hero) and for not being able to accommodate the attendant difficulty of domestic life if one does marry (being Arnold). Caught between selfishness and love, Larkin's bachelor becomes like the 'bleeder' who 'Can't manage either view' in his poem 'Love'.[12] The system of courtship annoys him in part because it seems calculated to expose a man's weakness; the poet in 'Wild Oats', for instance, accepts all the blame for the failure of a relationship and offers a tacit admission that he is 'too selfish, withdrawn, / And easily bored to love' (*CP*, 143).

Since Larkin often insists so strongly on the dichotomy of singleness as opposite to marriage, with sexual desire wreaking havoc in the middle, he seizes on the sexual revolution of the 1960s as an illustration of what can happen when several of these earlier restrictions are lifted. While this change could theoretically create a better system for men caught in this bind, the poet remains pessimistic about his own chances of happiness and envious of others who can seize pleasure without feeling guilty. Several poems from Larkin's final volume, *High Windows*, cast the middle-aged bachelor in a setting of sexual freedom; yet when the revolution comes, it proves a further source of bitterness and frustration. This is a brilliant subject for his poetry to address, since the new system is in many ways no improvement on the old, thus providing a new subject for satire; freedom in the sense of lack of commitment does not necessarily lead to intimacy or fulfilment. But seeing it – even seeing it as an illusion – played out by others, can reinforce his personal sense of deprivation still further.

In a broad sense, Larkin sees himself as a product of, and consequently a captive of, his time and generation. 'Annus Mirabilis' and 'High Windows' perceive the modern generation as having achieved freedom from entrapment because sex no longer necessarily leads to domestic responsibility entailed by the begetting of children. The kid can 'fuck' his girlfriend without the danger of begetting children thanks to the girl's (probable) pills or diaphragm (*CP*, 165). Similarly, the entire generation described in 'Annus Mirabilis' has entered a glorious revolution:

> Then all at once the quarrel sank:
> Everyone felt the same,
> And every life became
> A brilliant breaking of the bank,
> A quite unlosable game.
> (*CP*, 167)

Because of a change in the social structure and the advent of contraceptives, the middle-aged bachelor in 1963 has a much better chance of obtaining 'Sexual intercourse' with no strings attached – although, to his chagrin, he cannot partake in it (*CP*, 167). The times are now propitious, but liberation occurred 'just too late for me' (*CP*, 167).

The speaker is prevented from joining in the revolution less because of external constraints than because of internal scruples. Intellectually he perceives the advantages of free sex. Still, the protagonist has so completely internalised old-fashioned notions of moral restraint – no sex without marriage, or at least without shame – that he cannot now throw them off. He sees himself as a product of his time and generation, becoming like the man in 'Posterity', whom the contemptuous biographer characterises as 'Not out for kicks or something happening – / One of those old-type *natural* fouled-up guys' (*CP*, 170). Similarly, the poet in 'Annus Mirabilis' admires the sexual revolution impersonally, applauding its forthrightness, though he declares himself unable to benefit from it.

At the same time, something rings slightly false in his celebration of the miraculous event. For one thing, the change fails to eradicate the link between sex and money. Sex remains a business deal, and the optimistic hope that everyone will participate in breaking the bank seems a deliberate naïveté. Secondly, the choice of a specific date, 1963, seems suspiciously reductive. It is all too simple. The poet's description of life as a 'quite unlosable game' hints at parody; the tone of the entire poem is a puzzling mixture of sincerity and irony (*CP*, 167). It acknowledges envy and loss; but the modest self-deprecation ('rather late for me') is offered too readily, and suggests that the poet is disassociating himself from something he does not care much about (*CP*, 167). He may regret not having enjoyed more sexual freedom, yet he regrets it too politely to seem entirely convincing.

Several poems in *High Windows* are fuelled by envy; the successful figure of Horatio in 'Letter to a Friend about Girls' broadens to include an entire generation. In 'High Windows', it is 'everyone young' who is 'going down the long slide / To happiness, endlessly' (*CP*, 165). In 'Money', the poet's bank account becomes a siren ('I listen to money singing') who seems to promise pleasure, as did the girl on the poster in 'Sunny Prestatyn'. 'Money' begins:

> Quarterly, is it, money reproaches me:
>   'Why do you let me lie here wastefully?
> I am all you never had of goods and sex.
> You could get them still by writing a few cheques'.
> (*CP*, 198)

This too is a deceptive temptation. The poet's bitterness is increased by his observation that other people appear to manage their resources better: they have acquired 'a second house and car and wife' (*CP*, 198). Yet again, these are not something he wants, even though he could now afford them. From his view-point, the system has not changed significantly, not least because he does not feel that he can allow himself pleasure. In addition, the notion of having to pay for pleasure still haunts him; it still takes money to buy 'goods and sex', or at least to acquire a second wife (*CP*, 198). Even in this new, relatively enlightened system, sex is something that the poet cannot enjoy in a normal way. He mocks himself for his own inadequacy ('Not out of kicks or something happening'), though he also satirises the new system as well (*CP*, 170). The *long slide* to happiness sounds too facile to be real (*CP*, 165). One is left finally with the haunting sense of difficulty and pain which characterises the poet's view at the end of 'Money' and 'High Windows'. All that Larkin can do in response to the siren call of money or to his overwhelming envy of the younger generation is to take up a vantage point which he has taken up before, to distance himself behind a window, through which he watches the manic dance of life. And it can only be a partial solution to his pain; from this perspective, the poet's sense of despondency predominates: 'It is intensely sad' (*CP*, 198).

Yet given the fact that Larkin is primarily expressing a corporate masculine perspective on sexual matters, there still remains the problem of the misogyny his work expresses. One might well ask what Larkin is trying to achieve in these poems. One response to redeem the poet from a charge of misogyny might be that he is satirising men with these views and thus showing that women ought to be treated less as objects and more as people in their own right. However, this does not seem to be the case, since he might just as strongly appear to want women to stop tormenting men; it remains unclear just what difficulties the men in Larkin's poetry and fiction are projecting onto women out of their own internal struggles, and what external difficulties they have to contend with. In effect, Larkin never reaches a resolution to these questions, and they continue to spin in endless reworkings of the conflict. Another possible consideration is that Larkin is making women symbolic of the lure of romantic love in order to satirise the foolishness of excessive emotion; he is notably pessimistic on this subject, and women in his poetry and fiction might suffer in their representation from bearing the burden of expressing this disappointment and bitterness.

In poems such as 'I see a girl dragged by the wrists' and 'Deceptions', Larkin shows a tenderness, even a reverence toward women. The girl in the *North Ship* poem, 'I see a girl dragged by the wrists', possesses an elusive vitality and joy which the poet envies but feels that he cannot attain: 'To be that girl! – but that's impossible' (*CP*, 279). The struggle between two people which is pictured in this poem is one of relative gaiety; the girl laughs as she is being dragged along in the snow, and she is clearly willing and enjoying the relationship of being dominated by another.

In 'Deceptions' Larkin addressed the problems of violence and sex when a rape results, and the event here is not distanced by satire but rather brought close by focusing on its victim and her agony. The poet shows compassion for the girl's suffering; yet at the same time, the poem remains problematic because the poet also shows a great deal of sympathy with the man who has attacked her, and thus he ends the poem with a marked detachment from the woman's suffering, which he begins the piece in describing. This ambivalent view-point suggests a complex psychological structure underneath, where the poet can to some extent identify with the girl's victimisation – but only partially. He seems to show tenderness to her and participation in her sorrow *because* she has been hurt. To some extent, the poem suggests that the poet can neither imaginatively be nor understand the victimised Victorian girl; though he certainly shares some empathy with her by identifying with her pain: 'Even so distant, I can taste the grief, / Bitter and sharp with stalks, he made you gulp' (*CP*, 32). This description is also a grim kind of Freudian pun as well as a literal one, since the girl has been drugged before being violated. Yet in a way, the poet distances himself and admits that he cannot participate in that grief, though this too is a mark of respect for her: 'I would not dare / Console you if I could' (*CP*, 32). Ultimately, however, the poet dramatises the girl's agony in light of the rapist's dissatisfaction once the deed is done; the man, in his view, attains entrance only to 'fulfilment's desolate attic' by violating her (*CP*, 32). This understanding acknowledges that the rapist's sadistic violence cannot solve his desire for revenge against women, which has deeper roots. The girl has been punished as an innocent victim, and the poet expresses remorse for her ruin at the same time that he recognises some of the impulses which led to it.

One important aspect of the poem is its seeming reality, achieved through direct reference to an actual event. This is not at all the same as the adolescent fantasies such as those described in 'A Study of Reading Habits', where the poet exults in 'The women I clubbed with sex! / I broke them up like meringues' (*CP*, 131). This obviously came out of a book – or the poet's own imagination. In 'Deceptions', however, Larkin seems to insist upon our seeing the rape as a vivid, actual occurrence, by first quoting the girl's own words from Mayhew's account in his massive study, *London Labour and the London Poor*. Mayhew himself tried in his research and writing not to sentimentalise the poor or their problems; and yet Larkin almost exploits the scene by evoking the girl's words and her misery and then turning to the criminal's point of view. It appears almost frighteningly detached.[13]

Much – though not all – of the burden of difficulty here lies with several critics' readings of the poem, which tend to accept at face value the premise advanced in the poem that the rapist is somehow worse off than his victim. One result of summarising the prose content of the poem – especially given its basis in actual incident – is to make the poet and critic seem casual and heartless. A question such as 'Is it really worse for the rapist because he is less undeceived than the girl is?' seems academic and cruel on the critic's part, if this is indeed what the poet is proposing. Yet it is an assumption which generally remains unchallenged. One critic responds as follows: 'the only consolation he can offer the girl is that her suffering is "exact". She will spiritually grow by her knowledge; the "fulfilment" of the rapist is in reality not fulfilling, but disappointing, a blundering into empty confusion.'[14] Another reading suggests: 'Though the girl cannot be consoled for her various pains, she harboured no delusions as to what was happening. Because

Larkin thus uses the rapist's lust as an emblem of all human desires, his sense of shared self-deception allows him to go beyond pity for the girl or indignation against the rapist.[15] Yet this is surely a bit abstract. It is all very well to write sagely about suffering, but this poem seems less Hardyesque and fateful and immediate than it does detached almost to the point of sadism.

For one thing, this equable view of the rapist as personally 'unfulfilled' in his action ignores the sociological perspective having to do with cold cash, a connection of which Mayhew himself was keenly aware. Someone is eventually going to profit from the ruin of the girl, and from her abduction into prostitution. It also neglects to mention the aspect of domination which the violent act of the rapist clearly demonstrates. He may be spiritually unfulfilled, but he has physically brutalised her, an act which one may assume is not spiritually enlightening for her so much as it is damaging. Finally, this kind of reading ignores the extent of the girl's actual suffering – which is so great that she begs her captors to kill her – and fails to appreciate that she was deceived in large measure as well. She is sufficiently drugged during the rape as to discover that she has 'been ruined' (her words) only the next morning (*CP*, 32). In sum, I do not think that one can have it both ways: Larkin as detached poetic observer and Larkin as sympathetic to human suffering. While not ignoring the aesthetics of the poem, the callousness which it exhibits and the sadism which it in part condones ought at the least to be seen as problematic – and as a limitation in Larkin's art.

Although Larkin wrote non-satirical poems about men's relationships with women, the underlying subtext still seems to express resentment towards women. The burden of these poems seems to be the difficulty men experience in dealing with their sexual desire and in relating to women. A posthumously published but incomplete poem entitled 'The Dance' provides a fascinating example of this ambivalence, which Larkin apparently wrestled with over a long period. It describes a particular situation – a social dance – and the poet's feelings of paralysis, jealousy and longing as they occur during the course of the evening. The social outing combines three agreeable things, 'Drink, sex and jazz', which constitute a modernised version of the traditional elements of revelry, 'Wine, women and song' (*CP*, 154). Yet the abandonment to pleasure which the poet seeks through experiencing these things is not forthcoming; the dance described here primarily offers a stage for acute sexual and emotional anxiety. At the same time, this poem contains probably the most deeply considered and nearly positive view of love and desire of any of Larkin's works. It records a moment when the poet recognises that emotion might be possible, even permissible, and when he considers allowing his defences against it figuratively to 'topple' (*CP*, 157). The poem expresses genuine regret and real pain, and records an attempt to reach for the object of his desire, even as the poet regrets that attempt in the same breath, crying:

> How useless to invite
> The sickened breathlessness of being young
>
> Into my life again!
> 　　　　　　　　(*CP*, 157)

The negative elements found in Larkin's other poetry about sexual desire are strongly present in this piece – the poet still senses violence and mockery (in the outside world and in women themselves), and he feels aggrieved, self-conscious, and at times frantic to escape. Characteristically, his first response to the prospect of the dance includes strong overtones of guilt; he looks at himself in the mirror while dressing at home and he sees 'The shame of evening trousers, evening tie', and this ambivalence resonates throughout the poem, as in his designation of the dance as the woman's 'innocent-guilty-innocent night' (*CP*, 154, 156). The very fact that he must rationalise the dance as something 'normal and allowed' suggests his uneasiness in attending it (*CP*, 154). On first arriving, for instance, he senses hostility in the parked cars and feels he must traverse an alien landscape which seems both to mock and beckon him:

> Half willing, half abandoning the will,
> I let myself by specious steps be haled
> Across the wide circumference of my scorn.
> No escape now. Large cars parked round the lawn
> Scan my approach.
> 　　　　　　　　(*CP*, 154)

Still more menacing overtones greet him inside, in the form of threats from people or inanimate objects which seek to waylay him and prevent him from achieving his goal of pursuing the woman whom he has come to see. The dance floor 'reverberates as with alarm', the music is 'omen-laden', the parental figure in the portrait of the 'gilt-edged Founder' declines to offer 'protection', while a male rival (the 'weed from Plant Psychology') keeps on appearing to dance with the woman and to spark acute envy in the poet (CP, 154–6).

But the central emotional drama of the poem, apart from the threatening elements which distress him, is the poet's relationship with the woman herself. Much of his energy goes into attempting to interpret what she is communicating, as it earlier went into scanning the setting of the dance; and he fears to find her hostile as well. When they first dance together, she seems faintly antagonistic: 'Your look is challenging / And not especially friendly' (CP, 155). Yet this gives way to the distinct possibility of love, which the poet in turn clearly recognises – though it, like so many other things at the dance, contains the threat of potential violence:

> I feel
> The impact, open, raw,
> Of a tremendous answer banging back
>
> As if I'd asked a question. In the slug
> And snarl of music, under cover of
> A few permitted movements, you suggest
> A whole consenting language, that my chest
> Quickens and tightens at, descrying love –
> (CP, 155)

He still cannot decide whether or not to act upon this realisation, and to seize the possibility of love – and indeed, his meditation is largely directed towards questioning his own ability *to* love. He feels that he lacks the qualities which 'Moments like this demand' (CP, 155). He also mocks himself in these terms, as being too old to participate in emotional relationships: 'It's pathetic how / So much most people half my age have learned / Consumes me only as I watch you now' (CP, 156).

The extent of his anxiety is stressed by his seeming inability to manoeuvre to get what he wants. At one point he wavers:

> I ought to go,
> If going would do any good; instead,
> I let the barman tell me how it was
> Before the war
> (CP, 157)

Yet when the evening figuratively begins again, as he sits down at a table with the woman and her friends, the sinister elements of the dance have been transformed; and in dancing with her a second time he mercifully escapes notice. The two of them 'take the floor/ Quite unremarked-on', and in this setting of relative security and freedom he again contemplates her invitation to love, or her 'silent beckoning' (*CP*, 157). In sum, 'The Dance' suggests that the possibility of love and intimacy exists; that it is good and much to be desired; and that the poet wishes (at least to some extent) that he possessed the qualities necessary to be able to seize it. In the end, the conflict remained largely unresolved for Larkin – the poem was unfinished, and its last word, 'understand', continues to resonate without an answer (*CP*, 158).

For the most part, the very egocentrism, anger and frustration which Larkin articulates form the heart of his argument against women throughout his work. If life is painful, he insists on howling about it and on not allowing any dilution of his pain. To say that he has always got what he wanted constitutes 'A perfectly vile and foul / Inversion of all that's been' (*CP*, 202). He exaggerates a masculine, egotistical view: his heroes exult in 'The women [they] clubbed with sex' as a means of rebelling against the deprivation which they have experienced (*CP*, 131). From one point of view, the only way to counter feminine sexual allure as power is by means of retaliation and violence. Nonetheless, these outbursts are in part a rhetorical device designed to mock and satirise what was, to Larkin and others of his generation, a real dilemma; and to some extent, he seems to have solved the problem by devoting himself to writing and insisting on its superior importance, as he suggests in 'Reasons for Attendance'. He insists here that sexual fulfilment and artistic creativity are mutually exclusive entities. In splitting the two elements into opposing sides, 'Reasons for Attendance' thus creates a dichotomy between union and individuation, between absorption in another person and devotion to the 'rough-tongued bell' of Art (*CP*, 80). Accordingly, Larkin argues with himself endlessly: 'Sex, yes, but what / Is sex?' (*CP*, 80). The problem of assigning the proper value to it – as opposed to art – preoccupies him both in a broad, social and psychological context and in an intensely personal one. He insists on division: self as artist as opposed to Arnold as husband and father. In sustaining and separating these two views, he remains suspended indefinitely in an agony of indecision.

From Janice Rossen, *Philip Larkin: His Life's Work* (Hemel Hempstead, 1989), pp. 66–76, 80–93.

NOTES

[Janice Rossen's feminist criticism of Larkin's poetry brings the issue of misogyny into the foreground. Why is it, she asks, that so many of the women in Larkin's poems are imagined as 'distant' and 'other'? She concludes that Larkin's 'fury against women' is part of a battle raging within himself: an internal conflict between sexual fulfilment and artistic creativity, perceived by the poet as mutually exclusive entities. Rossen adds, however, that Larkin's largely negative and hostile representation of women is countered, to some extent, by a lyrical, romantic impulse to imagine women as inspirational and pure. Like Steve Clark (essay 6), she also suggests that Larkin's poetry has a positive, regenerative role in exposing how men habitually misrepresent women through myths and stereotypes. Ed.]

1. Larkin to Sutton, MS DP/174/2, 30 October 1951, Philip Larkin Archive, Brynmor Jones Library, University of Hull.

2. Ibid., 20 November 1949.

3. Ibid., 20 October 1941.

4. Ibid., 15 September 1948.

5. Ibid., 2 January 1951.

6. Drawing reproduced in description of Larkin letters to Sutton, *Christie's London* catalogue, Bouquet – 3858, 22 June 1988, p. 51.

7. Philip Larkin, *Required Writing: Miscellaneous Pieces 1955–82* (London, 1983), p. 261. Further references will be abbreviated as *RW* and included in the text.

8. Larkin to Sutton, MS DP/174/2, 30 October 1951.

9. Jean Hartley, in the BBC Radio programme 'The bicycle-clipped misanthropist', produced by Alistair Wilson (1986).

10. Terry Whalen, *Philip Larkin and English Poetry* (London, 1986), p. 43.

11. Ibid., p. 44.

12. This line appears in the version of the poem published in *Critical Quarterly*, 8: 2 (1966), and is altered in the *Collected Poems*.

13. Mayhew describes his book as 'the first attempt to publish the history of a people, from the lips of the people themselves – giving a literal description of their labour, their earnings, their trials, and their suffer-

ings, in their own "unvarnished" language'. He goes on to stress that he hopes not to sentimentalise the distress under which the poor suffer, but rather to give the rich a more intimate knowledge of their sufferings. Henry Mayhew, *London Labour and the London Poor*, Vol. 1 (London, 1861), pp. iii–iv.

14. David Timms, *Philip Larkin* (Edinburgh, 1973), p. 59.

15. Bruce Martin, *Philip Larkin* (Boston, 1978), p. 48. Lolette Kuby also writes somewhat dismissively of the girl's misery, claiming that 'Her suffering excludes frustrated expectation and disillusionment. The man, on the other hand, the victimiser ruthlessly fulfilling his will, is nature's fool because it is not his will. His readings had become "erratic" (and erotic), a wandering from reason and humanity, a misreading'. Still, this reading of the man's misreading seems excessively abstract and distanced. See Lolette Kuby, *Philip Larkin: An Uncommon Poet for the Common Man* (The Hague, 1974), p. 47.

# 8

# Into the Heart of Englishness

*TOM PAULIN*

Social history and the lyric poem appear to be poles apart. Politics and culture are always melting into different shapes, but the lyric speaks for unchanging human nature, that timeless essence beyond fashion and economics. Reading the opening lines of Larkin's 'Afternoons':

> Summer is fading:
> The leaves fall in ones and twos
> From trees bordering
> The new recreation ground.
> (*CP*, 121)

we catch the characteristic accent of the medieval English lyric and are reassured by something that endures beyond the sadness of leaves falling. The new recreation ground and 'estateful of washing' fade into the background, and out of an elegiac sense of time passing a permanent and essential quality emerges – that devout, rather bony Englishness Larkin celebrates or questions in many of his poems. The sad lyricism is rooted in a culture, but the poem's plaintive terseness encourages us to elevate the emotion into a universal value and to miss Larkin's real theme – national decline. The autumn leaves fall in ones and twos, rather like colonies dropping out of the empire, while the poem's tonal melancholy evokes the seeming permanence of a personal emotion that also happens to be universal. After many an autumn, we watch another fading season and feel sad.

The young mothers whose beauty has thickened feel that 'something' is pushing them to the side of their own lives, and this is a metaphor for a sense of diminished purpose and fading imperial power. Incipient middle age is like a return to the middle ages, to the English people's faint, marginal, early history. The poem's lonely voice promises an exit from history into personal emotion, but that private space turns out to be social after all. This lyric poem is therefore a subtly disguised public poem, for it comments on a social experience.

Larkin wrote 'Afternoons' in late 1959 and it is an elegy both for a decade and for an historical experience. The wind that is ruining the young women's 'courting-places' in a Hull park is a trope, just like Macmillan's use of the same figure in his famous 'wind of change' speech, except that Larkin's attitude is opposed to the historical process the Conservative Prime Minister was describing. Larkin loves the unchanging, and in his Jubilee quatrain he locates its symbolic presence with devotion:

> In times when nothing stood
> but worsened, or grew strange,
> there was one constant good:
>     she did not change.
>         (CP, 210)

Facing this poem in the *Collected Poems* is a lacklustre complaint about ageing entitled 'The Winter Palace' which makes the disguised metaphors of 'Afternoons' explicit. Ageing is like being a monarch besieged by revolutionaries. Change is a revolutionary process, the completed revolution is death. But the lyric voice – 'Summer is fading', 'Westron winde, when wilt thou blow' – remains constant within mutability, like the monarch. Much as Larkin was bored by *The Faerie Queene*, he has more in common with Spenser than might appear. Both are English Protestant royalists whose nationalism was intensified by their experience of Ireland.

In the deep, or not so deep, recesses of Larkin's imagination, there is a rock-solid sense of national glory which reveals itself in 'The March Past', a poem about a military band which he wrote in Belfast in 1951. The loud martial music produces:

                    a sudden flock of visions:
        Honeycombs of heroic separations,
        Pure marchings, pure apparitions...

The poet is overcome by a 'blind',

        Astonishing remorse for things now ended
        That of themselves were also rich and splendid
        (But unsupported broke, and were not mended) –
                                        (CP, 55)

The Yeatsian word 'remorse' (Larkin quotes 'When such as I cast out remorse' in his introduction to *The North Ship*) points to the synergy of nationalism and lyricism in his imagination. It is, of course, a transposed nationalism – fiercely pro-imperial, unlike Yeats's anti-colonial lyrics. And yet for all his repudiation of Yeats, Larkin's career is a version of the old magician's – instead of flowing hair and bow tie, baldness and bicycle clips and the Library Association tie. Instead of the Abbey Theatre, Hull University Library.

Public Larkin acts a part, cultivating a sober-suited persona with a gloomy-tender private side. But that private side is another form of concealment, for it enables him to issue public statements disguised as lyric poems. The skilled and self-conscious performer makes institutional life appear heroic, because life in the 'first slum of Europe' has to retain a vision of that greatness, those pure marchings and apparitions, which a now-drab island once gave to the world. Because things rich and splendid are now at an end, life on the island is unheroic, routine, toadlike. The present – October 1953 in 'Triple Time' – is 'traditionally soured', a time 'unrecommended by event'. Beyond it stretch 'our last / Threadbare perspectives, seasonal decrease' (*CP*, 73).

Characteristically, Larkin naturalises his embittered sense of cultural decline as seasonal, the falling of leaves. Where he feels an optimism or joy in the present, nature is socialised through traditionally English imagery – trees thresh like 'unresting castles', white blossoms create lost lanes of 'Queen Anne's lace'. Most daringly, the 'sense of falling' in 'The Whitsun Weddings' becomes an 'arrow-shower' like the clothyard arrows in Olivier's film of *Henry V*. The poem summons both the play's patriotism and that of the film (it was made during the Second World War), but the reference is typically oblique. Perhaps only readers of a certain generation – those brought up on Victorian children's literature – will recognise that bows and arrows, just as much as cricket bats and oak trees, are icons of patriotic devotion in English culture.

In 'Long lion days' the midday 'hammer of heat' is a martial memory of imperial high noon, not just a poetic apostrophe to a heatwave. And this resembles the fusion of sunshine, empire and Edwardian nostalgia in 'At Grass':

> Silks at the start: against the sky
> Numbers and parasols: outside,
> Squadrons of empty cars, and heat,
> And littered grass: then the long cry
> Hanging unhushed till it subside
> To stop-press columns on the street.
> (CP, 29)

This is on one level a field of battle – squadrons, littered grass, the long cry of victory travelling across time and distance into newspapers and history books. The horses are emblems of the heroic as they are in Yeats and in his brother Jack's drawings and paintings, but in the poem's present – January 1950 – they are observed almost by a sniper's eye:

> The eye can hardly pick them out
> From the cold shade they shelter in,
> Till wind distresses tail and mane;
> Then one crops grass, and moves about
> – The other seeming to look on –
> And stands anonymous again.
> (CP, 29)

The phrase 'cold shade', like 'distresses', is classical – this is the underworld of dreary shades that move through the waste dominions of the dead in the *Aeneid*. The horses are heroic ancestors – famous generals, perhaps, who can now 'stand at ease' but who are also vulnerable, anonymous and largely neglected. Only the groom and his boy tend them now. Like the last vestiges of traditional hierarchy, these servants 'with bridles in the evening come' – the closing line's elegiac, slightly archaic cadencing beautifully imparts a strange sense of threat.

As Janice Rossen points out in *Philip Larkin: His Life's Work*, this poem marks a turning-point in Larkin's style, but unfortunately she is unable to see his style as more than the product of personal neurosis. She states that the racehorses symbolise 'something' about success and failure, and neglects to notice that the threatening atmosphere of the closing lines is Larkin's response to modern social democracy. His elitist distaste for British mass society shows in the contrast he draws between the 'slovenly crowd' in *A Girl in Winter* and the 'more highly strung' horses which seem to belong to 'a higher breed altogether'. Where Yeats's crowd in 'At Galway Races' is 'all of the one mind', like a completely cohesive society united by a single belief, Larkin's crowd is only 'half-attentive'. It is this lack of unity of social being which he mourns in 'At Grass' – it exists somewhere in the Edwardian past, an idealised memory against which 1950s England appears dull, pinched, banal and second-rate. And despite his notorious dislike of 'abroad', Larkin's celebrations of island life are shot through with an intense loathing of his own insularity. That insularity – its sealed cosiness, its bleak disgusted bareness – is not a subject the poems appear to address because Larkin disguises it as a form of self-consciousness, the poetry of the autonomous self.

The connection between the personal and the national life is made through the idea of power and its loss. The self desires full and undivided sovereignty but fears a diminution of its personal freedom through marriage. Larkin's long, nagging, troubled argument against marriage is almost like a public agonising about national sovereignty. He sets out to defend his personal autonomy – the 'realm of me', to adapt Emily Dickinson – and he employs the different attics, flats and single rooms he inhabits as symbols of that sacred privacy. But by carrying his search for autonomy to the limit, he subjects it to potentially destructive stresses. At first autonomy wins, and in 'Dry-Point' he exclaims against marriage:

> What ashen hills! what salted, shrunken lakes!
> How leaden the ring looks,
> Birmingham magic all discredited,
>
> And how remote that bare and sunscrubbed room,
> Intensely far, that padlocked cube of light
> We neither define nor prove,
> Where you, we dream, obtain no right of entry.
> (*CP*, 37)

This clean, sunny, secure room is the ideal autonomous self, but in 'Mr Bleaney' the ugly functionalism which the adjective 'padlocked' carries in 'Dry-Point' becomes the metaphoric coffin of 'one hired box'. This is not simply a prolepsis for death – it defines the queasy lonely discomfort of the self that doubts the value of its independence.

If Dickinson's poetry may be read as a struggle to achieve and preserve female autonomy, Larkin's poems are often sceptical assertions of male autonomy, a state 'we' neither define nor prove because as males we have always enjoyed it. Or have we enjoyed it? Isn't there something frowsty or fusty or just downright awful about the little cell where each of us preserves his ego?

Larkin raised this question jokily in a letter to Barbara Pym: 'why are single rooms so much worse than double ones? Fewer, further, frowstier? Damper, darker, dingier? Noisier, narrower, nastier?' This complaint was made in 1969, but in 'Counting', written in the mid-1950s, he is more triumphalist in his assertion of 'one':

> Thinking in terms of one
> Is easily done –
> One room, one bed, one chair,
> One person there,
> Makes perfect sense; one set
> Of wishes can be met,
> One coffin filled.
>
> But counting up to two
> Is harder to do;
> For one must be denied
> Before it's tried.
>                         (*CP*, 108)

One is ace and masculine, two is trouble and female, though singleness is rejected – at least temporarily – in 'Poetry of Departures':

> I detest my room,
> Its specially-chosen junk,
> The good books, the good bed,
> And my life, in perfect order...
>                         (*CP*, 85)

This self-hatred is prompted by a spasm of admiration for someone else's 'audacious' rejection of job and career, but that admiration is then cancelled in favour of what can only be construed as a camp gesture:

> But I'd go today,
>
> Yes, swagger the nut-strewn roads,
> Crouch in the fo'c'sle
> Stubbly with goodness, if
> It weren't so artificial,
> Such a deliberate step backwards
> To create an object:
> Books; china; a life
> Reprehensibly perfect.
>                    (CP, 85–6)

Here Larkin fuses his art and his life – his solitude is an 'artificial' gesture, a self-conscious and deliberately reactionary conclusion which reworks the earlier statement 'I detest my room' and quietly exults in the reproofs it aims to provoke. The poem doesn't so much develop an argument as retrace its steps in order ironically to adopt a more complex and more honest perspective. But the honesty of that perspective is really a form of lesser deception, for Larkin comes clean by admitting that his solitariness is a pose. He has merely substituted one mask for another.

In an early notebook poem which Rossen quotes, Larkin speaks of 'art's plain room' and this is another version of his favourite symbol, the sunscrubbed room that excludes 'you', the other, the threat. The symbol is more than simply personal and more than campily self-conscious, because to the outsider it is bound to appear as the expression of a culture and a history. Larkin speaks not for the imperial male – too transcendental a subject that – but for the English male, middle-class, professional, outwardly confident, con-trolled and in control. The history of that distinctive personality has yet to be written, but anyone who has observed it as a phenomenon, as a distinctive pattern of behaviour and attitude, is bound to see Larkin as a secret witness to what it feels like to be imprisoned in a personality that 'something hidden from us chose'. Thus Larkin's favourite romantic value, 'solitude', designates the consciousness of the autonomous English male professional. It refers not to physical isolation, but to a consciousness which has been moulded by up-bringing and education to manage and govern. Such personalities, with their committee skills, power lusts and filing-cabinet voices, are seldom attractive, but what is so lovable about Larkin's persona is the evident discomfort he feels with the shape of the personality he has been given. Angry at not being allowed to show emotion, he writhes with anxiety inside that sealed bunker which is the English ethic of privacy. He journeys into the interior, into the unknown heart – the maybe missing centre – of Englishness.

This exploration of a way of feeling – or not feeling – is the subject of *A Girl in Winter*, where he places the foreigner, Katherine, inside a middle-class southern English family in order to explore the limitations of the culture he loved. Katherine is intimidated by the sixteen-year-old Robin's 'almost supernatural maturity', by the finished quality of his public-school manners which overwhelm her with 'a sense of barren perfection'. This is a version of the reprehensible perfection of 'Poetry of Departures', and it is developed through Katherine's reaction to the welcome Robin's family give her on arrival. They welcome her 'undramatically, even casually, as if she had come from the next village'. Disappointed, Katherine feels that there is no 'intimacy' among them: 'the whole thing resembled a scene in a hotel lounge'.

As an outsider from a European country Larkin never names and shows no interest in evoking, Katherine is puzzled by Robin's personality and by his motives in asking her to visit:

> It couldn't be natural for anyone of sixteen to behave like a Prince Regent and foreign ambassador combined. It just wasn't possible. Besides, if (ghastly thought!) by the thousandth chance it *was* natural, it would mean that he would never have asked her. They would be so entirely opposite in every way that – And again, to be so entirely independent, yet so gracious – and Robin's movements were always beautifully finished and calm – well, it would mean that *people*, mere friends, mere other personalities, would hold no interest at all for him.[1]

This must be what the use of 'natural' means in 'Posterity' – 'One of those old-type *natural* fouled-up guys' – where there is again a foreign perspective on an English personality. Here 'natural' means in reality 'artificial', because it describes a code of manners, a way of acting in public which leaves the private human being utterly enigmatic and detached.

Larkin's unusually ruffled, spontaneous prose sets Katherine's consciousness, her unstudied passion, against Robin's English reserve which she tries to understand for the mask it is: 'And therefore this reserve, this sandpapering of every word and gesture until it exactly fitted its place in the conversation, this gracious carriage of the personality – this was not natural, or at the most it was a manner, so familiar by now that his thoughts and motives could change freely behind it' (*GW*, 91). Katherine wants to see what is behind the mask, she wants to understand the core of his privacy and to know what his detached, enigmatic freedom really is. She has perceived that in any social situation he is never wholly present. This distinctively English combination of presence and detachment is well described by Roy Harris in a recent essay on the state of the English language. Harris notes: 'For the British, communal life is bearable only on the understanding that one may withdraw from it, temporarily or permanently, into another world of inviolable, timeless privacy.' The natural reserve of the English male (British is too wide a term) expresses the sense that any communal activity – say a family gathered to greet a foreign guest – is both temporary and inferior compared to that inviolable, because padlocked, cube of light which is completely self-sufficient. The French call this quality *morgue anglaise*, and in the novel Katherine identifies it almost as a puzzle, a logical construct which conceals either emotion or the absence of emotion.

As a novelist, Larkin wants to explore this enigma, but as a poet he knows this is the form of consciousness he's stuck with. He is caught in the trap of being unable to adopt an alternative way of feeling because to do so would mean relinquishing his native language and his Englishness. In *A Girl in Winter* he tries to solve this problem by giving a foreign perspective on English 'natural' reserve, but he refuses to give Katherine any foreign words or to describe the events that subsequently bring her back to England as a wartime refugee. She thinks, feels and speaks entirely in English. There are hints that she is German, but she may be connected with a poem Larkin wrote during the war:

> Like the train's beat
> Swift language flutters the lips
> Of the Polish airgirl in the corner seat.
> The swinging and narrowing sun
> Lights her eyelashes, shapes
> Her sharp vivacity of bone.
> Hair, wild and controlled, runs back:
> And gestures like these English oaks
> Flash past the windows of her foreign talk.
> (*CP*, 288)

These lines from poem XII in *The North Ship* express more than sexual attraction. It is as if the English oaks are being left behind by the Polish airgirl's fast, vivacious talk, as if she speaks a language of the passions that Larkin is unable to understand. His later hostility to foreign languages ('deep down I think foreign languages irrelevant' he told one interviewer) isn't present in this poem, which expresses something of the emotional release he found in listening to jazz and blues records. But it would never do, he told his Hull friend Jean Hartley, 'to marry a foreigner'. It was difficult enough to understand the minds and hearts of fellow members of the English middle class. Difficult and also unsatisfying, because of the English prejudice against emotions, the belief that they are somehow foreign.

In Larkin's personal mythology, black American musicians become icons of the emotions and cheer his glum, solitary rationality. In 'The Persistence of the Blues' he remarks that somehow 'in this most characteristic music of the American Negro has been imprisoned an inexhaustible emotional energy. You can go on playing or listening to the blues all night.' In a brilliant phrase, he calls Billie Holliday's latterday voice 'at once charred and scorching', and he rejects the idea that black Americans had the blues because they were 'naturally melancholy'. They had the blues because they were 'cheated and bullied and starved'. Nevertheless, they have a 'relaxed vitality' white America lacks. This may seem to express a sense of his own inferiority, except that Larkin believes that black musicians exist to entertain the whites: 'the tension between artist and audience in jazz slackened when the Negro stopped wanting to entertain the white man', he argues in *All What Jazz*. The white audience must be in control, because if they are not, modernism and Black Power will inevitably follow.

This deep-seated idea of control emerges briefly in *Jill*, when the lovesick John Kemp looks out of a train window at trees being tossed 'recklessly' by the wind. He meditates on love fulfilled and unfulfilled and looks again at the tree tops: 'What control could he hope to have over the maddened surface of things?' Larkin wants everything to submit to the rational exercise of power, but the result is a desperate attraction to something which is apparently other than that power, to the wildness *and* control of the Polish airgirl's flowing hair. Listening to jazz records he is able to indulge emotion like a private hobby, rather as if he is the Housman of Auden's sonnet, who keeps tears like dirty postcards in a drawer. In this way he can both enjoy a snug security and have access to mechanically reproduced emotion – emotion that can be switched off and on at will and so be controlled in the way that trees in a high wind and personal relationships cannot be.

In *Jill*, John Kemp hopes that he will be able to have that essential space for the establishment of personal autonomy, a room of his own: 'with a fire and the curtains drawn, where he could arrange his few books neatly, fill a drawer with his notes and essays (in black ink with red corrections, held together by brass pins), and live undisturbed through the autumn into the winter'. Unfortunately, he has to share a room with an upper-class lout whose 'panoplied and trampling' existence he comes to admire but who disturbs his dream of hibernating in his study. Examining the symbol of solitary room with jazz record playing, we can see that this is a version of Defoe's profound cultural myth of Crusoe and Friday on the island. Elizabeth Bishop recognised this, and her subtly ironic long poem 'Crusoe in England' affectionately mocks Larkin:

> I often gave way to self-pity.
> 'Do I deserve this? I suppose I must.
> I wouldn't be here otherwise. Was there
> a moment when I actually chose this?
> I don't remember, but there could have been.'
> What's wrong about self-pity, anyway?
> With my legs dangling down familiarly
> over a crater's edge, I told myself
> 'Pity should begin at home'. So the more
> pity I felt, the more I felt at home.[2]

The glum, tetchy, agonised questions, the self-conscious self-pity, the drably and quizzically fatalistic 'I suppose I must' sound like Larkin at his most insular. Bishop's foreign perspective anatomises a type of terminal Englishness that feels lost and tired and out of date.

Larkin likes to set up apparent opposites – room with fire blazing, cold wind and darkness outside – and this appears to express his insularity and independence. In *A Girl in Winter* Robin and Katherine meet during the war – he is thrawn, nervous, edgy, while she feels only an 'abstract kindliness' towards him. Her solitary bedsit is described like this: 'there was a fire, that he paid to keep burning; she had hot coffee she could give him; there was so much laconic mutual help, while outside lay the plains, the absence of the moon, the complete enmity of darkness' (*GW*, 237). A fire and hot coffee, outside the cold plains. It is a lyric moment that offers an epiphany for the natural fouled-up personality the older Robin has revealed – his emotional nullness and undeveloped heart. The cold plains of his personality are inside the room.

A similar vision appears many years later in Larkin's discussion of Emily Dickinson's poems: 'somewhere within them there is a deep fracture, that chills the harmless properties into a wide and arctic plain where they are wedged together eternally to represent a life gone irrevocably wrong'.[3] As the ships' horns cry in 'Arrivals, Departures': '*come and choose wrong*'. The source of this primal sense of mistaken choice – a secular version of original sin – is hard to identify, but it is addressed in an unpublished poem which begins with the vulnerable, rather overprecise line: 'Love again: wanking at ten past three'. He then tries to discover why love 'never worked for me':

> Something to do with violence
> A long way back, and wrong rewards,
> And arrogant eternity.
>
> (*CP*, 215)

It is difficult to decide what these lines refer to, and though it is tempting to read them as invoking a Hughesian primitivism as a metaphor for historic violence, this seems unlikely. The urge towards self-knowledge is blocked off even as it is apparently obeyed, and the poem oddly combines an admission of masturbation with reticence, as if there is something that can't be faced.

Perhaps the phrase 'arrogant eternity' can be linked to the image of deep blue air in 'High Windows' – an image which sets the windows of Larkin's top-floor flat against the imagined paradise of youthful sexuality. The idea of arrogant eternity is a version of Larkin's secret idea of the poet, an idea that runs counter to the argument he advances several times in his critical prose that poets should have a 'direct relationship' with the reading public, as Kipling, Housman and Betjeman had. This relationship depends on 'normal' vision, syntax, language, because poetry is 'an affair of sanity, of seeing things as they are'. The days when 'one could claim to be the priest of a mystery are gone'. Larkin's rational commonsense materialism, his insistence that poems should give pleasure, appears both modest and polemically anti-modernist, but he has an altogether more ambitious concept of the poet that Milton, Shelley and Yeats would have approved.

From Milton's 'high lonely tower' to Shelley's starlit 'evening tower' to Yeats's self-conscious recuperation of Milton and Shelley in *The Tower*, the line is clear and apparently terminal. No poet since Yeats has laid claim to the mystic symbol of platonic poet in his ancient tower. No one has had the nerve, except Larkin. Typically, he disguises his appropriation of the symbol by appearing to invoke another kind of building in these lines:

> By day, a lifted study-storehouse; night
>   Converts it to a flattened cube of light.
> Whichever's shown, the symbol is the same:
>   Knowledge; a University; a name.
>                        (*CP*, 220)

From the library of which he was custodian to that emblem of personal privacy in 'Dry-Point', the symbol remains constant – each is a cube of light. The poet and the librarian are one, the library and the rented flat are identified.

In the early 'Best Society' Larkin again occupies the symbol:

> Viciously, then, I lock my door.
> The gas-fire breathes. The wind outside
> Ushers in evening rain. Once more
> Uncontradicting solitude
> Supports me on its giant palm;
> And like a sea-anemone
> Or simple snail, there cautiously
> Unfolds, emerges, what I am.
>                        (*CP*, 56–7)

These lines are reworked in 'Vers de Société', which again rehearses the argument in 'Best Society' that virtue is social, solitude selfish. In the later poem, Larkin rejects the time he's spent in society, time that should have been 'repaid':

> Under a lamp, hearing the noise of wind,
> And looking out to see the moon thinned
> To an air-sharpened blade.
>                        (*CP*, 181)

The lunar blade is a daring echo of Yeats in his visionary tower, a version of Sato's sword in 'The Table':

> Chaucer had not drawn breath
> When it was forged. In Sato's house,
> Curved like new moon luminous, moon-luminous,
> It lay five hundred years.[4]

Like Yeats, Larkin wants to make his pen into a sword and fuse violence with 'arrogant eternity'. His sometimes violent rancour is a version of Yeats's passionate hatred and is webbed in with his youthful ambition to be a 'great' writer.

In 'Best Society' the autonomous, fully empowered self unfolds like a sea anemone or a snail, and this marine imagery anticipates his cunning use of the tower symbol in the second poem in 'Livings', where the keeper of the light rejoices in his solitude:

> Rocks writhe back to sight.
> Mussels, limpets,
> Husband their tenacity
> In the freezing slither –
> Creatures, I cherish you!
> (*CP*, 187)

Here, the disguised platonist exults in his freedom. The poet in the seaport of Hull is reincarnated as a custodian of light who is also 'guarded by brilliance', another version of the padlocked light-cube. The high windows of the poet's flat and his library are also a version of the lighthouse-tower, as is the 'high room' in the unfinished 'At thirty-one, when some are rich'.

Larkin reworks the symbol in 'The Old Fools' – 'Perhaps being old is having lighted rooms / Inside your head' – and alters it slightly in 'Friday Night in the Royal Station Hotel':

> In shoeless corridors, the lights burn. How
> Isolated, like a fort, it is –
> The headed paper, made for writing home
> (If home existed) letters of exile: *Now*
> *Night comes on. Waves fold behind villages.*
> (*CP*, 163)

The hotel is like a fort in some nameless colony or like a lighthouse above darkening waves. The poem displaces an English provincial city and makes its author momentarily into an exile. This bold deployment of *ostranenye* which transforms the Victorian hotel into a place of mystery and danger is essentially colonial, rather than European.

The maritime fastness of Hull, its bracing dinginess and unique atmosphere of being somehow Yorkshire and north European and entire unto itself, is essential to Larkin's public–private persona:

> Isolate city spread alongside water,
> Posted with white towers, she keeps her face
> Half-turned to Europe, lonely northern daughter,
> Holding through centuries her separate place.
> (CP, 203)

This deeply-felt cantata celebrates the great, graceful, pointless Humber Bridge, which every day sends a few cars out into Lincolnshire. Larkin obviously had his doubts about the structure – 'this stride into our solitude', he calls it – but he uses the opportunity to express his sense of his own poetic mission, his commitment to what Coleridge in his poem to Wordsworth terms 'the dread watch-tower of man's absolute self'. The strangeness and the isolation and the white towers in Larkin's cantata reach back to Milton's star-gazing platonist and to the visionary Protestantism both poets share. In 'Bridge for the Living' Larkin casts himself as a watchman in Zion who longs to echo Isaiah's words: 'My lord, I stand continually upon the watchtower in the daytime, and I am set in my ward whole nights.' On watch, a prophet, he speaks for the nation:

> And past the poppies bluish neutral distance
> Ends the land suddenly beyond a beach
> Of shapes and shingle. Here is unfenced existence:
> Facing the sun, untalkative, out of reach.
> (CP, 136–7)

These lines from 'Here' identify the value of solitude with a vision of the North Sea, so that Hull – a 'terminate and fishy-smelling / Pastoral of ships up streets' – and the hinterland of Spurn Head build an emblem of England.

In Larkin's tower-poem, 'Livings II', there is a bracing and delighted sense of being completely isolated, totally islanded:

> Barometers falling,
> Ports wind-shuttered,

> Fleets pent like hounds,
> Fires in humped inns
> Kippering sea-pictures –
> (*CP*, 187)

The lighthouse is exchanged in 'The Card-Players' for the 'lamplit cave' of another kippered inn, where Jan van Hogspeuw, Old Prijck and Dirk Dogstoerd celebrate the 'secret, bestial peace!' Like the royalist and misogynistic dons in 'Livings III', the three grotesques are cronies who symbolically express a type of desolate selfish comfort which Larkin is torn between hating and hugging. Like Bleaney they embody a revulsion against his own insularity with its prejudices and recessive professional Englishness, but as their caricatured names are Dutch rather than English Larkin is able to off-load his self-disgust on to the foreign.

For all this poem's invocation to rain, wind and fire, no one reading Larkin can fail to notice that there is a gruelling, punitive, desperately joyless quality to his imagination. Though he can be warmly reverential, often the England he addresses is a cold country inhabited entirely by hard-working Anglo-Saxon Protestants who wear cheap, ugly clothes and drink beer. This is the England of 'Show Saturday', a place of small towns and allotments where it is forever 1947, though sometimes it feels like 1347; and as Rossen points out, the alliterative line 'Watchful as weasels, car-tuning curt-haired sons' might be a line from *Piers Plowman*. She suggests that this resemblance to Langland makes the image appear 'timeless' and so fails to notice that Larkin is in fact offering a distinctively nationalist point of view. Often the poems provide images for the sentiments Norman Tebbit expressed at the start of his political career:

> Nor as a small densely populated island with a closely integrated population living cheek by jowl sharing common ethics, ambitions and standards – and prejudices too – can we afford to import large numbers of immigrants who neither share nor care for those ethics, ambitions or standards – and with prejudices of their own – nor can we allow them to set up foreign enclaves in our country.

Larkin's snarl, his populism and his calculated philistinism all speak for Tebbit's England and for that gnarled and angry puritanism which is so deeply ingrained in the culture. Recognising this, Larkin called himself 'one of nature's Orangemen', adopting the mask of an Ulster Protestant, a sort of Belfast Dirk Dogstoerd, in order to ironise his own philistinism. Yet that attitude was itself a strategy because it enabled him to conceal the knowledge that he had created many outstandingly beautiful poems. In that distinctively embarrassed English manner he had to bury his pride in his artistic creations under several sackfuls of ugly prejudices.

One of his deepest prejudices was against women, and in a rigorous account of 'Deceptions' Rossen analyses Larkin's most famous attic image:

> For you would hardly care
> That you were less deceived, out on that bed,
> Than he was, stumbling up the breathless stair
> To burst into fulfilment's desolate attic.
> (CP, 32)

Rossen argues that this 'equable' view of the rapist as personally unfulfilled ignores the fact that the source in Mayhew's *London Labour and the London Poor* clearly shows that someone is eventually going to profit from the girl's ruin and abduction into prostitution. The poem also neglects to mention the rapist's violence and domination, and Rossen further argues that the 'callousness' it exhibits and the 'sadism' it in part condones ought to be seen as a limitation in Larkin's art.[5]

Rossen's study is valuable for this insight into Larkin's misogyny and for the many quotations from his unpublished letters and notebooks which she discusses. Larkin wrote to Barbara Pym that he felt deeply humiliated at living in a country which spent more on education than defence, and this emotion must underlie his assertion of male autonomy in the poems. Although Rossen is unsympathetic in her attempts to understand the roots of the writer's block Larkin suffered, she shrewdly notes that in addressing his stalled creativity as a subject for poems he began to forge 'a distinctive, ingenious sort of pessimism'. Her biographical speculations are often clumsy and her critical comments usually amount to dull descriptive paraphrase, but by drawing on so much unpublished material she is able to extend our understanding of the very cunning and very wounded personality of a poet whose sometimes rancid prejudices are part of his condition, part of the wound. Watching the east coast of England from his lighted tower, he dreams of escaping from that imprisoning self: 'Such attics cleared of me! Such absences!'

From the *Times Literary Supplement*, 20–26 July 1990, pp. 779–80.

## NOTES

[Tom Paulin's criticism of Larkin's work continues to provoke a fierce debate. Very few essays on Larkin have had such a powerful and controversial effect as this one. 'Into the Heart of Englishness' first appeared in the *Times Literary Supplement* (July 1990) as a review of Janice Rossen's *Philip Larkin: His Life's Work*. It was subsequently reprinted with the title 'She Did Not Change: Philip Larkin' in Paulin's *Minotaur: Poetry and the Nation State* (London and Boston, 1992), pp. 233–51. The essays in *Minotaur* combine a deeply felt appreciation of poetic form with a probing political intelligence: they show how seemingly 'innocent' texts embody particular power relations, often associated with questions of nationhood and national identity. Paulin's incisive historicist method is evident in his reading of Larkin's poems. He argues that Larkin's plangent lyricism is rooted in the cultural history of post-war England, and that a dominant theme of the poetry is national decline. The melancholy that pervades such poems as 'The March Past' and 'At Grass' betrays 'a sense of diminished purpose and fading imperial glory'. Paulin's critical methods have much in common with those of cultural materialism and new historicism, but he remains staunchly independent of theoretical 'camps' and brilliantly unpredictable. Ed.]

1. Philip Larkin, *A Girl in Winter* (London, 1947; 1975), pp. 90–1. Further references will be abbreviated as *GW* and included in the text.

2. Elizabeth Bishop, 'Crusoe in England', *Complete Poems* (London, 1991), p. 163.

3. Philip Larkin, *Required Writing* (London, 1983), p. 193.

4. W. B. Yeats, *The Poems*, ed. Daniel Albright (London, 1994), p. 248.

5. Janice Rossen, *Philip Larkin: His Life's Work* (Hemel Hempstead, 1989) p. 89. [See p. 154 in this volume. Ed.]

# 9

# Margins of Tolerance: Responses to Post-war Decline

*STAN SMITH*

'Provinciality' perhaps always contains within it the sting of distance. The individual whose centre is always elsewhere, whether in Heaven or in London, inserts his own distance into the landscape, a distance he carries everywhere with him. Yet most of the poetry in the English tradition has had a strong provincial rootedness. In the poetry of the post-war period, however, whether the landscape is native or not, it has usually been at one remove, seen, as so often in Philip Larkin's poetry, through the window of a train, or even of a house in which one is almost equally transient. Coventry, glimpsed from a train in 'I Remember, I Remember', though the poet's birthplace, is not where he has his 'roots', 'only where my childhood was unspent, ... just where I started' (*CP*, 81), to be dismissed in a doggedly negative listing of all the things that didn't happen there. The poetry of place is, in fact, usually a poetry of displacements lovingly cultivated.

Distance is a recurring and complex concept in Larkin's poetry. In 'Arrivals, Departures' (*CP*, 65) it constitutes a reassurance to the sleepy resident who hears 'Arrivals lowing in a doleful distance' from the docks, though he is 'nudged from comfort' by the final stanza. In 'At Grass', it is the very stuff of nostalgia, as the poem opens with a view of one-time racehorses reduced to anonymity by retirement. Spatial distance places the observer in a secure frame: 'The eye can hardly pick them out'. As the poem develops the image, by recalling a time when these horses were 'picked out' both by binoculars and by fame, it compounds spatial and temporal distance with a further concept, that of a distinguishing excellence:

> Yet fifteen years ago, perhaps
> Two dozen distances sufficed
> To fable them....
>> (CP, 29)

'Whatever Happened?' makes distance the very ground of freedom, as the individual extricates himself from dangerous and compromising circumstances, leaving 'whatever happened' transplanted into the ironically significant perspective where 'All's kodak-distant'. 'Places, Loved Ones' keeps the same ambivalent composure: the lack of a 'proper ground', a settled commitment, frees the self from responsibility, 'Should the town turn dreary, / The girl a dolt'. The mediations of distance rescue one from the compromising immediacy of the *instant*, 'that special one / Who has an instant claim / On everything I own / Down to my name' (CP, 99). Propriety and property, self-possession, as for Eliot's early anti-heroes, is at a premium in this poetry. 'Reasons for Attendance' defines the social space of this distance: the speaker looks in through a lighted window where dancers, all under twenty-five, dance to the sound of a trumpet. It is the music which convinces him of his own reality as an 'individual'. But individuality seems to posit distance as its *sine qua non*, though it carries with it, too, that omen of death and dispossession which concludes 'Dry-Point', 'Next, Please' and 'Going'.

'Deceptions', which provides the title for *The Less Deceived* (1955), where all the foregoing poems appeared, makes distance the very ground of our humanity. The poem opens with what seems like a qualification. As it evolves, this is transformed into ultimate consolation: all alike, victim and rapist and pitying poetic voyeur of Mayhew's Victorian anecdote, are equally pitiable, for everything passes. It is a subtle modulation from a time-transcending sympathy –

> Even so distant, I can taste the grief,
> Bitter and sharp with stalks, he made you gulp.

– with all its touching cumulative detail, through the 'Slums, years, [that] have buried you', the rejection of anything so impertinent as consolation, the somewhat abstract meditation on suffering, to the strangely equivocal separation of violator's and poet's and girl's responses in the last lines –

> For you would hardly care
> That you were less deceived, out on that bed,
> Than he was, stumbling up the breathless stair
> To burst into fulfilment's desolate attic.
> (CP, 32)

But it is perhaps the opening poem of the volume which presents most clearly the function of retrospective distances in Larkin's poetry. The title, 'Lines on a Young Lady's Photograph Album', itself establishes an ironic distance, calling up conventional album verse, many previous poems, by Hardy, MacNeice, Day Lewis on the same theme, and, more naughtily, other famous meditations on the relation between art, time and history. Gaining access to the album is presented as an act of sexual triumph cognate to that implied, negatively, in Keats's description of the Grecian urn as a 'still unravished bride': the two opening lines set up a coy counterpoint:

> At last you yielded up the album, which,
> Once open, sent me distracted. All your ages
> Matt and glossy on the thick black pages!
> Too much confectionery, too rich:
> I choke on such nutritious images.
> (CP, 71)

Far from preserving detachment, the eye here becomes a predator, 'hunger[ing] from pose to pose' as it scans these trophies of time and change, photographs of childhood, adolescence and 'these disquieting chaps who loll / At ease about your earlier days'. The 'Faithful and disappointing' art of photography, 'that records / Dull days as dull, and hold-it smiles as frauds' seems to persuade us overwhelmingly 'That this is a real girl in a real place, / In every sense empirically true'. But it is precisely the art as *illusion* which appeals to the poet. The captured present is in actuality past, and *it always has been*. The window of the photograph through which we look here is a window on a time that was *always* out-of-date, transformed so in the very process of being committed to print. Distance always involves time for Larkin; but here, the snapshots enable the past to enter into its true element, as an *immediate* fiction. Time, whether personal, or public, is reduced to unreality by its own passage, as in 'Deceptions'. And with such illusions, we can never be disillusioned, for all their candid multiplicity of detail is mere rhetoric, the small change of artistic 'persuasion':

> Or is it just the *past?* Those flowers, that gate,
> These misty parks and motors, lacerate
> Simply by being over; you
> Contract my heart by looking out of date.
>
> Yes, true; but in the end, surely, we cry
> Not only at exclusion, but because
> It leaves us free to cry. We know *what was*
> Won't call on us to justify
> Our grief, however hard we yowl across
>
> The gap from eye to page....
>
> (CP, 72)

This distant instance, or instant distance, gives away the secret of art's transformations. For though the heart may be doubly contracted (both shrunken and committed) by this image, it is at the same time set free by its exclusion from event. The yowling across the gap is, then, a mere self-indulgence, another kind of treat, harking back to the gluttonous delight of the opening stanza. These photographs 'condense, / In short, a past that no one now can share, / No matter whose your future', holding her 'like a heaven' where she *lies* (the word picking up all those ambiguities of truth, falsehood and fictionality the whole poem has juggled with) 'Unvariably lovely ..., / Smaller and clearer as the years go by'. The function of such images, in fact, is not to record the past, and hint at the abandoned futures, but to liberate the *present* from contracts and obligations. Distance, in Larkin's poetry, is a way of renouncing 'responsibility for time'.

Larkin's poetry insists on the specificity of its local colour, but there is a sense in which this provides the same kind of deception. The poem which opens *The Whitsun Weddings* (1964) is ostensibly about Hull, in all its picturesque matter-of-factness. But it is called 'Here', and the town is nowhere mentioned by name. In reality, the poem is about the general condition of 'hereness', that contingency in which a given world forces itself upon our attention in all its provincial otherness. All the details of the poem are in fact pseudo-specificities, generalities listed in their impinging commonplaceness, as in the second stanza, where the cataloguing eye runs the environment, the people and its commodities into one vast shopping-list, consummated in the phrase 'A cut-price crowd, urban yet simple, dwelling / Where only salesmen and relations come' (*CP*, 136). As the third stanza hints, what we are dealing with here is not a slice of life but a 'pastoral', caught in the 'bluish neutral distance' (stanza four) not of space but of mind. If this landscape is provincial, it is not because it is a place 'where removed lives / Loneliness clarifies'; nor because it is remote from London. Rather, it is provincial because it is far removed from the metropolis of the heart, the true centre of being.

Even when, as in the title poem, the entrained Larkin is homing in on London, this sense of exile persists. On the one hand, he is excluded from the unique particularities of other lives, 'someone running up to bowl', the 'hothouse [which] flashed uniquely'. On the other hand, nostalgia for this empirical immediacy is actually intensified by the recognition that such items are not unique at all, but endlessly repeated, as 'the next town, new and nondescript, / Approached with acres of dismantled cars' (*CP*, 114). The wedding parties, gathering at each new station, all seem unchallengingly unique for their participants, but the travelling poet sees 'it all again in different terms', terms which he then lovingly catalogues in all their tawdry yet touching generality. That these dozen marriages come to share the poet's itinerant watching of the landscape, in 'this frail / Travelling coincidence', may momentarily include them within the poet's compassion: there is a noticeable opening up of sympathy once they become paid-up fellow-travellers on his journey. Nevertheless, the words 'jewellery substitutes' and the image of the girls 'Marked off unreally from the rest', imply a conviction similar to Eliot's: 'Humankind cannot bear very much reality'. It is as if these particular lives are unreal precisely because they are stereotyped: the general category negates, for Larkin, the value and uniqueness of the individual life. Only the abstracted, distanced observer really preserves his individuality: there is no one else like him on the train.

This condescension, turning to resentment before the actual typicality of what is supposed to be uniquely individual life, pervades the poetry of the post-war period. It expresses the renewed anxiety of a traditional liberal-individualism that has survived into an era of welfare-state social democracy, where mass tastes and values prevail, and the charming yokels of an earlier pastoral have turned into menacingly actual travelling-companions, claiming equal rights with the egregious and refined spectator of their shoddy ordinariness. Larkin usually manages to maintain an equivocal balance in his responses to such a world, poised between annoyance and deference. In more recent work, such as the poems in *High Windows* (1974), this balance has gone, and the mood is a more tight-lipped one, of disdain sharpening to odium. 'Going, Going' is a testimony here, with its lament for an England that he no longer thinks will last out his time – the traditional England of pastoral, where the village louts know their places (climbing 'Such trees as were not cut down'). Though the fifth stanza focuses on the spectacled grins of the Business Pages, which lie behind the commercial despoliations that are turning England into the 'First slum of Europe', such figures are oddly unspecific besides the venomous caricature of the preceding stanza, which seems to finger the real culprits:

.... The crowd
Is young in the M1 café;
Their kids are screaming for more –
More houses, more parking allowed,
More caravan sites, more pay.
(CP, 189)

More for all means less for the privileged sensibility of the threnodist; and the expansion in quantity means a diminution in quality – a quality with which the poetic voice is unmistakably identified. Poets of course, do not have to be democrats, nor should they be denied the right to indulge middle-aged pique. Larkin's poetry is valuable both in itself and as a symptomatic document of a cultural decline in which it is fundamentally implicated. One can, however, justifiably feel a little uncomfortable with sentiments that refuse to acknowledge their own complicity in that which they lacerate. The 'long perspectives' of which he spoke in 'Reference Back' no longer 'link us to our losses', but enable us to exculpate and extricate ourselves from their compromising contingency. The poet presumably has himself to be in the M1 café, even as a dubious beneficiary of its cuisine, in order to observe all these others. Tourists always complain that the tourists are spoiling the view.

In such situations, a frequent trick of Larkin's is to bridge the gap between refined sensibility and admass culture by a fetchingly idiomatic turn of phrase which reassures that the poet is himself really one of the boys, not a supercilious aesthete. In 'Going, Going' this is effected in the eighth stanza, with the plaintive admission that he feels, for the first time, 'That before I snuff it, the whole / Boiling will be bricked in / Except for the tourist parts' (*CP*, 190). 'This Be The Verse' justifies its Housmanish world-weariness by its opening bluff colloquialism, as if paying in advance for the mawkishness of what follows: 'They fuck you up, your mum and dad' (*CP*, 180). But it is perhaps in the magnificent title-poem of *High Windows* that the strategy pays off most impressively.

Here, a translucent nihilism in the concluding lines of the poem is saved from mere afflatus by the careful preparations of its opening. The self-consciously casual and dismissive vulgarity of this opening stanza clears the way for the Dantesque vision of paradisal beauty in the last. The movement from the squalidly tangible world of the opening to the airy lucidities without form or substance in the last enacts, in paradigmatic form, that process of abstraction, of disengagement, which underlies most of Larkin's poems. The careful enjambement at the end of the first stanza, isolating the loose usage of 'paradise' as the last word in a colloquial crescendo, prepares for the two-facedness of that rapid shift to 'everyone young going down the long slide / To happiness, endlessly' and points towards the authentic paradise of the last lines, where 'endless' means not 'perpetually repeated' but 'without bounds'.

> When I see a couple of kids
> And guess he's fucking her and she's
> Taking pills or wearing a diaphragm,
> I know this is paradise
>
> Everyone old has dreamed of all their lives –
> (*CP*, 165)

But before the expansive dénouement can be reached, there has to be a reprise of this movement, in which the poet projects back into the past a response similar to his own, of which an imaginary earlier self was the recipient, not the source. This at once affirms continuity, qualifies the sourness of the present self, and *consoles* him with the possibility that this is no more accurate for the two 'kids' than it was for him. Anyone looking at him, forty years ago, may have thought the same, 'That'll be the life':

> .... *He*
> *And his lot will go down the long slide*
> *Like free bloody birds.* And immediately
>
> Rather than words comes the thought of high windows:
> The sun-comprehending glass,
> And beyond it, the deep blue air, that shows
> Nothing, and is nowhere, and is endless.

Such are the consolations of philosophy that the retrojected words bring express relief, freeing the self from the oppression of exclusion, and cancelling the coarseness as – in its gratuitous appearance, as if from nowhere (its proper home) – it bypasses logic. Such almost tangible negativity is the heart's true metropolis.

Larkin may find Modernism distasteful, but when he has to deal with a real, contingent world, his response is Eliot's. In the rancorous lampoon of a poem such as 'Posterity' he assumes a Prufrockian, self-deprecating irony which actually preserves its little lyric secrets from the contempt of others. 'Homage to a Government' calls up echoes of Housman (particularly his 'Epitaph on an Army of Mercenaries'), but *its* occasion is precise and specific: the Wilson government's decision, in 1969 (the poem provides its own date) to withdraw its troops from 'East of Suez', for financial reasons. For Larkin, this is some kind of betrayal, as if, presumably, the troops had not been stationed out there for what, in the long term, were financial reasons: to preserve the investments, raw materials, and cheap labour of an imperialist economy. The condescension Larkin evinces towards ordinary mortals, incapable of self-government or self-direction, mere walking embodiments of some prototype discerned by the generalising intelligence of the observer / poet, is displayed here as a possibly disingenuous naïvety. This Prufrockian 'naïvety' dissociates the whole question of decolonisation from its confused and complex history, and presents it as simply one more venal betrayal in the story of a vulgar and degrading social democracy. Once again, the true culprit is that unspeakable *menu peuple* whose motives are gestured at in the twist of line five into line six:

> Next year we are to bring the soldiers home
> For lack of money, and it is all right.
> Places they guarded, or kept orderly,

> Must guard themselves, and keep themselves orderly.
> We want the money for ourselves at home
> Instead of working. And this is all right.
>
> (CP, 171)

For Larkin, this shabby sell-out by a government intent on pla-cating a restive electorate devalues not only the present but the past and the future. The statues which record an imperial heritage will be standing in the same squares; they will 'look nearly the same'. The subterfuge which, almost unnoticed, erodes a history is skil-fully caught in that adverb. But the same poet who in 'This Be The Verse' advises that the only answer to the 'fuck-ups' of life is to 'Get out as early as you can, / And don't have any kids yourself', now evokes posterity as if it were the real and only tribunal before which to judge the perfidies of the present:

> Our children will not know it's a different country.
> All we can hope to leave them now is money.

By the same polemic device, children were once cast to ask their fathers (at least on hoardings): 'What did you do in the Great War, daddy?'

From Stan Smith, *Inviolable Voice: History and Twentieth-Century Poetry* (Dublin, 1982), pp. 171–80.

## NOTES

[Stan Smith's historicist reading of Larkin's poems is taken from his *Inviolable Voice: History and Twentieth-Century Poetry* (1982), still one of the finest studies of modern poetry, though sadly out of print. It shares with Tom Paulin's essay a fundamental conviction that Larkin's poems are deeply implicated in post-war cultural decline, as well as a shrewd and discerning sense of poetic language and form. One of the most distinctive features of this essay, however, is its method of approaching 'history' through images of spatial and temporal 'distance'. Smith also draws more obviously than Paulin does on the methods and insights of Marxist critical theory, especially in his analysis of social class. His reading of 'The Whitsun Weddings', in particular, extends the emphasis on 'distance' to show how the poem's way of seeing people turns from disengagement to condescension. Ed.]

# 10

# Philip Larkin: Lyricism, Englishness and Postcoloniality

*JAMES BOOTH*

Philip Larkin is by common consent a very English writer. But to what extent is this Englishness a limiting factor in his work? Larkin himself rejected the suggestion that his poems could be read as 'standing for' any place or principle. He would have denied that his work embodied anything as ideological as imperialism, Toryism, patriarchy, Englishness. He wrote, rather, about 'the experience. The beauty'.[1] His themes as he defined them in a letter to Patsy Strang of July 1953 are the universal commonplaces of lyric poetry:

> I should like to write about 75–100 new poems, all rather better than anything I've ever done before, and dealing with such subjects as Life, Death, Time, Love, and Scenery in such a manner as would render further attention to them by other poets superfluous.[2]

Nevertheless many readers, both critics and admirers, insist on searching beneath Larkin's lyricism, for the unconscious political key to his work. Lisa Jardine states: 'The work is the product of its times; its author's preoccupations are those of a generation, a class and a nation'.[3] Stephen Regan, though more appreciative of Larkin's poetry than Jardine, argues similarly that his works are best read as 'the products of a particular society at a particular time'. Regan reproaches aesthetic, 'formalist' readings with ignoring 'history'. The 'realities' with which poetry is concerned are 'social and historical'.[4] In Regan's view, poems apparently concerned with 'timeless', universal themes such as Life, Death, Time, Love or Scenery are more accurately to be read as concerned with particular working-class, or Victorian, or masculine, or postcolonial versions of Life, Death, Time, Love or Scenery.[5]

During his lifetime Larkin was most frequently ideologised as a harmless British eccentric bachelor, a decent, agnostic, welfare-state 'poet of the common man'. Seamus Heaney characterised him in 1976 as a poet of 'composed and tempered English nationalism ... the not untrue, not unkind voice of post-war England'.[6] In order to protect his privacy the poet cooperated with this fiction, particularly in the BBC Monitor programme of 1964, *The Bicycle-clipped Misanthropist*. It is one of the positive results of the publication of Larkin's *Selected Letters* in 1992 and Andrew Motion's biography in 1993 that this figment has been dispelled for ever. However, one ideological myth has been banished only to be replaced by another. Many have concluded on reading the letters that Larkin's literary conservatism was merely the acceptable face of a more profound reactionary chauvinism. Worse still, the materialist, neo-Marxist critics tell us, all art is propaganda, the personal is always political; and the ideological wickedness revealed in the *Letters* was there, all the time, hidden between the lines of apparently innocent lyrics about Life, Death, Time, Love, and Scenery.

Lisa Jardine, writing in the *Guardian* shortly after the appearance of the *Letters*, neatly registers the abrupt displacement in the popular imagination of one ideologically coherent Larkin by another:

> Philip Larkin ... is not the benevolent, modest, librarian with an extraordinary ear for a quintessentially British kind of detail of A-level anthologies, but rather a casual, habitual racist, and an easy misogynist.

She goes on to reject Larkin as a fit subject for the serious attention of her students. His poems are irrelevant to a postcolonial, multi-cultural Britain:

> Actually, we don't tend to teach Larkin much now in my Department of English. The Little Englandism he celebrates sits uneasily within our revised curriculum, which seeks to give all of our students, regardless of background, race or creed, a voice within British culture.[7]

She and her colleagues refer to Larkin's poems only to teach their students 'to see through the even texture of Larkin's verse, to the parochial beliefs which lie behind them'. More emotively Tom Paulin refers to 'the sewer under the national monument' revealed by Larkin's *Letters*.[8]

It cannot be denied that there is an ideological provocativeness, amounting at times to self-parody, about the figure which Larkin takes care to cut in his later letters: an extreme Tory immigrant-basher with a hatred of trendy lefties:

> Prison for strikers,
> Bring back the cat,
> Kick out the niggers –
> How about that?
>     (*Letters*, 493)

He lets rip with deliberate offensiveness against the noisy West Indian crowd at Lords cricket ground:

> And as for those black scum kicking up a din on the boundary – a squad of South African police would have sorted them out to my satisfaction.
>     (*Letters*, 719)

And here he is in a letter to Kingsley Amis, lashing out in the same breath against fashionable women writers, immigrants, and the state subsidy of leftist subversives:

> I am extricating myself from the Arts Council Literature Advisory Panel – not my cup of piss. Just sitting there while lady novelists shoot their mouths off. Fay Weldon wyyaaarch Margaret Foster (Forster?) yuuuuck. And Chas Os. [Charles Osborne] sittin and grinnin and fixing it all up afterwards the way he wants it. I agree with you that it should all be scrapped. No subsidies for Gay Sweatshirt or the Runcorn Socialist Workers Peoples Poetry Workshop. Or wogs like Salmagundi or whatever his name is.
>     (*Letters*, 664–5)

In his later years Larkin dedicated himself to becoming as reactionary as humanly possible. When he found himself acting in a politically correct way he expressed horrified surprise. In a letter to Thwaite he admitted to having taken the 'ethnic' side in the discussion at an earlier Arts Council meeting: 'I thought I might see you at the Arts Co. Lit. Pan. yesterday – aren't you on it? – but no such luck. You should have heard me pleading for ethnic culture' (*Letters*, 629). Confronted with such a strenuous display of ideological self-definition, it is not surprising perhaps that readers should turn a sceptical eye on Larkin's art.

The counter to the ideological version of Larkin is simple. Two days after the appearance of Jardine's attack the *Guardian* printed three letters reasserting the aestheticist position. Whatever Larkin's limitations as a private individual, it was argued, he deliberately transcended them as a poet. David Townsend, Director of Social Services in Croydon, wrote offering to eat his copies of *High Windows*, *The Whitsun Weddings* and *The Less Deceived* if Jardine could point to any expression of misogyny or racism in them. Claire Tomalin pointed out that 'T. S. Eliot was anti-semitic. D. H. Lawrence made racist remarks. Evelyn Waugh's social attitudes are deplorable. Tolstoy had some poisonous beliefs. So did Flaubert' (for gender balance she could have added Virginia Woolf). The prejudices of these writers, it was argued, are separable from, and irrelevant to, their artistic achievement. A cartoon neatly underlined the point, depicting one woman reader saying to another: 'I find I simply can't *touch* a poet who isn't a vegetarian'.[9]

I propose to examine the question of Larkin's Englishness from three different angles. Firstly I will analyse one of his most purely lyric poems, 'Livings II', in order to compare the relative value of the aesthetic and ideological approaches to his national identity. I will then treat two specific aspects of the ideological attack on Larkin's work. Larkin's supposedly misogynistic addiction to masturbation, a 'vice' conventionally associated with the repressed English schoolboy, will be compared with Alice Walker's feminist treatment of the same topic. Then Larkin's racism will be examined in the light of his enthusiasm for black jazz, and his cultural assumptions will be compared with those of his fellow British writer, Salman Rushdie.

## I

The three pieces collectively titled 'Livings' (completed in 1971) seem, on the face of it, very much poems to be read aesthetically rather than ideologically. Their concern is 'Life' at an existentially pure extreme. The noun 'Life', indeed, is too static in its overtones to describe the poet's elusive subject. Rather these poems treat the unstable process of 'living'. The title is a kind of pun. On the prosaic level each of the three speakers describes how he makes his living, in the sense of earning his keep. But the epiphany towards which each poem builds indicates that the real subject transcends material contingencies. All the speakers are men, caught at a moment of solitary reflection on their lives. But there is no moral or political pattern to be detected in the juxtaposition of their soliloquies. Their circumstances are as randomly diverse as possible: a young commercial traveller idly contemplates a change in his routine on the eve of the Great Crash of 1929; a lighthouse-keeper enjoys his isolation in his tower above the sea; a member of an Oxbridge college settles in for a cosy evening drinking port with his cronies two or three centuries ago. There is little doubt that had Larkin's fading inspiration permitted him to continue the series (as he intended) this randomness would have proliferated. The poet's deliberate aim seems to be to evade Regan's context of 'history'. The common factor between these speakers is simply that they are 'living'.

The central poem of the triptych is the most intensely lyrical. In it the ageing Larkin reverts to the extravagant symbolism of his youthful first volume, *The North Ship* ('The third ship drove towards the north, / Over the sea, the darkening sea'). But now, a quarter of a century later, the rich evocativeness of his early style has been replaced by a mannered, elliptical terseness reminiscent of Imagism. The poem takes the form of the lighthouse-keeper's fierce celebration of his solitude:

> By day, sky builds
> Grape-dark over the salt
> Unsown stirring fields.
> Radio rubs its legs,
> Telling me of elsewhere:
>
> Barometers falling,
> Ports wind-shuttered,
> Fleets pent like hounds,
> Fires in humped inns
> Kippering sea-pictures –
>
> Keep it all off!
>      (*CP*, 187)

The brusque virtuosity of the style serves in itself as a metaphor for the lighthouse-keeper's sense of freedom. Elaborate and highly 'poetic' though it is, the poem still gives the impression of a real person speaking spontaneously. The short trimeters shift between iambs and trochees, making the lines halt and break into clipped nervous phrases. The images meander through a cadenza of discords and surprising contradictions. The 'Grape-dark' sky gathers over 'salt ... fields', with a sharp clash of taste associations. The fields are 'Unsown', indicating sterility, but they are 'stirring', indicating restless life. The radio, like a cricket which has strayed inside from these inhospitable 'fields' 'rubs its legs', thus keeping the speaker company, without burdening him with another human presence.

This far-fetched conceit of the radio as cricket-on-the-hearth introduces a sequence of images which clash sentimental cosiness with the lighthouse-keeper's purer, more absolute security at the top of his 70-foot tower. With violent paradox the image of 'elsewhere' which most reassures him of his own precious, existential 'here' is the traditional cosy retreat in a warm inn. There is something claustrophobic about the humped inns of his imagination, whose sea-pictures, humorously 'kippering' in the smoke, keep the sea at a safe, reassuring distance. In contrast, his own position out above the sea's exploding, slavering suds, gives him a sense of security far beyond such banal sentimentalism. Even the sea-going fleets, which also occur to his mind's eye, are enclosed and cramped, as they huddle 'wind-shuttered' (suggesting inn-shutters), and 'pent like hounds'. These hounds, however, are prevented, to the speaker's satisfaction, from venturing out over the 'fields' of the sea. (It is perhaps not irrelevant here that Larkin was passionately opposed to blood sports.) The lighthouse-keeper exults in the storm, in the swerving snow and the 'Leather-black waters' which confirm his immunity from human intrusion. His retreat is no warm sociable inn; it is a fiercely anti-social cell of solitude:

> Guarded by brilliance
> I set plate and spoon,
> And after, divining-cards.
> Lit shelved liners
> Grope like mad worlds westward.
> (*CP*, 188)

There is much wit and artistry in this poem which can be enjoyed in and for itself. The reader may also hear intertextual echoes from the earlier lyric tradition. The speaker is perhaps a deliberate variant on Yeats's 'Platonist' in his tower. But Larkin's solitary is very different from Yeats's. He is not engaged in any spiritual quest; he is simply earning his living. All he does in his elevated isolation is eat frugally, and pass the time reading divining-cards. His solitude is enjoyed for its own sake; it is not grandly philosophised.

A closer parallel with Larkin's poem is perhaps the mystical but secular privacy described in 'The Garden', by Andrew Marvell. To Marvell, as to the lighthouse-keeper, 'Society is all but rude, / To this delicious Solitude'. Marvell's imagery is pastoral rather than extravagantly romantic, but it generates a similarly intense anti-socialness to Larkin's – and the same euphoric negativity: 'Annihilating all that's made / To a green Thought in a green Shade'. For the seventeenth-century poet privacy is an Edenic garden; for his twentieth-century successor it is the lighthouse-keeper's lonely cell. But the two poets' passion for solitude is essentially the same. The whimsical eccentric of 'The Garden' loves trees rather than people: 'Fair Trees! where s'eer your barkes I wound, / No Name shall but your own be found'.[10] The lighthouse-keeper of 'Livings' passionately loves the mussels and limpets clinging to the rocks: 'Creatures, I cherish you!'

Larkin frequently expresses a desire to escape from the pressures of 'society' by effacing himself – or his self ('Such attics cleared of me!'). In a letter of 1966 he even longs drolly, like Marvell, for the quiescence of inanimate nature: 'Yes, life is pretty grey up in Hull. Maeve wants to marry me, Monica wants to chuck me. I feel I want to become something other than a man – a rosebush, or some ivy, or something. Something noncontroversial' (*Letters*, 382). Some readers might feel that Marvell's and Larkin's elaborately witty projections of their private worlds place them in a distinctly English tradition. They can be seen, perhaps, to celebrate a characteristically English sense of privacy ('an Englishman's home is his castle').

It is here that we re-enter the ideological debate. Should the critic follow this hint further by translating aesthetics into ideology? Is the truest interpretation of poems like 'Livings' a political one? Tom Paulin believes so. In his view Larkin is not the pure aesthete he claims to be; rather he is 'concerned to issue public statements disguised as lyric poems'. Larkin's solitary English eccentric is less an aesthetic and cultural creation than a political one. 'Larkin speaks not for the imperial male – too transcendental a subject that – but for the English male, middle-class, professional, outwardly confident, controlled and in control'.[11] The lonely, brilliant room in which the lighthouse-keeper has his being is to be read as a mystification of Larkin's socio-political Englishness. 'The poet in the seaport of Hull is reincarnated as a custodian of light ...'.[12]

Paulin's Larkin is however too complex to be a comfortable Little Englander. His is a personality 'wounded' by English constraints and inhibitions. He celebrates his Englishness, but he also resents it. He is constantly pushing against the meanness of spirit which it imposes on him, and his poetry rises from this psychological tension. Larkin himself would seem to concur, to an extent, with this analysis. He remarked that his poetry was 'nothing if not personal',[13] and was only too ready to convict himself of poverty of spirit and selfishness: 'How meanly I doled myself out, doubting and counting'.[14] But in Paulin's view to interpret the poet's attitudes simply in terms of 'personal neurosis' is as inadequate as the purely aesthetic reading. The wounds in his personality are caused by his Englishness, and the key to his neurosis lies in his national, political ideology:

> Angry at not being allowed to show emotion, he writhes with anxiety inside that sealed bunker which is the English ethic of privacy. He journeys into the interior, into the unknown heart – the maybe missing centre – of Englishness.[15]

As Paulin notes, Larkin once described himself as 'one of Nature's Orangemen', and it is the Orangeman's edgy, insecure nationalism which he sublimates in his poetry.

The problem with Paulin's analysis, perceptive and accurate though it is, is its moralism. The grinding of his Irish axe deafens Paulin to the lyric mode of Larkin's work, and everything he says remains beside the point. Paulin confuses the circumstances of the poet's time and place with his lyric theme. No doubt the author of 'Livings II' is, as Paulin says, English, he is male, he belongs to the professional classes, and he has a strong sense of privacy. He might also be said to have a 'wounded personality'. But the same could be said for innumerable other men of Larkin's generation who wrote no poetry or bad poetry. The *poetry* cannot be explained by this analysis. And Larkin is a poet, not a propagandist. He quite lacks the ideological assertiveness which Paulin attributes to him. He is not a spokesman. This poem, for instance, is in no sense the manifesto (nor the confession) of 'the autonomous English male professional'. Nor is the 'privacy' which it so ambiguously celebrates an 'ethic'.

It is characteristic of lyric poetry that the poet's rhetorical strategy should reduce ideological and political specifics to mere contingency. The reader does not need to identify with (or even be aware of) the poet's Englishness, his maleness, or his middle-classness, in order to respond to the lighthouse-keeper's celebration of solitude. Nor would the poem be 'truer' if the poet abandoned the pretence of speaking in the person of a lighthouse-keeper, and told us instead of the anxieties of an English middle-class librarian. Larkin has not cast the poem in this highly-wrought symbolic mode in order to conceal or mystify his own 'real' ideological concerns, but in order to transcend them. There is such a thing as 'Life' (or 'living'); and this poem is about it.

Paulin detects a 'synergy of nationalism and lyricism' in Larkin's imagination.[16] This is quite wrong. Intensely English though he was, Larkin's lyricism is profoundly at odds with his nationalism. The only work in which he consciously attempted such a synergy (apart from the jokey doggerel fragments of the letters) is 'Homage to a Government', a poem about which he was extremely uncomfortable. In an interview he even disowned any political motive in writing it, pleading lamely and nonsensically: 'Well, that's really history rather than politics' (*RW*, 52). He seems to have recognised that this exceptional foray into political polemic was a mistake. Elsewhere, in poems intended for publication, he avoids politics completely.

Paulin's inability to distinguish Larkin the man from Larkin the lyric poet can sometimes lead him into patent absurdities. Thus for Paulin the 'real theme' of 'Afternoons' is not the universal 'elegiac sense of time passing', but 'national decline':

> Summer is fading:
> The leaves fall in ones and twos
> From trees bordering
> The new recreation ground.
> (*CP*, 121)

Paulin explains:

> The autumn leaves fall in ones and twos, rather like colonies drop-
> ping out of the empire ... The young mothers whose beauty has
> thickened feel that 'something' is pushing them to the side of their
> own lives, and this is a metaphor for a sense of diminished purpose
> and fading imperial power.[17]

There is a desperate ring about his confident assertion 'and this is a
metaphor for ...'. These mothers in the children's playground are,
surely, the most inappropriate emblem of declining imperial power
imaginable. They are women; they are working class. When did
such people ever represent England's imperial glory?

Despite Paulin's efforts, the lyric, aesthetic reading of Larkin
remains more rewarding. This is not 'a subtly disguised public
poem' requiring elucidation by an ideological inquisitor. The
subject of 'Afternoons' is Time, a natural subject for a poet approaching 40. With a sure lyric instinct Larkin expresses his personal
emotion through an 'objective correlative' carefully distanced from
his own socio-political situation. As in the case of 'Livings' the
social specifics are at a tangent to those of the middle-class bachelor
librarian Larkin. The albums, lettered *Our Wedding*, lie, touching
and pathetic, near the television. The women's beauty has 'thickened' and their children are growing up. The poem closes with a
comment on the ageing process which is as relevant to the poet and
the reader as to the young mothers:

> Something is pushing them
> To the side of their own lives.
> (*CP*, 121)

These women do not embody Larkin's social or political prejudices
(nor do they express his personal prejudice against marriage). They
are certainly not a metaphor for empire, any more than are the
worn out old horses in 'At Grass', which Paulin ingeniously inter-
prets as metaphorical 'retired Generals'.

Larkin's Englishness may be intense, but it is not a matter of coherent ideology. His poems present lyric universals with an English
accent. This is why his work is so popular abroad.[18] In Paulin's
hands Larkin's beautiful, static, depersonalised lyrics are perversely
returned to the parochial kinetics from which they have been so art-
istically disengaged – as though the critic's duty were to uncover

what Larkin's poetry would have been like had he *not* been a great poet.

## II

It might be objected that this argument is somewhat evasive. 'Livings' and 'Afternoons' are particularly 'pure' lyrics, which perhaps do not confront us with the most problematic elements of Larkin's personality: his alleged misogyny for instance. In 'Livings II' the lighthouse-keeper plays cards with himself. In the earlier, more overtly personal poem, 'Best Society', the imagery delicately hints that the speaker plays with himself in a more literal sense:

> Our virtues are all social ...
>
> Viciously, then, I lock my door.
> The gas-fire breathes. The wind outside
> Ushers in evening rain. Once more
> Uncontradicting solitude
> Supports me on its giant palm;
> And like a sea-anemone
> Or simple snail, there cautiously
> Unfolds, emerges, what I am.
>
> (*CP*, 56–7)

Here surely, in this 'sceptical assertion of male autonomy',[19] there is conclusive evidence of a synergy between Larkin's 'wounded personality' and his lyricism. His specifically English masculinity limits his vision and spoils the aesthetic transcendence at which he aims. Sex is viewed in this poem, as in the more negative 'Dry-Point', solely as a matter between the male poet and his own body. Women, marriage and the social virtues are deliberately locked out. This, the extremest manifestation of privacy in his work, rooted in English puritanism and the single-sex school system, surely has no universal implication. It is uncomfortably, embarrassingly culture-specific, particularly when such poems are read in the light of the jokey reference to the young poet's 'flogging chart' (*Letters*, 42), or his shameless auto-erotic jokes: 'I don't – *I don't* – want to ... spend circa £5 [on taking a girl out] when I can toss off in five minutes, free, and have the rest of the evening to myself';[20] 'sexual intercourse ... like asking someone else to blow your own nose for you'.[21]

In contrast with Larkin's white, English, male view of masturbation, that of the black, American woman, Alice Walker, appears unmistakably politically correct. A central image in Walker's novel *Possessing the Secret of Joy* is the small female idol which the protagonists find in the midwife's hut:

> ... the little figure from M'Lissa's hut, smiling broadly, eyes closed, and touching her genitals. If the word 'MINE' were engraved on her finger, her meaning could not be more clear. She is remarkably alive.[22]

Walker, concerned with the barbarous practice of clitoridectomy, by which women are dispossessed of their sexual selves in the interests of social control, sees the idol and its 'self-possession' as a moving symbol of women's potential freedom. For her, masturbation is a means by which women can reclaim their bodies from patriarchal oppression. In this context of sexual politics autoeroticism takes on an ideological meaning apparently vastly different from Larkin's crude 'tossing off'.

The difference between Larkin and Walker lies in sexual politics. But is it an essential difference? Larkin, like Walker, preserves his self against the demands of society by the act of possessing his own body in 'secret'. Like Walker Larkin attempts to create a private space in which his sexuality will not function as a means of social repression. Both Walker and Larkin seek through auto-eroticism to evade the jealous patriarchal system determined to destroy their independence and dominate them. Paulin talks of Larkin's 'defence of male autonomy'. But, as Walker shows us, such autonomy is not specifically male, and Larkin's defence of it is ultimately not ideologically gendered. He is not defending male autonomy; he is defending *his* autonomy. Larkin happens to be a male, so he expresses this desire for freedom and self-possession in male imagery, just as Walker expresses it in female imagery.

Some commentators associate Larkin's masturbation with what they see as his sexism. Indeed, on the evidence of Motion's biography he did behave rather badly towards some of the women in his life (though not as badly as Tolstoy or Picasso). As Monica Jones poignantly remarked: 'He lied to me, the bugger, but I loved him'.[23] It is important to recognise however that the attitudes towards women which he expresses in both letters and poems is not predatory, but defensive. It would be a mistake to read his jokes about having the evening to himself rather than spending it with a woman as the arrogant misogyny of his generation and class. He is no more anti-women than Walker is anti-men.

The early letters concerned with his engagement show him constantly embarrassed, struggling not to hurt Ruth Bowman's feelings, while at the same time remaining true to himself. It is the possessiveness of marriage to which he objects:

> Further, women don't just sit still & back you up. They want children: they like scenes: they want a chance of parading all the emotional haberdashery they are stocked with. Above all they like feeling they 'own' you – or that you 'own' them – a thing I hate.
>
> (*Letters*, 158)

Larkin is no aggressor in the war of the sexes. He objects as passionately to owning a woman as to being owned by her. In this respect his hatred of patriarchy is as strong as Walker's. Moreover this attitude transcends gender. His novel *A Girl in Winter* follows the pattern of a classic boy-meets-girl story. But when at its close Robin succeeds in going to bed with Katherine, the result is neither sentimental togetherness, nor male triumph. Instead, the man is contemptuously ignored and we are left with the woman's feelings of aloneness and sterility. The denial of the usual sexual politics is extraordinary for a writer of Larkin's generation, and contrasts strongly with the attitudes of his contemporary, Kingsley Amis.

Larkin's account of his feelings in a letter to James Sutton of October 1945 is characteristically awkward and self-critical:

> It is rather a disturbing experience to have someone utterly dependent on you, it puts one's least thoughts and actions under a microscope (at any rate, to oneself) and short-circuits one's processes. One has no elbow-room. I feel as if my wings were in danger of being clipped. And it worries me also to find that I am a long way off being capable of any emotion as simple as what is called love. It seems limiting and maneating [*recte* 'insulating'] to me.
>
> (*Letters*, 110)

There is a distinct note of shamefacedness about his stubborn self-possession in the face of his fiancée's emotional demands. The misreading of 'insulating' as 'maneating' in the *Selected Letters* serves to point up how little of the sexual-political there really is in Larkin's attitude. The heavily gendered irritation with female importunacy implied by the word 'maneating' jars against the reflective, serious tone of the rest of the passage. The young poet's genuine fear that domesticity will blunt or 'insulate' his poetic sensibility is transformed into a simple masculine fear of women.[24]

In Alice Walker also, the issue of 'self-possession' transcends sexual politics. In *Possessing the Secret of Joy* masturbation is not merely a blow against patriarchal oppression. Through the figure of Queen Anne (nicknamed after the flower Queen Anne's Lace) it is also projected in more universal terms:

> She rode bareback, always ... She experienced orgasm while riding the horse ...
> She'd been brought up by pagan parents, earth worshippers, on a little island somewhere in Hawaii. She could experience orgasm doing almost anything. She said that at home there were favorite trees she loved that she rubbed against. She could orgasm against warm, smooth boulders ... she could come against the earth itself if it rose a bit to meet her. However ... she'd never been with a man.
> (*Possessing the Secret of Joy*, 169–70)

Pierre, who relates the story of Queen Anne, finds himself pondering on the differences between male and female sexuality: 'Is it only woman who would make love to everything? Man, too, after all, has external sexual organs. But does man seek oneness with the earth by having sex with it?' (171). The question is left unanswered. (Walker is presumably unfamiliar with Marvell's rejection of the love of women in favour of the love of trees: 'No white nor red was ever seen / So am'rous as this lovely green'.) Most significantly, it is precisely Queen Anne's self-possession which makes Pierre fall in love with her. Indeed he insists she was the 'only girl he ever loved' (169). *He* has no desire to possess *her*.

This passage in Walker's novel is rendered in a lyrical register, suggesting the fashionable 'forest-fucker' mysticism of the Sixties. Larkin's lyricism in 'Best Society' is more controlled and original. But it serves the same purpose as Walker's – to present 'self-possession' as a profound existential satisfaction:

> Once more
> Uncontradicting solitude
> Supports me on its giant palm;
> And like a sea-anemone
> Or simple snail, there cautiously
> Unfolds, emerges, what I am.
> (*CP*, 56–7)

Larkin's images of nature ('sea-anemone', 'simple snail') are exquisite metaphors for physiological/psychological sensation, while Walker's ('trees', 'warm, smooth boulders', 'the earth') boldly symbolise a pantheistic oneness with Nature. But despite the differences, the rhetoric of both writers serves to imply that self-fulfilment is a natural and organic thing. Larkin and Walker are perhaps the only recent writers of any prominence who project auto-eroticism as a means of taking control of one's own destiny, rather than as a failure of relatedness. The black American woman and the white British man are not so different from each other as they might at first seem.

## III

There is no hint of racism in any poem which Larkin wrote for publication. The racism of the letters, however, must be deplored. But, even in the letters it is greatly complicated by contradictory elements. Larkin made no attempt to be ideologically consistent on any issue. Though he affected patriotism in later life, as a young man he was eager to evade service in the wartime army, feeling that it would interfere with his development as an artist. Though he became a respectable librarian, he stole books from libraries and at least one bookshop. Throughout his life his response to figures of authority was highly ambiguous. In 1978, his poetic inspiration gone, he wrote a feebly pious quatrain for the Queen's Jubilee:

> In times when nothing stood
> but worsened, or grew strange,
> there was one constant good:
> she did not change.[25]
> (*CP*, 210)

In earlier days he showed a raucous disrespect for royalty. In a letter to Norman Iles of 8 November 1942 he remarked:

> I see we have finally 'finished' Rommel in Africa. Philip [Brown] & I stood to attention when the midnight bulletin was read out & sang 'God Rape the King'. (I hope some fucking censor reads this.)
> (*Letters*, 47)

On VE day, 1945, alone with the radio, he wrote to James Sutton: 'I listened to Churchill blathering out of turn this afternoon, and the King this evening'.[26]

Larkin's racism is no more consistent than his royalism. His later letters show him as a comic stereotype of the anti-immigrant Tory, complaining about 'the rising tide of niggers', referring casually to the 'bloody Paki next door', and fearing 'all manner of germs brought into the country by immigrants etc. (Powell For Premier)' (*Letters*, 557, 673, 421). He was, nevertheless, as we have seen, quite capable of 'pleading for ethnic culture' on the Arts Council Literature Advisory Panel (*Letters*, 629). On the personal level he remained on good terms with R. K. Biswas, an Indian colleague at Leicester University (*Letters*, 445). Biswas, indeed, was among those who came to Larkin's defence during the *furore* following the publication of the *Letters*.

More significantly Larkin's racism coexisted with a lifelong passion for black jazz music, and his attitudes towards race are seen at their most complex in this context, where his feelings were most deeply involved. In a long letter to Charles Monteith of Faber written in 1971 he discusses the editor's plans to commission a book on Louis Armstrong. Here we find, not racial prejudice, but a positive acknowledgement of the 'hybridity' celebrated by such recent postcolonial theorists as Homi Bhabha:

> Or there might be a cultural work, taking Armstrong as a kind of Trojan horse of Negro values sent into white civilisation under the cover of entertainment.
>
> (*Letters*, 444)

There is no hint in Larkin's tone of the racist's fear of adulteration. Indeed he seems to welcome Armstrong's subversion of 'white civilisation'. Later in the same letter he recommends that Monteith choose an author:

> prepared to spend a good deal of time assembling not only a reasonably definitive life of Armstrong but to attempt to place him as a cultural phenomenon in the twentieth century, not overlooking the part he has played (with, of course, other artists such as Duke Ellington, Fats Waller and so on) in 'Negroising' western culture.
>
> (*Letters*, 445)

Here, in speaking of the music he loves, his superficial racism drops away to reveal an appreciation of the black element in his own culture.

It is perhaps unfortunate that most readers derive their notion of Larkin's attitudes on this subject from the Introduction to *All What Jazz*, where his real enthusiasm for the 'Negroising' of Western culture by jazz is overshadowed by anti-modernist polemic. He remarks, for instance, that 'The tension between artist and audience in jazz slackened when the Negro stopped wanting to entertain the white man' (*RW*, 294). In the context of this 'not wholly defensible' *jeu d'esprit*[27] this sounds cruder than it actually is. As a description of one moment in the historical development of jazz, it is in fact perceptive and thought-provoking. Larkin certainly does not intend it as a prescription for the correct relationship between races. His detection of the slackening cultural 'tension' between black musician and white audience is trivialised when it is interpreted to imply that 'The white audience *must be* in control' or that 'black musicians exist to entertain the whites'.[28] In fact Larkin's love of jazz expresses more than racial condescension. In Larkin's generation of white Britons the passion for black American jazz grew out of a sense of increasing cultural complexity. For the schoolboy in Coventry, as for many others of his time, black American jazz offered an escape from, and a protest against, the conventional constraints of his home. Its exotic, 'Negroising' influence initiated them into a culture emotionally richer and less inhibited than that of their parochial British environment.

With this in mind even Larkin's most apparently condescending remarks about black music may appear less offensive. 'The Negro was a wonderful entertainer, but he isn't any good as an artist' he wrote, and enthuses in an early letter about 'the negro's childlike beauty' (*Letters*, 20). But, in Larkin's defence, it should be remembered that this version of 'the Negro' as a spontaneous, unspoilt child of nature, a creature of emotion and rhythm rather than of self-conscious European calculation, is common in much pioneering writing by blacks in the 1930s, the time when the young Larkin was first encountering the 'Negroising' effect of jazz. The Francophone West Indian poet, Aimé Césaire, who coined the term 'Négritude', writes:

> Eia ...
> For those who explored nothing
> For those who never mastered
>
> Eia for joy
> Eia for love[29]

And Léopold Sédar Senghor, who was later to become President of Senegal, shows attitudes not dissimilar to Larkin's:

> Emotion is completely Negro as reason is Greek. Water rippled by every breeze? Unsheltered soul blown by every wind, whose fruit often drops before it is ripe? Yes, in one way, the Negro is richer in gifts than in works.[30]

## IV

This issue of race and culture may be refocused, perhaps, by means of another politically incorrect comparison. At present the two writers who, paradoxically, stand as most intensely representative of 'British' culture are Philip Larkin and Salman Rushdie. At first sight this seems a mere trick of words, confusing two distinct layers in the word 'British'. When speaking of Larkin the meaning of 'British' which comes to mind is ancient and semi-racial. He is English perhaps, rather than British; or British simply because he is English. This definition of Britishness is, in the most literal sense, 'insular': 'this island race' is English, and its culture is rooted in 'our island story'. When speaking of Rushdie, however, a non-insular definition of 'Britishness' must be invoked, based on the recent history of far-flung Empire and the immigration which followed decolonisation. Rushdie is British because he satisfies the legal criteria for citizenship, which do not depend on race or 'culture'. He has a British passport. In fact of course the two definitions of Britishness are not fundamentally different. The English are also immigrants in Britain, and Celtic hackles may still sometimes rise at the appropriation of 'Britishness' by the English newcomers. Nevertheless Larkin was 'born British'; Rushdie was not.

By this argument Larkin's Britishness is old-fashioned and 'post-imperial'; Rushdie's is modern and 'postcolonial'. Larkin's poetry is frequently, if inaccurately, interpreted as expressing nostalgia for the glories of Empire. Seamus Heaney gives a relatively benign version of this post-imperial Larkin. He quotes 'Going, Going',[31] and comments:

> The loss of imperial power, the failure of economic nerve, the diminished influence of Britain inside Europe, all this has led to a new sense of the shires, a new valuing of the native English experience.[32]

Larkin then is a 'native' Englishman, with a British xenophobia against the 'lesser tribes' of the Empire: 'wogs like Salmagundi or whatever his name is'. Rushdie, in contrast, is a 'native' subject of Empire who, in a postcolonial world, has become British. As government ministers repeatedly stressed in the days following the *fatwa*, Rushdie must be protected from terrorism because he is 'a British novelist'. More profoundly Rushdie symbolises a new identity forged out of the postcolonial mix of modern Britain. He is, by ethnic and cultural origin, 'hybrid' in a sense which Larkin is not. Larkin is thus excluded from the multicultural 'revised curriculum', while Rushdie is central to it. This euphoric ideological antithesis seems to prove that, though they are both 'British', Larkin and Rushdie really have nothing in common.

A less ideologically judgemental approach, however, offers different perspectives. In fact Larkin and Rushdie both participate, if to different degrees, in that hybridising process which has, for many centuries, been the central characteristic of British culture.[33] Once one steps back from their self-conscious provocations – Larkin's anti-immigrant remarks, Rushdie's satire on 'Mrs Torture's' police state – suggestive similarities emerge. Their sensibilities are pluralist, secular, individualist, and their cultural assumptions are in certain fundamental respects the same. Both, for instance, constantly evade or defy institutional authority. Each projects a culturally diverse, fragmented, postmodern sensibility through dramatised *personae* ('They fuck you up, your mum and dad', 'Books are a load of crap'). Larkin said 'I think one has to dramatise oneself a little',[34] and hoped that he was 'quite funny' (*RW*, 47). Rushdie writes: 'perhaps, if one wishes to remain an individual in the midst of the teeming multitudes, one must make oneself grotesque'.[35]

The young Larkin even expresses the literal blasphemy for which Rushdie is at present suffering. In a letter to Sutton of December 1940 he advises his friend to prefer exotic non-Christian imagery in his paintings: 'No fucking Christianity'.[36] Late in his life he reread the Bible, commenting: 'It's absolutely bloody amazing to think that anyone ever believed any of that. Really, it's absolute balls. Beautiful, of course. But balls.'[37] More generally, the young Larkin's remark 'I hope some fucking censor reads this' would be a most appropriate epigraph for all Rushdie's work, from *Grimus* to *The Satanic Verses*. It is a measure of the Britishness of Rushdie's sensibility, perhaps, that he was genuinely surprised and indignant when the Islamic censor so forcibly reminded him of the non-British element in his hybrid personality.

It is also no accident that Baal in *The Satanic Verses* is, like Larkin, a lyric poet. When he is finally unmasked to face the judgement of Mahound, the poet defiantly asserts his individual perceptions against the totalitarian collectivity: 'I am Baal', he announces; 'I recognize no jurisdiction except that of my Muse; or, to be exact, my dozen Muses'.[38] Like Larkin who, when asked what he wrote about, replied simply 'the experience. The Beauty', Baal is fiercely, empirically, anti-ideological. Stylistically they may lie at opposite poles of concision and prolixity. But the poet's precise nuances and the novelist's riotous multiplicities express a common conviction that their individual responses, however awkward and embarrassing, are the only touchstone of authenticity. Larkin and Rushdie are both passionate in rejecting the bad faith of official or 'correct' language, and this extremism has led to similar problems for their readers. Rushdie flouts the pious taboo of Islam which demands absolute respect even for the Prophet's name, and boldly adopts the offensively garbled Arabic 'Mahound', used by the foreign enemies of Islam in the Middle Ages. Larkin flouts the pious taboos of contemporary multiculturalism which demand extreme politeness across racial and linguistic barriers, and offensively garbles the Indian name of the man he sees as the standard-bearer of 'ethnic culture': 'wogs like Salmagundi or whatever his name is'.

More particularly both Larkin and Rushdie show an intensely intimate, but highly ambiguous attitude towards specific icons of Britishness. 'Poetry and sovereignty are very primitive things', said Larkin, in support of the institution of the Laureateship (*RW*, 75). Nevertheless he himself declined the position. Rushdie satirises the racism of 'Ellowen Deeowen' and lays into 'Mrs Torture', but is then compelled ruefully to acknowledge his gratefulness to the government for ensuring his protection from terrorism. Larkin effuses 'I adore Mrs Thatcher', but when he met his idol in person he could not stop himself from sparring with her, on the characteristic Larkinesque ground of awkward, bloodyminded honesty:

'Surely', Larkin suddenly said, 'you don't want to see a united Germany?' 'Well, no', Mrs Thatcher answered, 'perhaps not.' 'Well then', Larkin asked her, 'what's all this hypocrisy about wanting the wall down then?'[39]

When she misquoted a line from 'Deceptions': 'Her mind was full of knives', he commented: 'she might think a mind full of knives rather along her own lines', adding hastily 'not that I don't kiss the ground she treads' (*Letters*, 751).

It would be a foolish exercise in essentialism, and counter to the whole drift of my argument, to argue that Larkin and Rushdie share a precisely definable British quality. Nevertheless some of their basic attitudes are surprisingly similar. It may be that the common culture implied by their shared 'Britishness', though it does not fit the currently fashionable ideological categories, is not therefore a mere figment. As Rushdie said, 'You don't have to be just one thing if you describe yourself as British'.[40] Perhaps, after all, Larkin and Rushdie do not belong to two opposed Britains: Larkin's one of 'comfortable insularity' and Little England parochialism; Rushdie's one of postcoloniality and multicultural diversity. For all their differences, the country of the mind which they imaginatively inhabit is recognisably the same place.

From Michael Baron (ed.), *Larkin With Poetry* (Leicester, 1997), pp. 9–30.

## NOTES

[This essay was presented in a slightly different form at an English Association Conference on Philip Larkin at the British Academy in July 1994, along with papers from Blake Morrison, Stephen Regan, Marion Lomax and Andrew Swarbrick. Returning to the arguments first rehearsed in his highly praised *Philip Larkin: Writer* (1992), James Booth disputes the idea that Larkin's 'Englishness' is a limiting factor in his work, and questions any suggestion that Larkin's lyricism is shaped and conditioned by his nationalism. What Booth values in Larkin's work are 'the universal commonplaces of lyric poetry'. He makes a firm distinction between his own 'aestheticist' or 'formalist' position and the 'ideological' or 'political' criticism of Tom Paulin and others. The most surprising and unusual aspect of Booth's essay is its comparative study of Larkin's work and writings by Alice Walker and Salman Rushdie. In showing how Larkin's interests as a writer converge with those of Walker and Rushdie, Booth seeks to defend his poetry from charges of misogyny and racism. Ed.]

1. Philip Larkin, *Required Writing: Miscellaneous Pieces 1955–82* (London, 1983), p. 68. Further references will be abbreviated as *RW* and included in the text.

2. *Selected Letters of Philip Larkin 1940–1985*, ed. Anthony Thwaite (London, 1992), p. 202. Further references will be abbreviated as *Letters* and included in the text.

3. Lisa Jardine, 'Saxon Violence', *Guardian*, 8 December 1992, Section 2, p. 4.

4. Stephen Regan, *Philip Larkin* (Basingstoke, 1992), pp. 57, 37.

5. Ibid., p. 66.

6. Seamus Heaney, 'Englands of the Mind', in *Preoccupations: Selected Prose 1968–1978* (London, 1980), p. 167.

7. Jardine, 'Saxon Violence'.

8. Tom Paulin, *Times Literary Supplement*, 6 November 1992, p. 15.

9. *Guardian*, 12 December 1992.

10. Andrew Marvell, *The Poems*, ed. Hugh MacDonald (London, 1956), pp. 51–2.

11. Tom Paulin, 'She Did Not Change: Philip Larkin', in *Minotaur: Poetry and the Nation State* (London, 1992), pp. 239–40. This essay was first published as 'Into the Heart of Englishness', *Times Literary Supplement*, 20–26 July 1990. [Reprinted in this volume – see pp. 160–77. Ed.]

12. Ibid., p. 247.

13. Jean Hartley, *Philip Larkin, The Marvell Press and Me* (Manchester, 1989), p. 62.

14. Philip Larkin, 'Single to Belfast', in Andrew Motion, *Philip Larkin: A Writer's Life* (London, 1993), p. 197.

15. Paulin, *Minotaur*, p. 240.

16. Ibid., p. 235.

17. Ibid., p. 233.

18. During the discussion of this paper at the British Academy on 1 July 1994, a French participant suggested that Larkin's defensive insularity would readily appeal to a French reader concerned for the fate of Gallic culture, embattled in an increasingly Anglophone world. An intriguing paradox! Jardine refuses to teach Larkin's poetry on the

ground that her students (even the male Anglo-Saxons among them) 'belong to a generation whose face is turned towards the new Europe, and for whom comfortable British insularity holds no romance' (*Guardian*, 8 December 1992). She seems unaware that many French and Italian students are enthusiastic about Larkin's poetry. In 1994 Larkin was a set author for *Agrégation* candidates in France. The students I encountered there all found Larkin peculiarly English. But, lacking British inhibitions, they experienced no difficulty in hearing the universal inflection in his English voice. To them the 'Englishness' of Larkin was as interesting and complex as say the Spanishness of Picasso, the Russianness of Tolstoy, the Americanness of Ezra Pound. See also *Etudes britanniques contemporaines, Numéro special: Philip Larkin*, January 1994.

19. Paulin, *Minotaur*, p. 238.

20. Kingsley Amis, *Memoirs* (London, 1991), p. 61.

21. Andrew Motion, *Philip Larkin: A Writer's Life* (London, 1993), p. 119.

22. Alice Walker, *Possessing the Secret of Joy* (London, 1992), p. 189. Further page references will be given in the text.

23. Motion, *Philip Larkin: A Writer's Life*, pp. 310–11.

24. Other misreadings (or misprints) in the *Selected Letters* are: 'the style of the shit-houses': *recte* 'styte' (p. 73), and 'on live': *recte* 'on line' (p. 635). Larkin's handwriting is not always clear.

25. It is thoroughly characteristic that Larkin should also have written a less respectable version of the same poem:

> After Healey's trading figures,
>     After Wilson's squalid crew,
> And the rising tide of niggers –
>     What a treat to look at you!
>         (*Letters*, p. 557)

26. James Booth, *Philip Larkin: Writer* (Hemel Hempstead, 1992), p. 17.

27. Motion, *Philip Larkin: A Writer's Life*, p. 396.

28. Paulin, *Minotaur*, p. 243.

29. Aimé Césaire, *Cahier d'un Retour au Pays Natal (Return to My Native Land)*, translated by Emile Snyder (Paris, 1971), p. 120.

30. Wole Soyinka, *Myth, Literature and the African World* (Cambridge, 1976), p. 129.

31. 'Going, Going', despite its felicities, falls into the category of 'required' rather than 'inspired' writing, having been commissioned by the

Department of the Environment. In private Larkin casually belittled even his best work, but his description of this poem as 'thin ranting conventional gruel' carries conviction (*Letters*, p. 452).

32. Heaney, 'Englands of the Mind', in *Preoccupations*, p. 169.

33. Seamus Heaney also points to a postcolonial element in Larkin – but in rather a different sense. Ted Hughes, Geoffrey Hill and Larkin, he suggests, are all 'possessed of that defensive love of their territory which was once shared only by those poets whom we might call colonial – Yeats, MacDiarmid, Carlos Williams' (pp. 150–1).

34. Ian Hamilton, 'Four Conversations', *London Magazine*, N.S. 4: 6 (Nov. 1964), p. 74.

35. Salman Rushdie, *Midnight's Children* (London, 1982), p. 109.

36. Letter to James Sutton, 16 December 1940.

37. Motion, *Philip Larkin: A Writer's Life*, p. 486.

38. Salman Rushdie, *The Satanic Verses* (London, 1988), p. 391.

39. Motion, *Philip Larkin: A Writer's Life*, p. 497.

40. Jane Bryce, 'Commonwealth Literature: 25 Years', *Wasafiri*, 11 (1990), 3.

# 11

# Larkin's Identities

*ANDREW SWARBRICK*

The few visitors to Philip Larkin's top-floor flat in 32 Pearson Park, Hull, where Larkin lived for eighteen years, might have noticed in the bathroom a montage 'juxtaposing Blake's "Union of Body And Soul" with a Punch-type cartoon of the front and back legs of a pantomime horse pulling in opposite directions against one another and captioned "Ah, at last I've found you!"'.[1] For an intensely private man, Larkin was strangely willing to offer public portraits of himself, however self-parodyingly laconic. The most public revelations of his self-protecting privacy are, of course, the poems. The pursed-up bachelor in 'Spring', the cynically debunking revenant of 'I Remember, I Remember', the sniggering agnostic of 'Church Going', the rootless, childless, provincial librarian, the nostalgic elegist: Larkin's poems seem to come to us very appealingly as the expression of a personality disclosing itself with self-deprecating honesty. Just how much lay hidden behind the disclosures and how self-revealing those masks were has been thoroughly explored by Andrew Motion in his biography of Larkin.[2] This present study is not so much interested in the 'personality' of Larkin as in the rhetorical constructions of his poems and the ways in which they aspire to things 'out of reach'. In Larkin's case, this meant a yearning for metaphysical absolutes, for states of being imagined, as it were, beyond the reach of language. He once told an interviewer, 'One longs for infinity and absence, the beauty of somewhere you're not'.[3] His poems are attempts to occupy the imaginative space of 'somewhere you're not' and are ultimately

211

concerned with existential questions of identity, choice and chance, isolation and communality.

On this showing, Larkin is a more adventurous, challenging and provocatively 'modern' writer than his critics, and some of his admirers, have been prepared to concede. The moments of most intense assent in Larkin, his own 'enormous yes', come with the vocabulary of nullity: nowhere, absences, oblivion, the 'dear translucent bergs: / Silence and space' ('Age' [*CP*, 95]). The terror of death is matched by the yearning for annihilation, the fear of non-existence by the desire for anonymity. The ultimate aspiration is for 'unfenced existence', and in Larkin's work elemental presences take on a metaphysical significance, suggesting everything that is consolingly non-self, the Other. Thus, 'Myxomatosis' is an existentialist statement about life as meaningless endurance, and 'Nothing To Be Said' a ludic saying something out of nothing. It should come as no surprise that Christopher Ricks, in *Beckett's Dying Words*, finds common ground between Samuel Beckett and Philip Larkin.[4]

Larkin's bathroom collage identifies the abiding conflicts from which his poetry emerged, the visionary integration of the spiritual and the corporeal mockingly juxtaposed with the comic disintegration of the pantomime horse. Every impulse in Larkin was met and matched by its opposite, and the collage reveals the fundamental collision in Larkin which determined the nature of his work. In his poetry we find expressed a lifelong argument between the artist and the philistine, between aspiring aestheticism (here represented by Blake) and the iconoclastic mockery of the cartoon. Larkin's work is very far removed from 'genteel bellyaching' and provincial unadventurousness. It emerges from the delicate negotiation of two powerful forces in Larkin: the passionate desire to live a life devoted to writing, and the iconoclastic fury of having that desire thwarted. The result is an art suspicious of its own claims, resisting its own rhetorical persuasiveness. (D. J. Enright early noted of Larkin that 'he doesn't altogether trust poetry, not even his own',[5] and another critic wrote a piece on Larkin entitled 'Against Imagination'.[6]) In Larkin we find exemplified the Yeatsian choice between perfection of the work or perfection of the life. His writing is driven by a sense of failure in both.

Anthony Thwaite assembled a *Collected Poems* in 1988, gathering fugitive published poems, printing some of the longer fragments from Larkin's manuscript notebooks and making a selection from the unpublished poems Larkin wrote before *The North Ship* and

*The Less Deceived*. It suddenly offered a rather different impression of Larkin from the one he had carefully cultivated. He was revealed as having written much more than had been assumed, with nearly eighty unfamiliar poems appearing in addition to the newly published juvenilia. Thwaite's chronological arrangement (with the earliest work appended), though it met with hostility from reviewers who thought Larkin's own ordering of poems should have been preserved, allowed otherwise buried patterns to surface. Newly visible were the relatively productive periods and phases of particular preoccupations. It also allowed readers to see at what point the familiar Larkin began to emerge. In his review of the *Collected Poems*, Blake Morrison noted of 'If, My Darling': 'It's the first poem in which Larkin shows signs of dramatising himself ... Once he could wear his defeat like an overcoat, not hide beneath it, Larkin was away.' Morrison summarised his general impression thus: 'what we have should be enough to ensure that Larkin will never again be patronised as a dried-up toad squatting on modernism, but be seen as an original, obsessive, deep-feeling poet who consistently refused the consolations of conventional belief.'[7]

But Morrison's judgement proved optimistic. The publication of Larkin's *Selected Letters* in 1992 met with widespread consternation.[8] The volume was accused of revealing an intemperate, foul-mouthed misogynist and racist bigot whose 'gouts of bile' (as Larkin himself admitted) passed for political opinion. Larkin's most hostile critics seized on these revelations as the values underpinning the whole of Larkin's work and reputation: the sewer, as Tom Paulin put it (fearing the worst of Thwaite's editorial cuts) underneath the national monument. Affronted in the letters by 'a steady stream of casual obscenity, throwaway derogatory remarks about women, and arrogant disdain for those of different skin colour or nationality', Professor Lisa Jardine reassured *Guardian* readers that, in the interests of pluralism, 'we don't tend to teach Larkin much now in my Department'.[9] Later, Bryan Appleyard offered a portrait of Larkin's 'repellent, smelly, inadequate masculinity', parading him as 'a drab symptom of a peculiar contemporary national impulse to refuse all ambition'.[10] There was more general dismay at the unrelieved intensity of Larkin's misery, the inconsolable desolation conveyed in some of his letters. There was a feeling, too, that without a biographical context, the letters left Larkin perilously exposed (though it was odd of some reviewers to find this culpable whilst simultaneously pointing to the nakedness).

The very earliest criticism of Larkin's work had condemned its 'tenderly nursed sense of defeat'; now the life was to be conflated with the work, as if Larkin's writing, even in the letters, was a simple reflex of personality. In truth, the relationship between Larkin's life and work is highly problematic and teasingly oblique. Andrew Motion's biography, published shortly after the letters, revealed more of Larkin's deviousness, not only in his relationships with women, but in the strategies by which he presented himself to the world. There is now a danger of our taking the poems less seriously than the letters, though it is a danger Larkin courted. Ian Hamilton pointed out that the Larkin 'revealed' in the letters had been before us all the time in the poems, 'but these were usually so well judged, as dramas or confessions, that we could speak also of a Larkinesque "persona" – a self-projection that might in part be a disguise'. Because of the performative element in the poems, they hover between autobiographical confession and the contrivances of personae. 'We knew he was "fucked up" because he told us so, in poem after poem, but the Larkin we admired *was* "supposed to ... find it funny or not to care", or at any rate to have the gift of transmuting daily glooms into great haunting statements about love and death – ours as well as his.'[11] Hamilton returns us to the problem of Larkin's 'masks' and ventriloquisms, and the rhetorical strategies which make his poems simultaneously self-revealing and self-protective.

'Posterity' is a poem which positively invites this kind of scrutiny, written as it is on the boundary between the public and the private. Here, Larkin can pretend to construct his own epitaph. Its ostensible joke is that the poem's speaker will be posthumously saddled with an uncomprehending American biographer, just as the American will have to tolerate this boring Englishman. Otherwise so different, they are the same in feeling thwarted and forced to settle for second-best. Within this irony, Larkin plays with self-revelation, just as the opening plays with self-referentialism ('Jake Balokowsky, my biographer, / Has this page microfilmed' [*CP*, 170]). Balokowsky is in the same tradition as the self-seeking academic in 'Naturally the Foundation will Bear Your Expenses' and seems paraded mockingly before us as the biographer who will fail to pluck the heart of the poet's mystery, getting only as far as the uncomprehending intemperateness of 'Oh, you know the thing ... One of those old-type *natural* fouled-up guys'.

But the question remains: how far do we imagine that the poet agrees with this conclusion about himself? Again, the ostensible joke is that he doesn't at all. The point of the poem seems to rest in the feeling that the American has got it all callously wrong. But this in turn makes the poem too sentimental, smug and vain, and the poem simply does not leave its speaker with that kind of triumph. For Balokowsky's uninhibited idiom dominates the poem, and in the characteristically cautious English irony is expressed admiring envy that 'he's no call to hide / Some slight impatience with his destiny'. At the end, the speaker does suffer a defeat. Not only are he and Balokowsky more alike than they seem, but Balokowsky's complacent cliché might well describe the poem's speaker perfectly. The poem cuts both ways. As a poem bent on non-disclosure, it wants to say that its speaker reckons to rise above the sweeping, simple-minded psychoanalysing of an unsympathetic biographer. But the non-disclosure is suddenly the poem's most revealing aspect: Balokowsky's diagnosis is grotesquely right.

The same sort of reversal is evident in another biographical sketch, 'Self's the Man'. It looks to be an attack on the idiocy of marriage by a relieved bachelor who suddenly confesses to uncertainty. But the real confession in the poem is its rebarbative smugness in arguing that 'self's the man' for everybody. Other poems disintegrate more calculatedly into self-subversive doubt: am I better than those I accuse? They do so by exploiting a multiplicity of tonal registers which undermine authorial stability. In a simple sense Larkin's poems, together and separately, are multivocal. Explicitly or implicitly, an 'I' addresses a 'you' and they thus take on the condition of speech-acts. They are 'performative' in being constructed with an explicit consciousness of the impression they are creating; their 'voices' express attitudes sometimes ecstatic (as in 'Solar' and 'Water'), often mocking, and frequently epigrammatic in pursuing a philosophical 'truth'. Even at their most declarative (as in their use of coarse language), the poems carry a highly self-conscious rhetorical persuasiveness.

The English philosopher J. L. Austin thought of all language as 'performative', that is, not so much involved in making statements as in making gestures of intention and producing calculated effects. Terry Eagleton paraphrases: 'Literature may appear to be describing the world, and sometimes actually does so, but its real function is performative: it uses language within certain conventions in order to bring about certain effects in a reader. It achieves something *in* the saying: it is language as a kind of material practice in itself, discourse as social action.'[12] Or, in Larkin's case, discourse as social interaction. The personae or 'masks' by which Larkin ventriloquises attitudes evolve from his command of idiom, often of caricature: the landlady's chatter in 'Mr Bleaney', the *'Then she undid her dress'* of popular fiction, the newly-wed's excited *'I nearly died'*, the academic's complacent hypocrisies in 'Naturally the Foundation will Bear Your Expenses', Balokowsky's Americanisms and finally the whole argot of advertising imagery. Populated by social types and embodiments of stereotypical attitudes, Larkin's poems foreground the metonymic aspect of language, the capacity to suggest the whole by the representative part. They are the dramatised speech-acts of a speaker who, seeming to participate in, actually manipulates, the drama of his poems. George Watson has defined in terms applicable to Larkin what he calls the 'eccentric stance' in poetry:

> It arises out of a highly insular tradition of conversation: amusingly semi-learned talk, richly allusive, vivified by a speaker into social performance – the British, as foreigners often remark, tending to be actors, or at least mimics – and by a speaker conscious of himself as a character and eager to impart that consciousness to others, whether as entertainment, self-defensive deceit, or both ...[13]

Larkin once ended an interview by saying of his poems, 'Don't judge me by them. Some are better than me, but I add up to more than they do.'[14]

Fundamentally, the construction of 'selves' is a function of the way language operates in Larkin's poetry and his work represents a striking instance of Mikhail Bakhtin's descriptions of dialogic discourse. Bakhtin wanted to evolve a poetics of the novel which would account for its historical rise to pre-eminence as a genre, but the terms he used offer a helpful approach to Larkin, particularly when we remember that Larkin began to write the poems by which he came to be known at just the point he was abandoning his novels.

David Lodge has explained that for Bakhtin literary discourse is performative, that a word is not so much a two-sided sign as, in Bakhtin's words, a 'two-sided *act* ... It is determined equally by whose word it is and for whom it is meant ... A word is territory *shared* by both addresser and addressee, by the speaker and his interlocutor'.[15] For Bakhtin, this multivocal polyphony is the medium of the novel:

Herein lies the profound distinction between prose style and poetic style ... for the prose artist the world is full of other people's words, among which he must orient himself and whose speech characteristics he must be able to perceive with a very keen ear. He must introduce them into the plane of his own discourse, but in such a way that this plane is not destroyed. He works with a very rich verbal palette.[16]

The peculiar triumph of Larkin's lyricism is precisely to incorporate 'other people's words' in just the way described by Bakhtin. Moreover, the use of direct speech in the poems works in the way described by Lodge:

Characters, and the persona of the authorial narrator ... are constituted not simply by their own linguistic registers or idiolects, but by the discourses they quote and allude to.

A corollary of Bakhtin's insight is that language which in itself is flat, banal, clichéd and generally automatised can become vividly expressive when mimicked, heightened, stylised, parodied and played off against other kinds of language in the polyphonic discourse of the novel.[17]

'*My wife and I have asked a crowd of craps / To come and waste their time and ours: perhaps / You'd care to join us? / In a pig's arse, friend*' (*CP*, 181). This is polyphonic enough, the framing automatised formality of the social invitation synchronised with its opposite idiom, the recipient's far from automatised feelings (attributed by him to the host or actually belonging to the host?) and merging in the anti-social mutuality of 'friend' (addressed to Warlock-Williams, or to the reader, or to both?). Lodge shows how Bakhtin came to doubt that any literary text could be purely monologic, and to conclude that all literary discourse is to some extent inherently dialogic. He quotes this passage from Bakhtin:

Doesn't the author always find himself *outside* of language in its capacity as the material of the literary work? Isn't every writer (even the purest lyric poet) always a 'playwright' insofar as he distributes all the discourses among alien voices, including that of the 'image of the author' (as well as the author's other *personae*)? It may be that every single-voiced and nonobjectal discourse is naïve and inappropriate to authentic creation. The authentically creative voice can only be a *second* voice in the discourse. Only the second voice – *pure relation*, can remain nonobjectal to the end and cast no substantial and phenomenal shadow. The writer is a person who knows how to

> work language while remaining outside of it; he has the gift of indi-
> rect speech.[18]

The development of Larkin's poetry can be seen as the progress towards manipulating language 'while remaining outside of it', when the embarrassed aestheticism of the early lyrics gives way to the dramatisation of unaesthetic experience; when the novelist's ear for other people's words is used to construct idiolects not in plots, but in the suddenly intense moments of poems.

Bakhtin's remarks are useful because they distinguish between the writer and what he writes by reminding us of the materiality of the writer's medium. Moreover, they offer an approach to Larkin's poems which begins to get us away from the familiar Larkin criticism which describes his 'themes' (the more 'unchanging' – love, time, death, etc. – the better) or analyses his poetic style in terms of its faithfully mimetic representation of an unmediated 'reality'. Instead, Bakhtin's remarks ask us to focus on Larkin's rhetoric, on the ways in which his poems construct themselves as speech-acts in order to persuade the reader into one point of view or another. The fundamental 'theme' of identity arises naturally from Larkin's situation as a writer 'outside' his language. His poems are not 'confessional', because they know the fictiveness of 'self-revelation'. But they represent the effort to achieve self-definition. Balokowsky is right: the speaker's fouled-upness is *natural*. Larkin's poetry is constantly striving for what is always 'out of reach': the ultimate expression of an absolute selfhood.

'Posterity' is an Englishman's view of an American's view of an Englishman. It collides attitudes by dealing in stereotypes: the American's jeans and sneakers; the Coke machine; the Englishman's periphrastic irony ('Some slight impatience with his destiny') compared with the American's frank colloquialisms ('I'm stuck with this old fart' – but not as stuck as the old fart himself is). At the centre of Larkin's poetry is the pursuit of self-definition, a self which feels threatened by the proximity of others but which fears that without relationship with otherness the self has no validity. Though the argument often takes the form of solitariness and selfishness set against sociability and selflessness, it is not really an argument about the profit and pains of loneliness. Fundamentally, Larkin's is an existential argument about the nature of individual identity, about the existential authority of choice and chance, about the articulation of an absolute self. Larkin approached these issues through the vocabulary of separateness, of exclusion and difference, establishing a kind of negative self-definition. His sense of identity is often expressed in the vocabulary of nullity and anonymity, suggesting both the ultimate desire for oblivion and an absolute terror of death. In the face of these teasing negatives and the vocabulary of denial, critics have been happier to construct a national identity for Larkin, perceiving in him a defining voice of Englishness.

In 'Englands of the Mind', Seamus Heaney adduced Larkin as representing a national attitude. 'The loss of imperial power, the failure of economic nerve, the diminished influence of Britain inside Europe, all this has led to a new sense of the shires, a new valuing of the native English experience.'[19] The particular 'England' represented in Larkin is identified in the ancestry of Larkin's language:

> What we hear is a stripped standard English voice, a voice indeed with a unique break and remorseful tone, but a voice that leads back neither to the thumping beat of Anglo-Saxon nor the Gregorian chant of the Middle Ages. Its ancestry begins, in fact, when the Middle Ages are turning secular, and plays begin to take their place beside the Mass as a form of communal telling and knowing.[20]

Heaney goes on to identify Larkin's social representativeness and tolerance more generously than some other recent critics. 'He is a poet, indeed, of composed and tempered English nationalism, and his voice is the not untrue, not unkind voice of post-war England ...'[21]

But the nationalism Heaney has in mind is the 'defensive love of their territory which was once shared only by those poets whom we might call colonial',[22] for Larkin committed himself to a provincial identity which is the paradigm of the insider/outsider figure so common in his poetry. Robert Crawford has located features of modernism in Larkin, especially in his use of demotic language: 'so often Larkin achieves his lyricism by an aggressively anti-literary opening that deploys the demotic which Modernism had brought into high art'.[23] Furthermore, 'Larkin, like so many of the Modernist writers, is a "provincial", rather than simply a poet of the English cultural centre.'[24] Living on the margins was not only a geographical fact for Larkin, but an imaginative site as well, where 'here' met 'elsewhere' and beyond the margin lay endlessness. Tomlinson's old charge of 'parochialism' actually begins to identify one of Larkin's most aspiring situations: at the limit, exposed to the beyond.

One of the most intelligent analyses of Larkin's national identity has come from Neil Corcoran, who finds in Larkin's poems about social ritual and national culture not only the obviously displaced feelings of religious devotion but a much more problematic assent than at first appears. 'The Importance of Elsewhere' explores the loss of a self-validating sense of difference on the poet's return from Belfast to England. Corcoran goes on to suggest that the imperialistic militarism of the band in 'The March Past' which brings 'a blind/ Astonishing remorse for things now ended' (*CP*, 55) belongs to 'a conception of an Englishness as the repository of value and identity for this poet who could find precious little of either anywhere else'. Corcoran translates this, and the unironic treatment of 'The differently-dressed servants' in 'MCMXIV', into a kind of willed nostalgia: 'the compulsions of nostalgia betray Larkin himself into an odd kind of historical "innocence"'.[25] On the other hand, Corcoran (and Tom Paulin too) might note that 'The March Past' is written as a swirl of confused and intense visions – the 'blind' remorse is also blinded – of which the poem can make little sense, and which are just as likely to relate to Larkin's having parted from his former fiancée as anything else. Corcoran is in danger of forcing an assumptive reading on to a poem which takes care to deal in an indefinite experience.

Corcoran argues that nostalgia overwhelms historical accuracy in such poems as 'To the Sea', 'Show Saturday' and 'The Explosion'. He emphasises the disjunction between the speaker and the community in the first two poems, and notes their creation of a pastoral 'no-time'. Of 'The Explosion', he asks: 'Did miners ever engage in this kind of activity on the way *to* work?' Thus, these poems represent 'fantasies of an impossibly idealised community',[26] idealised because the speaker separates himself from them. That separation is not necessarily a fictionalising, artificial de-historicising of England, but part of a wider argument about separateness and communality, about the individual self as a perpetual outsider. Of Larkin's nationalism, Corcoran could not have known what Andrew Motion's biography parenthetically revealed. One of the best known photographs of Larkin shows him sitting demurely on the large sign which says 'England' at Coldstream on the English/Scottish border. But, 'immediately before posing he had urinated copiously just behind the word'.[27]

As language becomes more multivocal in Larkin's poems, so they become more rhetorically devious in portraying versions of himself. Anxiously preoccupied with marriage and death, with solitude and communality, the poems pursue the nature of identity by nurturing a precious reticence. 'Something to do with violence / A long way back, and wrong rewards, / And arrogant eternity' ('Love Again' [*CP*, 215]): disclosure gratefully evaporates in the frustrated vagueness of 'Something to do with'. Tom Paulin has perceived in Larkin's reticence a quintessentially English strategy and emotional woundedness.

> Larkin speaks not for the imperial male – too transcendental a subject that – but for the English male, middle-class, professional, outwardly confident, controlled and in control. The history of that distinctive personality has yet to be written, but anyone who has observed it as a phenomenon, as a distinctive pattern of behaviour and attitude, is bound to see Larkin as a secret witness to what it feels like to be imprisoned in a personality that 'something hidden from us chose'. Thus Larkin's favourite romantic value, 'solitude', designates the consciousness of the autonomous English male professional. It refers not to physical isolation, but to a consciousness which has been moulded by upbringing and education to manage and govern. Such personalities ... are seldom attractive, but what is so lovable about Larkin's persona is the evident discomfort he feels with the shape of the personality he has been given. Angry at not being allowed to show emotion, he writhes with anxiety inside that sealed bunker which is the English ethic of privacy. He journeys into the interior, into the unknown heart – the maybe missing centre – of Englishness.[28]

For Paulin, part of Larkin's Englishness is an imperialist nostalgia. Larkin's lyricism persuades us 'to miss Larkin's real theme – national decline'. From this perspective, 'The March Past' is an English Protestant royalist's fiercely pro-imperial lament, and 'At Grass' tells of the threat felt by an imagination nostalgically Edwardian in the face of modern social democracy. The argument against marriage thus becomes a plea for an autonomy equivalent to national sovereignty. By thus identifying Larkin with a set of English nationalistic nostalgias, Paulin can use one stick to beat the other: Larkin represents a damaging sort of English culture, and a particular element of the English Establishment has taken Larkin to its heart as one of its own.

Paulin's interpretation rests on a determinedly ideological view of language and on a questionable allegorising: 'The autumn leaves fall in ones and twos, rather like colonies dropping out of the empire.' 'Rather like' begs a good deal of indulgence. For Paulin, the lyric voice 'promises an exit from history into personal emotion', but his argument turns on there being no escape from 'social experience'.[29] So for Paulin, Larkin's imagined sites of solitude, the 'padlocked cube of light', the isolated fortress of the lighthouse, the high windows of the bachelor flat and library office, are versions of Yeats's mystic symbol of the platonic poet in his ancient tower. But English reticence cannot reveal that kind of romanticism, and so Larkin conceals his innermost sense of himself behind masks of pretended disclosure and self-disgust. The poems protect an ultimate privacy, 'his commitment to what Coleridge in his poem to Wordsworth terms" the dread watch-tower of man's absolute self"'.[30] So Paulin concludes that 'In that distinctively embarrassed English manner he had to bury his pride in his artistic creations under several sackfuls of ugly prejudices.'

Paulin's powerful argument reminds us of the struggle between the aesthete and the philistine in Larkin, the aesthete secretly committed to a solitary Yeatsian vocation, the philistine having to be reticently sociable, speaking for 'that gnarled and angry puritanism which is so deeply ingrained in the culture'.[31] Paulin wants to use Larkin to attack a certain kind of Englishness and, in turn, a certain kind of Englishness to attack Larkin, so that he sees behind the poems 'the very cunning and very wounded personality of a poet whose sometimes rancid prejudices are part of his condition, part of the wound'.[32] The 'padlocked cube of light' is the Englishman's fastness, the ultimate privacy to which he can retreat in solitude. Paulin thus says that for Larkin, solitude has a 'romantic value'. But the poem from which this image comes, 'Dry-Point', in truth offers no such romanticism. The cube of light is not only padlocked, but allows 'no right of entry'. It is inviolable, because existentially beyond us. It does not protect the costive Englishman from 'the other'; it *is* the other. It is that condition of desirelessness, of emptiness, of anonymity, of sentient oblivion which in Larkin's work is felt as an existential absolute. It is Paulin who romanticises Larkin's yearnings into the reflexes of a national identity. For Larkin, the attempt to define himself, whether by relating the 'self' to marriage, or other people, or death, was a more purely existential problem. It meant asking what about the self was unique or universal, contingent or absolute, isolated or connected.

The ending of Larkin's 'Love Again', which characteristically reveals by withdrawing, carries something else hidden too. The manuscript draft ended:

Something to do with difference
A long way back ...

with 'difference' amended to 'violence'.[33] 'Violence' is more mysterious and apparently disclosing; but the erased 'difference' tells a
truer story. Larkin's poetry is the pursuit of difference, the thing
just out of reach, the being different from yourself. In demarcating
difference, in remaining the privileged outsider, Larkin was tracing,
in Richard Rorty's words, 'what made his I different from all the
other I's'.[34] His outsiderness was an outsiderness to language as
well, manipulating it as a dialogic negotiation with otherness: personae, caricatures, the reader. Ultimately, his poems create a community of difference: uncles shouting smut, mothers loud and fat,
girls marked off unreally from the rest, grim head-scarved wives,
young mothers at swing and sandpit, the men you meet of an afternoon, Dockery and son, and, fundamentally, writer and reader.
They pay tribute to the universality of uniqueness, expressing a
tender regard for the other individual selves in relation to which his
own self is defined. When his poetry turns away from society, it is
to confront those abiding elemental presences which clarify loneliness as 'oneness'. Its yearning for 'nowhere', 'unfenced existence',
the annihilation of self in an infinity of vacancy, is the expression of
a desire to merge difference in an absolute unity. In an early poem
called 'Continuing to Live', Larkin wondered about the value of
defining his own identity:

> And what's the profit? Only that, in time,
> We half-identify the blind impress
> All our behavings bear, may trace it home.
>    But to confess,
>
> On that green evening when our death begins,
> Just what it was, is hardly satisfying,
> Since it applied only to one man once,
>    And that one dying.
>                    (CP, 94)

Hence, the effort in Larkin's poems is to find continuities, the something rather than the nothing to be said. Finding continuities
becomes a way of defining the self not in terms of separateness, but
in its sensitiveness to otherness. Thus, Larkin's poems speak to us
and for us in their unique and representative individuality, in their

need to define 'the blind impress which chance has given him, to make a self for himself by redescribing that impress in terms which are, if only marginally, his own'.[35]

From Andrew Swarbrick, *Out of Reach: The Poetry of Philip Larkin* (Basingstoke, 1995), pp. 1–8, 154–8, 168–74.

## NOTES

[Andrew Swarbrick's *Out of Reach: The Poetry of Philip Larkin* was one of the first critical studies of Larkin's poetry to draw on previously unpublished manuscript material, as well as on new biographical information. Avoiding any simple correlation between the life and the work, it considers the poems as dramatised speech-acts and examines the rhetorical devices which enable the poems to construct a range of possible voices and 'selves'. This essay encapsulates one of the major insights of the book: it shows how Larkin's speakers strive for 'the ultimate expression of an absolute selfhood' while recognising that this is always 'out of reach'. In analysing the poems as speech-acts, the essay makes extensive use of discourse theory, especially Mikhail Bakhtin's proposition that all literary discourse is 'dialogic' or 'many-voiced'. Ed.]

1. Harry Chambers, 'Meeting Philip Larkin', in *Larkin at Sixty*, ed. Anthony Thwaite (London, 1982), p. 62.

2. Andrew Motion, *Philip Larkin: A Writer's Life* (London, 1993).

3. John Haffenden, *Viewpoints: Poets in Conversation* (London, 1981), p. 127.

4. Christopher Ricks, *Beckett's Dying Words* (Oxford, 1993).

5. D. J. Enright, 'Down Cemetery Road: the Poetry of Philip Larkin', in *Conspirators and Poets* (London, 1966), p. 142.

6. Hugo Roeffaers, 'Schriven tegen de Verbeelding', *Streven*, 47 (1979), 209–22.

7. Blake Morrison, 'In the grip of darkness', *Times Literary Supplement*, 14–20 October 1988, p. 1152.

8. *Selected Letters of Philip Larkin 1940–1985*, ed. Anthony Thwaite (London, 1992).

9. Lisa Jardine, 'Saxon Violence', *Guardian*, 8 December 1992, Section 2, p. 4.

10. Bryan Appleyard, 'The dreary laureate of our provincialism', *Independent*, 18 March 1993.

11. Ian Hamilton, 'Self's the man', *Times Literary Supplement*, 2 April 1993, p. 3.

12. Terry Eagleton, *Literary Theory: An Introduction* (Oxford, 1983), p. 118.

13. George Watson, *British Literature since 1945* (Basingstoke, 1991), p. 132.

14. Haffenden, *Viewpoints*, p. 129.

15. David Lodge, *After Bakhtin: Essays on Fiction and Criticism* (London, 1990), p. 90.

16. Ibid., p. 91.

17. Ibid., pp. 92–3.

18. Ibid., pp. 97–8.

19. Seamus Heaney, *Preoccupations: Selected Prose 1968–78* (London, 1980), p. 169.

20. Ibid., p. 165.

21. Ibid., p. 167.

22. Ibid., pp. 150–1.

23. Robert Crawford, *Devolving English Literature* (Oxford, 1992), p. 275.

24. Ibid., p. 276.

25. Neil Corcoran, *English Poetry Since 1940* (Harlow, 1993), p. 92.

26. Ibid., p. 94.

27. Motion, *Philip Larkin: A Writer's Life*, p. 372.

28. Tom Paulin, *Minotaur: Poetry and the Nation State* (London, 1992), pp. 239–40. [Reprinted in this volume – see pp. 160–77, Ed.]

29. Ibid., pp. 233–4.

30. Ibid., p. 248.

31. Ibid., p. 250.

32. Ibid., p. 251.

33. File DPL 11 in the Philip Larkin Archive lodged in the Brynmor Jones Library, University of Hull.

34. Richard Rorty, *Contingency, Irony and Solidarity* (Cambridge, 1989), p. 23.

35. Ibid., p. 43.

# 12

## Alas! Deceived

*ALAN BENNETT*

'My mother is such a bloody rambling fool', wrote Philip Larkin in 1965, 'that half the time I doubt her sanity. Two things she said today, for instance, were that she had "thought of getting a job in Woolworth's" and that she wanted to win the football pools so that she could "give cocktail parties".' Eva Larkin was seventy-nine at the time, so to see herself presiding over the Pick'n'Mix counter was a little unrealistic, and her chances of winning the football pools were remote as she didn't go in for them. Still, mothers do get ideas about cocktail parties, or mine did anyway, who'd never had a cocktail in her life and couldn't even pronounce the word, always laying the emphasis (maybe out of prudery) on the tail rather than the cock. I always assumed she got these longings from women's magazines or off the television, and maybe Mrs Larkin did too, though 'she never got used to the television' – which in view of her son's distrust of it is hardly surprising.

Mrs Larkin went into a home in 1971, a few months after her son had finished his most notorious poem, 'They fuck you up, your mum and dad'. She never read it (Larkin didn't want to 'confuse her with information about books'), but, bloody rambling fool or not, she shared more of her son's life and thoughts than do most mothers, or at any rate the version he gave her of them in his regular letters, still writing to her daily when she was in her eighties. By turns guilty and grumbling ('a perpetual burning bush of fury in my chest'), Larkin's attitude towards her doesn't seem particularly unusual, though his dutifulness does. Even so, Woolworth's would hardly have been her cup of tea. The other long-standing lady in

Larkin's life (and who stood for a good deal), Monica Jones, remarks that to the Larkins the least expenditure of effort was 'something heroic': 'Mrs Larkin's home was one in which if you'd cooked lunch you had to lie down afterwards to recover.' Monica, one feels, was more of a Woolworth's supervisor than a counter assistant. 'I suppose', wrote Larkin, 'I shall become free [of mother] at 60, three years before the cancer starts. What a bloody, sodding awful life.' His of course, not hers. Eva died in 1977 aged ninety-one, after which the poems more or less stopped coming. Andrew Motion thinks this is no coincidence.

Larkin pinpointed sixty-three as his probable departure date because that was when his father went, turned by his mother into 'the sort of closed, reserved man who would die of something internal'. Sydney Larkin was the City Treasurer of Coventry. He was also a veteran of several Nuremberg rallies, a pen-pal of Schacht's, and had a statue of Hitler on the mantelpiece that gave the Nazi salute. Sydney made no secret of his sympathies down at the office: 'I see that Mr Larkin's got one of them swastika things up on his wall now. Whatever next?' Next was a snip in the shape of some cardboard coffins that Sydney had cannily invested in and which came in handy when Coventry got blitzed, the Nazi insignia down from the wall by this time (a quiet word from the Town Clerk). But he didn't change his tune, still less swap the swastika for a snap of Churchill, who had, he thought, 'the face of a criminal in the dock'.

To describe a childhood with this grotesque figure at the centre of it as 'a forgotten boredom' seems ungrateful of Larkin, if not untypical, even though the phrase comes from a poem ('Coming') not an interview, so Larkin is telling the truth rather than the facts. Besides, it would have been difficult to accommodate Sydney in a standard Larkin poem, giving an account of his peculiar personality before rolling it up into a general statement in the way Larkin liked to do. Sylvia Plath had a stab at that kind of thing with her 'Daddy', though she had to pretend he was a Nazi, while Larkin's dad was the real thing. Still, to anyone (I mean me) whose childhood was more sparsely accoutred with characters, Larkin's insistence on its dullness is galling, if only on the 'I should be so lucky' principle.

As a script, the City Treasurer and his family feels already half-written by J. B. Priestley; were it a film, Sydney (played by Raymond Huntley) would be a domestic tyrant, making the life of his liberal and sensitive son a misery, thereby driving him to Art. Not a bit of it. For a start the son was never liberal ('true blue' all his life, Monica says), and had a soft spot for Hitler himself. Nor was the father a tyrant; he introduced his son to the works of Hardy and, more surprisingly, Joyce, did not regard jazz as the work of the devil, bought him a subscription to the magazine *Downbeat* (a signpost here), and also helped him invest in a drum-kit. What if anything he bought his daughter Kitty and what Mrs Larkin thought of it all is not recorded. Perhaps she was lying down. The women in the Larkin household always took second place, which, in Motion's view, is half the trouble. Kitty, Larkin's older sister ('the one person in the world I am confident I am superior to'), scarcely figures at all. Hers would, I imagine, be a dissenting voice, more brunt-bearing than her brother where Mrs Larkin was concerned and as undeceived about the poet as were most of the women in his life.

Whatever reservations Larkin had about his parents ('days spent in black, twitching, boiling HATE!'), by Oxford and adulthood they had modulated, says Motion, into 'controlled but bitter resentment'. This doesn't stop Larkin sending poems to his father ('I crave / The gift of your courage and indifference') and sharing his thoughts with his mother ('that obsessive snivelling pest') on all manner of things; in a word, treating them as people rather than parents. It's nothing if not 'civilised' but still slightly creepy, and it might have come as a surprise to Kingsley Amis, in view of their intimate oath-larded letters to one another, that Larkin, disappointed of a visit, should promptly have complained about him ('He is a wretched type') to his *mother*.

'Fearsome and hard-driving', Larkin senior is said never to have missed the chance of slipping an arm round a secretary, and though Larkin junior took a little longer about it (twenty-odd years in one case), it is just one of the ways he comes to resemble his father as he grows older, in the process getting to look less like Raymond Huntley and more like Francis L. Sullivan and 'the sort of person that democracy doesn't suit'.

Larkin's choice of profession is unsurprising, because from an early age libraries had been irresistible:

> I was an especially irritating kind of borrower, who brought back in the evening the books he had borrowed in the morning and read in the afternoon. This was the old Coventry Central Library, nestling at the foot of the unbombed cathedral, filled with tall antiquated bookcases (blindstamped Coventry Central Libraries after the fashion of the time) with my ex-schoolfellow Ginger Thompson ... This was my

first experience of the addictive excitement a large open-access public library generates.[1]

When he jumped over the counter, as it were, things were rather different, though father's footsteps come into this too: if you can't be a gauleiter, being a librarian's the next best thing. When called upon to explain his success as a librarian, Larkin said, 'A librarian can be one of a number of things ... a pure scholar, a technician ... an administrator or he ... can be just a nice chap to have around, which is the role I vaguely thought I filled' (*WL*, 113). Motion calls this a 'typically self-effacing judgement', but it's also a bit of a self-deluding one. It's a short step from the jackboot to the book-jacket, and by all accounts Larkin the librarian could be a pretty daunting figure. Neville Smith remembers him at Hull stood at the entrance to the Brynmor Jones, scanning the faces of the incoming hordes, the face heavy and expressionless, the glasses gleaming and the hands, after the manner of a soccer player awaiting a free-kick on the edge of the penalty area, clasped over what is rumoured to have been a substantial package. 'FUCK OFF, LARKIN, YOU CUNT' might have been the cheery signing-off in a letter from Kingsley Amis: it was actually written up on the wall of the library lifts, presumably by one of those 'devious, lazy and stupid' students who persisted in infesting the librarian's proper domain and reading the books.

It hadn't always been like that, though, and Larkin's first stint, at Wellington in Shropshire, where in 1943 he was put in charge of the municipal library, was a kind of idyll. Bitterly cold, gas-lit and with a boiler Larkin himself had to stoke, the library had an eccentric collection of books and a readership to match. Here he does seem to have been the type of librarian who was 'a nice chap to have around', one who quietly got on with improving the stock while beginning to study for his professional qualifications by correspondence course. Expecting 'not to give a zebra's turd' for the job, he had hit upon his vocation.

Posts at Leicester and Belfast followed, until in 1955 he was appointed Librarian at the University of Hull with the job of reorganising the library and transferring it to new premises. Moan as Larkin inevitably did about his job, it was one he enjoyed and which he did exceptionally well. The students may have been intimidated by him but he was popular with his staff, and particularly with the women. Mary Judd, the librarian at the issue desk at

Hull, thought that 'most women liked him more than most men because he could talk to a woman and make her feel unique and valuable'. In last year's *Selected Letters* there is a photo of him with the staff of the Brynmor Jones and, Larkin apart, there is not a man in sight. Surrounded by his beaming middle-aged assistants – with two at least he was having or would have an affair – he looks like a walrus with his herd of contented cows. There was contentment here for him, too, and one of his last poems, written when deeply depressed, is about a library.

> New eyes each year
> Find old books here,
> And new books, too,
> Old eyes renew;
> So youth and age
> Like ink and page
> In this house join,
> Minting new coin.
> (CP, 212)

Much of Motion's story is about sex: not getting it, not getting enough of it, or getting it wrong. For a time it seemed Larkin could go either way, and there are a few messy homosexual encounters at Oxford – though not *Brideshead* by a long chalk, lungings more than longings, and not the stuff of poetry except as the tail-end of 'these incidents last night'. After Oxford, Larkin's homosexual feelings 'evaporated' (Motion's word) and were henceforth seemingly confined to his choice of socks.

At Wellington he started walking out with Ruth Bowman, 'a 16-year-old schoolgirl and regular borrower from the library'. This period of Larkin's life is quite touching and reads like a fifties novel of provincial life, though not one written by him so much as by John Wain or Keith Waterhouse. Indeed Ruth sounds (or Larkin makes her sound) like Billy Liar's unsatisfactory girlfriend, whose snog-inhibiting Jaffa Billy hurls to the other end of the cemetery. Having laid out a grand total of 15s. 7d. on an evening with Ruth, Larkin writes to Amis:

> Don't you think it's ABSOLUTELY SHAMEFUL that men have to pay for women without BEING ALLOWED TO SHAG the women afterwards AS A MATTER OF COURSE? I do: simply DISGUST-ING. It makes me ANGRY. Everything about the ree-lay-shun-ship

> between men and women makes me angry. It's all a fucking balls-up.
> It might have been planned by the army or the Ministry of Food.
>
> (*WL*, 143)

To be fair, Larkin's foreplay could be on the funereal side. In the middle of one date with Ruth, Larkin (twenty-two) lapsed into silence. Was it something she'd said? 'No, I have just thought what it would be like to be old and have no one to look after you.' This was what Larkin would later refer to as 'his startling youth'. 'He could', says Ruth, 'be a draining companion.'

In the end one's sympathies, as always in Larkin's affairs, go to the woman, and one is glad when Ruth finally has him sized up and decides that he's no hubby-to-be. And he's glad too, of course. Ruth has Amis well sussed besides. 'He wanted', she says, 'to turn Larkin into a "love 'em and lose 'em type",' and for a moment we see these two leading lights of literature as what they once were: the Likely Lads – Larkin as Bob, Amis as Terry, and Ruth at this juncture the terrible Thelma.

Looking back on it now Ruth says, 'I was his first love and there's something special about a first love, isn't there?' Except that 'love' is never quite the right word with Larkin, 'getting involved' for once not a euphemism for the tortuous process it always turns out to be. 'My relations with women', he wrote, 'are governed by a shrinking sensitivity, a morbid sense of sin, a furtive lechery. Women don't just sit still and back you up. They want children; they like scenes; they want a chance of parading all the empty haberdashery they are stocked with. Above all they like feeling they own you – or that you own them – a thing I hate' (*WL*, 190). A. C. Benson, whose medal Larkin was later to receive from the Royal Society of Literature, put it more succinctly, quoting (I think) Aristophanes: 'Don't make your house in my mind.' Though with Larkin it was 'Don't make your house in my house either,' his constant fear being that he will be moved in on, first by his mother and then, when she's safely in a home, by some other scheming woman. When towards the finish Monica Jones does manage to move in it's because she's ill and can't look after herself, and so the cause of a great deal more grumbling. With hindsight (Larkin's favourite vantage point) it would have been wiser to have persisted with the messy homosexual fumblings, one of the advantages of boys being that they're more anxious to move on than in. Not, of course, that one has a choice, 'something hidden from us' seeing to that.

Larkin's earliest poems were published by R. A. Caton of the Fortune Press. Caton's list might have been entitled 'Poetic Justice', as besides the poetry it included such titles as *Chastisement Across the Ages* and an account of corporal punishment as meted out to women in South German prisons; since Larkin's tastes ran to both poetry and porn there is poetic justice in that too. He found that he shared his interest in dirty books with 'the sensitive and worldly-wise' Robert Conquest, and together they went on expeditions, trawling the specialist shops for their respective bag in a partnership that seems both carefree and innocent. Unusual, too, as I had always thought that porn, looking for it and looking at it, was something solo. Conquest would also send him juicy material through the post, and on one occasion conned the fearful Larkin into thinking the law was on his tracks and ruin imminent; he made him sweat for two or three days before letting him off the hook. That Larkin forgave him and bore no ill-will seems to me one of the few occasions outside his poetry when he comes close to real generosity of spirit.

Timorous though Larkin was, he was not shamefaced and made no secret of his predilections. Just as Elsie, secretary to his father, took her bottom-pinching Führer-friendly boss in her stride, so Betty, the secretary to the son, never turned a hair when she came across his lunch-time reading in the shape of the splayed buttocks of some gym-slipped tot, just covering it briskly with a copy of the *Library Association Record* and carrying on cataloguing. One of the many virtues of Motion's book is that it celebrates the understanding and tolerance of the average British secretary and the forbearance of women generally. As, for instance, the friend to whom Larkin showed a large cupboard in his office, full of both literary and photographic porn. 'What is it for?' she asked. 'To wank to, or with, or at' was Larkin's reply (*WL*, 222), which Motion calls embarrassed, though it doesn't sound so, the question, or at any rate the answer, presumably giving him a bit of a thrill. Like the other documents of his life and his half-life, the magazines were carefully kept, if not catalogued, in his desolate attic, though after twenty-odd years' perusal they must have been about as stimulating as *Beowulf*.

One unremarked oddity in the *Selected Letters* is a note from Larkin to Conquest in 1976 mentioning a visit to Cardiff, where he had 'found a newsagent with a good line in Yank homo porn, in quite a classy district too. Didn't dare touch it.'[2] I had assumed that in the matter of dirty magazines, be it nurses, nuns or louts in leather, you found whatever knocked on your particular box and stuck to it. So what did Larkin want with 'this nice line in homo porn'? Swaps? Or hadn't all that messy homosexuality really evaporated? Certainly pictured holidaying on Sark in 1955 he looks anything but butch. One here for Jake Balokowsky.

I am writing this before the book is published, but Larkin's taste for pornography is already being touted by the newspapers as something shocking. It isn't, but, deluded liberal that I am, I persist in thinking that those with a streak of sexual unorthodoxy ought to be more tolerant of their fellows than those who lead an entirely godly, righteous and sober life. Illogically I tend to assume that if you dream of caning schoolgirls' bottoms it disqualifies you from dismissing half the nation as work-shy. It doesn't, of course – more often it's the other way round – but when Larkin and Conquest rant about the country going to the dogs there's a touch of hypocrisy about it. As an undergraduate Larkin had written two facetious novels set in a girls' school, under the pseudonym of Brunette Coleman. It's tempting to think that his much advertised adoration of Mrs Thatcher ('What a superb creature she is, right and beautiful!') owes something to the sadistic headmistress of St Bride's, Miss Holden.

> As Pam finally pulled Marie's tunic down over her black-stockinged legs Miss Holden, pausing only to snatch a cane from the cupboard in the wall, gripped Marie by her hair and, with strength lent by anger, forced down her head till she was bent nearly double. Then she began thrashing her unmercifully, her face a mask of ferocity, caring little where the blows fell, as long as they found a mark some-where on Marie's squirming body. At last a cry was wrung from her bloodless lips and Marie collapsed on the floor, twisting in agony, her face hidden by a flood of amber hair.
>
> (*WL*, 91)

Whether Mr Heseltine is ever known as Marie is a detail; that apart it could be a verbatim extract from A History of Cabinet Government 1979–90.

Meeting Larkin at Downing Street in 1980, Mrs Thatcher gushed that she liked his wonderful poem about a girl. 'You know', she said, '"Her mind was full of knives."' The line is actually 'All the unhurried day / Your mind lay open like a drawer of knives,' (*CP*, 32) but Larkin liked to think that Madam knew the poem or she would not have been able to misquote it. Inadequate briefing seems a likelier explanation and, anyway, since the line is about an open mind it's not surprising the superb creature got it wrong.

Mrs Thatcher's great virtue, Larkin told a journalist, 'is saying that two and two makes four, which is as unpopular nowadays as it always has been' (WL, 479). What Larkin did not see was that it was only by banking on two and two making five that institutions like the Brynmor Jones Library could survive. He lived long enough to see much of his work at the library dismantled; one of the meetings he was putting off before his death was with the Vice-Chancellor designate, who was seeking ways of saving a quarter of a million pounds and wanted to shrink the library by hiving off some of its rooms. That was two and two making four.

Andrew Motion makes most of these points himself, but without rancour or the impatience this reader certainly felt. Honest but not prurient, critical but also compassionate, Motion's book could not be bettered. It is above all patient, and with no trace of the condescension or irritation that are the hazards of biography. He is a sure guide when he relates the poetry to the life, even though the mystery of where the poetry came from, and why, and when, sometimes defeats him. But then it defeated Larkin, or his writing would not have petered out when it did. For all that, it's a sad read, and Motion's patience with his subject is often hard to match. Larkin being Larkin, though, there are lots of laughs and jokes never far away. Before he became a celebrity (and, wriggle though he did, that was what he became) and one heard gossip about Larkin it was generally his jokes and his crabbiness that were quoted. 'More creaking from an old gate', was his dedication in Patrick Garland's volume of *High Windows*, and there were the PCs (which were not PC at all) he used to send to Charles Monteith, including one not quoted here or in the *Selected Letters*. Along with other Faber authors, Larkin had been circularised asking what events, if any, he was prepared to take part in to mark National Libraries Week. Larkin wrote back saying that the letter reminded him of the story of Sir George Sitwell being stopped by someone selling flags in aid of National Self-Denial Week: 'For some of us', said Sir George, 'every week is self-denial week.' 'I feel', wrote Larkin, 'exactly the same about National Libraries Week.' The letters are full of jokes. 'I fully expect,' he says of 'They fuck you up, your mum and dad', 'to hear it recited by 1000 Girl Guides before I die'; he gets 'a letter from a whole form of Welsh schoolgirls, seemingly inviting mass coition. Where were they when I wanted them?' (*WL*, 494). And in the cause of jokes he was prepared to dramatise himself, heighten his circumstances, darken his despair, claim to have been a bastard in situations where he had actually been all charm. What one wants to go on feeling was that, the poems apart, the jokes were the man, and the saddest thing about this book and the *Selected Letters* is to find that they weren't, that beyond the jokes was a sphere of gloom, fear and self-pity that nothing and no one touched. And, so far from feeling compassion for him on this score, as Motion always manages to do, I just felt impatient and somehow conned.

Trying to locate why takes one back to Auden:

> A writer, or at least a poet, is always being asked by people who should know better: 'Whom do you write for?' The question is, of course, a silly one, but I can give it a silly answer. Occasionally I come across a book which I feel has been written especially for me and for me only. Like a jealous lover I don't want anybody else to hear of it. To have a million such readers, unaware of each other's existence, to be read with passion and never talked about, is the day-dream, surely, of every author.[3]

Larkin was like that, certainly after the publication of *The Less Deceived* and even for a few years after *The Whitsun Weddings* came out. Because his poems spoke in an ordinary voice and boasted his quiescence and self-deprecation, one felt that here was someone to like, to take to, and whose voice echoed one's inner thoughts, and that he was, as he is here engagingly indexed (under his initials), a PAL. So that in those days, certainly until the mid-seventies, Larkin seemed always a shared secret. The great and un-expected outpouring of regret when he died showed this sentiment to have been widespread and that through the public intimacy of his poetry he had acquired a constituency as Betjeman, partly through being less introspective and more available, never entirely did. And while we did not quite learn his language or make him our pattern to live and to die, what one is left with now is a sense of be-trayal which is quite difficult to locate and no less palpable for the fact that he never sought to mislead the public about his character, particularly as he got older.

They were deceived, though. When Anthony Thwaite published the *Selected Letters* last year, the balance of critical opinion was dis-posed to overlook – or at any rate excuse – his racist and reactionary sentiments as partly a joke, racism more pardonable these days in the backlash against political correctness. Besides, it was plain that in his letters Larkin exaggerated; he wasn't really like that. Motion's book closes down this escape route. 'You'll be pleased to see the black folk go from the house over the way,' he says in a 1970 letter, and were it written to Amis or Conquest it might get by as irony, wit even, a voice put on. But he is writing to his mother, for whom he did not put on a voice – or not that voice anyway. Did it come with the flimsiest of apologies it would help ('I'm sorry,' as I once heard someone say, 'but I have a blind spot with black people'). How were the blacks across the way different from 'those antique negroes' who blew their 'flock of notes' out of 'Chicago air into / A huge remembering pre-electric horn / The year after I was born'? (*CP*, 106) Well, they were in Loughborough for a start, not Chicago. Wanting so much for him to be other, one is forced against every inclination to conclude that, in trading bigotries with an eighty-year-old, Larkin was sincere; he was being really himself:

> I want to see them starving
> The so-called working class
> Their weekly wages halving
> Their women stewing grass.
>     (*Letters*, 451)

The man who penned that might have been pleased to come up with the slogan of the 1968 Smethwick by-election: 'If you want a nigger neighbour, Vote Labour.' Larkin refused the Laureateship because he couldn't turn out poetry to order. But if he could churn out this stuff for his letters and postcards he could have turned an honest penny on the *Sun* any day of the week.

Then there is Larkin the Hermit of Hull. Schweitzer in the Congo did not derive more moral credit than Larkin did for living in Hull. No matter that of the four places he spent most of his life – Hull, Coventry, Leicester and Belfast – Hull is probably the most pleasant; or that poets are not and never have been creatures of the capital: to the newspapers, as Motion says, remoteness is synonymous with integrity. But Hull isn't even particularly remote. Ted Hughes, living in Devon, is further from London (as the crow flies, of course) than Larkin ever was, but that he gets no credit for it is partly the place's fault, Devon to the metropolitan crowd having nothing on the horrors of Hull. Hughes, incidentally, gets much the same treatment here as he did in the *Selected Letters*, more pissed

on than the back wall of the Batley Working Men's club before a
Dusty Springfield concert.

Peter Cook once did a sketch in which, dressed as Garbo, he was
filmed touring the streets in an open-topped limousine shouting
through a megaphone 'I want to be alone'. Larkin wasn't quite as
obvious as that, but poetry is a public-address system too and that
his remoteness was so well publicised came about less from his
interviews or personal pronouncements than from the popularity of
poems like 'Here' and 'The Whitsun Weddings' which located
Larkin, put him on (and off) the map, and advertised his distance
from the centre of things.

That Hull was the back of beyond in the fifties wasn't simply a
London opinion: it prevailed in Hull itself. In 1959 I tentatively
applied there for a lectureship in medieval history, and the professor kicked off the interview by emphasising that train services were
now so good that Hull was scarcely four hours from King's Cross.
It wasn't that he'd sensed in me someone who'd feel cut off from
the vivifying currents of capital chic, rather that my field of study
was the medieval exchequer, the records of which were then at
Chancery Lane. Still, there was a definite sense that a slow and
stopping train southwards was some kind of lifeline and that come
a free moment, there one was going to be aimed. Even Larkin
himself was aimed there from time to time, and though his social
life was hardly a hectic round, he put himself about more than he
liked to think.

Until I read Motion's book I had imagined that Larkin was
someone who had largely opted out of the rituals of literary and
academic life, that he didn't subscribe to them and wasn't taken in
by them. Not a bit of it. There are umpteen formal functions, the
poet dutifully getting on the train to London for the annual dinner
of the Royal Academy, which involves a visit to Moss Bros ('and
untold expense'); there's at least one party at Buckingham Palace, a
Foyle's Literary Luncheon at which he has to give a speech, there
are dinners at his old college and at All Souls, and while he does not
quite go to a dinner up a yak's arse he does trundle along to the
annual festivities of the Hull Magic Circle. Well, the chairman of
the library committee was an enthusiastic conjuror, Larkin lamely
explains. When Motion says that Larkin had reluctantly to accept
that his emergence as a public man would involve more public

duties it's the 'reluctantly' one quibbles with. Of course there's no harm in any of these occasions if you're going to enjoy yourself. But Larkin seemingly never does, or never admits that he does. But if he didn't, why did he go? Because they are not difficult to duck. Amis has recorded how much pleasanter life became when he realised he could refuse invitations simply by saying 'don't do dinners' – a revelation comparable to Larkin's at Oxford when it dawned on him he could walk out of a play at the interval and not come back. But Larkin did do dinners, and not just dinners. He did the Booker Prize, he did the Royal Society of Literature, he did the Shakespeare Prize; he even did a dinner for the Coventry Award of Merit. Hermit of Hull or not, he dutifully turns up to collect whatever is offered to him, including a sackful of honours and seven honorary degrees. He was going to call a halt at six only Oxford then came through with 'the big one', the letter getting him seriously over-excited. 'He actually ran upstairs,' says Monica. And this is a recluse. Fame-seeking, reputation hugging, he's about as big a recluse as the late Bubbles Rothermere.

Motion says that institutional rewards for his work annoyed him, but there's not much evidence of it. Still, to parade in a silly hat, then stand on a platform to hear your virtues recited followed by at least one formal dinner is no fun at all, as Larkin is at pains to point out, particularly when you've got sweaty palms and are frightened you're going to pass out. His account of the Oxford ceremony makes it fun, of course. His new suit looks like 'a walrus maternity garment', and the Public Orator's speech was 'a bit like a review in *Poetry Tyneside*', so he gets by, as ever, on jokes. But if to be celebrated is such a burden why does he bother with it while still managing to suggest that his life is a kind of Grand Refusal? Because he's a public figure is Motion's kindly explanation. Because he's a man is nearer the point.

A crucial text here is 'The Life with a Hole in it' (1974):

> When I throw back my head and howl
> People (women mostly) say
> *But you've always done what you want,*
> *You always get your own way*
> – A perfectly vile and foul
> Inversion of all that's been.
> What the old ratbags mean
> Is I've never done what I don't.
>
> (*CP*, 202)

It's a set-up, though, that repeats itself so regularly in Larkin's life – Larkin wanting his cake but not wanting it to be thought he enjoys eating it – that it's hard to go on sympathising as Monica and Maeve (and indeed Motion) are expected to do, as well as any woman who would listen. Not the men, of course. Larkin knows that kind of stuff just bores the chaps, so they are fed the jokes, the good ladies his dizziness and sweaty palms, thus endearing him to them because it counts as 'opening up'.

About the only thing Larkin consistently didn't do were poetry readings ('I don't like going about pretending to be myself') and television. On the 1982 *South Bank Show* he allowed his voice to be recorded but refused to appear in person, and it's to Patrick Garland's credit that he managed to persuade the then virtually unknown Larkin to take part in a 1965 *Monitor* film, which happily survives. He was interviewed, or at any rate was talked at, by Betjeman, and typically, of course, it's Larkin who comes out of it as the better performer. Like other figures on the right – Paul Johnson, Michael Wharton and the *Spectator* crowd – Larkin regarded television as the work of the devil, or at any rate the Labour Party, and was as reluctant to be pictured as any primitive tribesman. Silly, I suppose I think this is, and also self-regarding. Hughes has done as little TV as Larkin and not made such a song and dance about it. There is always the danger for a writer of becoming a pundit, or turning into a character, putting on a performance of oneself as Betjeman did. But there was little danger of that with Larkin. He claimed he was nervous of TV because he didn't want to be recognised, but one appearance on the *South Bank Show* doesn't start a stampede in Safeways, as other authors could regretfully have told him.

If sticking in Hull seemed a deprivation but wasn't quite, so were the circumstances in which Larkin chose to live, a top-floor flat in Pearson Park rented from the university and then an 'utterly undistinguished modern house' he bought in 1974, 'not quite the bungalow on the by-pass' but 'not the kind of dwelling that is eloquent of the nobility of the human spirit' (*WL*, 440). It's tempting to think Larkin sought out these uninspiring places because for him they weren't uninspiring but settings appropriate to the kind of poems he wrote. But he seems never to have taken much pleasure in the look of things – furniture, pictures and so on. His quarters weren't particularly spartan or even Wittgenstein-minimalist (deck-chairs and porridge), just dull. The implication of living like this is that a choice has been made, another of life's pleasures foregone in the cause of Art, part of Larkin's strategy for a stripped-down sort of life, a traveller without luggage.

'I do believe', he wrote to Maeve Brennan, 'that the happiest way to get through life is to want things and get them; now I don't believe I've ever wanted anything in the sense of a ... Jaguar Mark IX ... I mean, although there's always plenty of things I couldn't do with, there's never been anything I couldn't do without and in consequence I "have" very little' (WL, 314–15). But the truth is, surely, he wasn't all that interested, and if he kept his flat like a dentist's waiting-room it was because he preferred it that way. He wanted his jazz records, after all, and he 'had' those. In one's own choosier circumstances it may be that reading of a life like this one feels by implication criticised and got at. And there is with Larkin an air of virtue about it, a sense that a sacrifice has been made. After all, Auden's idea of the cosy was other people's idea of the squalid but he never implied that living in a shit-heap was a precondition of his writing poetry; it just happened to be the way he liked it.

Still, Larkin never wanted to be one of those people with 'specially-chosen junk, / The good books, the good bed, / And my life, in perfect order' (CP, 85) or indeed to live, as he said practically everyone he knew did, in something called The Old Mill or The Old Forge or The Old Rectory. All of them, I imagine, with prams in the hall. Cyril Connolly's strictures on this point may have been one of the reasons Larkin claimed The Condemned Playground as his sacred book and which led him, meeting Connolly, uncharacteristically to blurt out, 'You formed me'. But if his definition of possessions seems a narrow one (hard to see how he could feel encumbered by a house, say, but not by half a dozen honorary degrees), his version of his life, which is to some extent Motion's also, was that if he had lived a more cluttered life then Art, 'that lifted rough tongued bell', would cease to chime. When it did cease to chime, rather earlier than he'd thought, ten years or so before he died, he went on living as he'd always lived, saying it was all he knew.

Striding down the library in the Monitor film Larkin thought he looked like a rapist. Garland reassured him, but walking by the canal in the same film there is no reassurance; he definitely does. Clad in his doleful raincoat with pebble glasses, cycle-clips and oceanic feet, he bears more than a passing resemblance to Reginald Halliday Christie. Haunting his cemeteries and churchyards he could be on the verge of exposing himself, and whether it's to a grim, head-scarved wife from Hessle or in a slim volume from Faber and Faber seems a bit of a toss-up. Had his diary survived, that 'sexual log-book', one might have learned whether this shy, tormented man ever came close to the dock, the poetry even a safety valve. As it was, lovers on the grass in Pearson Park would catch among the threshing chestnut trees the dull glint of binoculars, and on campus errant borrowers, interviewed by the Librarian, found themselves eyed up as well as dressed down.

> Day by day your estimation clocks up
> Who deserves a smile and who a frown,
> And girls you have to tell to pull their socks up
> Are those whose pants you'd most like to pull down.
>
> (*CP*, 161)

Motion's hardest task undoubtedly has been to cover, to understand and somehow enlist sympathy for Larkin and his women. Chief among them were his mother, whose joyless marriage put him off the institution long before poetry provided him with the excuse; Monica Jones, lecturer in English at Leicester, whom he first met in 1946 and who was living with him when he died; Maeve Brennan, an assistant librarian at Hull with whom he had a seventeen-year fling which overlapped with another, begun in 1975, with his long-time secretary at the library, Betty Mackereth. All of them (mother excepted) he clubbed with sex, though Maeve was for a long time reluctant to join the clubbed and Betty escaped his notice until, after seventeen years as his secretary, there was presumably one of those 'When-you-take-off-your-glasses-you're-actually-quite-pretty' moments. Though the library was the setting for so much of this heavy breathing, propriety seems to have been maintained and there was no slipping down to the stack for a spot of beef jerky.

Of the three, Monica, one feels, could look after herself, and though Larkin gave her the runaround over many years she was never in any doubt about the score. 'He cared', she told Motion, 'a tenth as much about what happened around him as what was happening inside him.' Betty, too, had him taped and besides had several other strings to her bow, including some spot-welding which she'd picked up in Leeds. It's only Maeve Brennan, among his later ladies anyway, for whom one feels sorry. Maeve knew nothing of the darker side of his nature – the porn, for instance, coming as a posthumous revelation, as did his affair with Betty. If only for her sake one should be thankful the diaries did not survive. A simpler woman than the other two, she was Larkin's sweetheart, her love for him romantic and innocent, his for her companionable and protective. Dull you might even say,

> If that is what a skilled,
> Vigilant, flexible,
> Unemphasised, enthralled
> Catching of happiness is called.
> (CP, 84)

A fervent Catholic (trust his luck), Maeve took a long time before she would sleep with him, keeping the poet-librarian at arm's length. Her arms were actually quite hairy – this, Motion says, adding to her attraction. Quite what she will feel when reading this is hard to figure, and she's perhaps even now belting down to Hull's Tao Clinic. While Maeve held him off the romance flourished, but as soon as she does start to sleep with him on a regular basis her days are numbered. Larkin, having made sure of his options with Betty, drops Maeve, who is desolate, and though he sees her every day in the library and they evolve 'a distant but friendly relationship' no proper explanation is ever offered.

There is, though, a lot of other explanation on the way – far too much for this reader – with Monica being pacified about Maeve, Maeve reassured about Monica, and Mother given edited versions of them both. And so much of it in letters. When the *Selected Letters* came out there was general gratitude that Larkin was old-fashioned enough still to write letters, but there's not much to be thankful for in his correspondence with Maeve and Monica. 'One could say', wrote Kafka, 'that all the misfortunes in my life stem from letters ... I have hardly ever been deceived by people, but letters have deceived me without fail ... not other people's letters, but my own.' So it is with Larkin, who as a young man took the piss out of all the twaddle he now in middle age writes about ree-lay-shun-ships.

The pity is that these three women never got together to compare notes on their lover, preferably in one of those siderooms in the library Mrs T.'s cuts meant had to be hived off. But then women never do get together, except in French comedies. Besides, the conference would have had to include the now senile Eva Larkin, whose spectre Larkin detected in all the women he had anything to do with, or had sex to do with. Motion identifies Larkin's mother as his muse, which I suppose one must take on trust if only out of gratitude to Motion for ploughing through all their correspondence.

What makes one impatient with a lot of the stuff Larkin writes to Monica and Maeve is that it's plain that what he really wants is just to get his end away on a regular basis and without obligation. 'Sex is so difficult', he complained to Jean Hartley. 'You ought to be able to get it and pay for it monthly like a laundry bill.' The impression the public had from the poems was that Larkin had missed out on sex, and this was corroborated by occasional interviews ('Sexual recreation was a socially remote thing, like baccarat or clog-dancing' [WL, 267]). But though Motion calls him 'a sexually disappointed Eeyore', in fact he seems to have had a pretty average time, comparing lives with Amis ('staggering skirmishes / in train, tutorial and telephone booth') the cause of much of his dissatisfaction. He needed someone to plug him into the fleshpots of Hull, the 'sensitive and worldly-wise Conquest' the likeliest candidate, except that Larkin didn't want Conquest coming to Hull, partly because he was conscious of the homeliness of Maeve. On the other hand, there must have been plenty of ladies who would have been willing to oblige, even in Hull; ready to drop everything and pop up to Pearson Park, sucking off the great poet at least a change from gutting herrings.

I imagine women will be less shocked by the Larkin story, find it less different from the norm than will men, who don't care to see their stratagems mapped out as sedulously as Motion has done with Larkin's. To will his own discomfort then complain about it, as Larkin persistently does, makes infuriating reading, but women see it every day. And if I have a criticism of this book it is that Motion attributes to Larkin the poet faults I would have said were to do with Larkin the man. It's true Larkin wanted to keep women at a distance, fend off family life, because he felt that writing poetry depended on it. But most men regard their life as a poem that women threaten. They may not have two spondees to rub together but they still want to pen their saga untrammelled by life-threatening activities like trailing round Sainsbury's, emptying the dishwasher or going to the nativity play. Larkin complains to Judy Egerton about Christmas and having to buy six simple inexpensive presents when there are rather more people about than usual ... No doubt in yours it means seeing your house given over to hordes of mannerless middle-class brats and your good food and drink vanishing into the quacking tooth-equipped jaws of their alleged parents. Yours is the harder course, I can see. On the other hand, mine is happening to me.

(WL, 289–90)

'And' (though he doesn't say this) 'I'm the poet.' Motion comments: 'As in "Self's the Man", Larkin here angrily acknowledges his selfishness hoping that by admitting it he will be forgiven.' 'Not that old trick!' wives will say, though sometimes they have to be grateful just for that, and few ordinary husbands would get away with it. But Larkin wasn't a husband, and that he did get away with it was partly because of that and because he had this fall-back position as Great Poet. Monica, Maeve and even Betty took more from him, gave him more rope, because this was someone with a line to posterity.

In all this the writer he most resembles – though, 'falling over backwards to be thought philistine' (as was said at All Souls), he would hardly relish the comparison – is Kafka. Here is the same looming father and timid, unprotesting mother, a day job meticulously performed with the writing done at night, and the same dithering on the brink of marriage with art the likely casualty. Larkin's letters analysing these difficulties with girls are as wearisome to read as Kafka's and as inconclusive. Both played games with death – Larkin hiding, Kafka seeking – and when they were called in it got them both by the throat.

Like Kafka, it was only as a failure that Larkin could be a success. 'Striving to succeed he had failed; accepting failure he had begun to triumph.' Not that this dispersed the gloom then, or ever. Motion calls him a Parnassian Ron Glum, and A. L. Rowse (not usually a fount of common sense) remarks, 'What the hell was the matter with him? He hadn't much to complain about. He was *tall*!' (WL, 404).

The publication of the *Selected Letters* and now the biography is not, I fear, the end of it. This is early days for Larkin plc as there's a hoard of material still unpublished, the correspondence already printed just a drop in the bucket, and with no widow standing guard packs of postgraduates must already be converging on the grave. May I toss them a bone?

In 1962 Monica Jones bought a holiday cottage at Haydon Bridge, near Hexham in Northumberland. Two up, two down, it's in a bleakish spot with the Tyne at the back and the main Newcastle–Carlisle road at the front, and in Motion's account of his visit there to rescue Larkin's letters it sounds particularly desolate. However, Jones and Larkin spent many happy holidays at the cottage, and on their first visit in 1962 they

> lazed, drank, read, pottered round the village and amused themselves with private games. Soon after the move, for instance, they began systematically defacing a copy of Iris Murdoch's novel *The Flight from the Enchanter*, taking it in turns to interpolate salacious remarks and corrupt the text. Many apparently innocent sentences are merely underlined ('Today it seemed likely to be especially hard'). Many more are altered ('her lips were parted and he had never seen her eyes so wide open' becomes 'her legs were parted and he had never seen her cunt so wide open'). Many of the numbered chapter-headings are changed ('Ten' is assimilated into I Fuck my STENographer). Even the list of books by the same author is changed to include UNDER THE NETher Garments.
>
> (WL, 319)

Something to look forward to after a breezy day on Hadrian's Wall or striding across the sands at Lindisfarne, this 'childishly naughty game' was continued over many years.

As a librarian, Larkin must have derived a special pleasure from the defacement of the text, but he and Miss Jones were not the first. Two other lovers had been at the same game a year or so earlier, only, more daring than our two pranksters, they had borrowed the books they planned to deface from a public library and then, despite the scrutiny of the staff, had managed to smuggle them back on to the shelves. But in 1962 their luck ran out and Joe Orton and Kenneth Halliwell were prosecuted for defacing the property of Islington Borough Council. Was it this case, plentifully written up in the national press, that gave Philip and Monica their wicked idea? Or did he take his cue from the more detailed account of the case published the following year in the *Library Association Record*, that delightful periodical which was his constant study? It's another one for Jake Balokowsky.

At forty-five Larkin had felt himself 'periodically washed over by waves of sadness, remorse, fear and all the rest of it, like the automatic flushing of a urinal' (WL, 369). By sixty the slide towards extinction is unremitting, made helpless by the dead weight of his own self. His life becomes so dark that it takes on a quality of inevitability: when a hedgehog turns up in the garden you know, as you would know in a film, that the creature is doomed. Sure enough he runs over it with the lawnmower, and comes running into the house wailing. He had always predicated he would die at sixty-three, as his father did, and when he falls ill at sixty-two it is of the cancer he is most afraid of. He goes into the Nuffield to be operated on, the surgeon telling him he will be a new man 'when I was quite fond of the old one'. One of the nurses is called Thatcher, another Scargill ('They wear labels'). A privilege of private medicine is that patients have ready access to drink, and it was a bottle of whisky from an unknown friend that is thought to have led him to swallow his own vomit and go into a coma. In a crisis in a private hospital the patient is generally transferred to a National Health unit, in this case the Hull Royal Infirmary, for them to clear up the mess. 'As usual' I was piously preparing to write, but then I read how Louis MacNeice died. He caught a chill down a pothole in Yorkshire while producing a documentary for the BBC and was taken into University College Hospital. He was accustomed at this time to drinking a bottle of whisky a day but, being an NHS patient, was not allowed even a sip; whereupon the chill turned to pneumonia and he died, his case almost the exact converse of Larkin's. Larkin came out of the coma, went home but not to work, and returned to hospital a few months later, dying on 2 December 1985.

Fear of death had been the subject of his last major poem, 'Aubade', finished in 1977, and when he died it was much quoted and by implication his views endorsed, particularly perhaps the lines

> ... Courage is no good:
> It means not scaring others. Being brave
> Lets no one off the grave.
> Death is no different whined at than withstood.
>
> (CP, 209)

The poem was read by Harold Pinter at a memorial meeting at Riverside Studios in the following March, which I wrote up in my diary:

> *3 March 1986.* A commemorative programme for Larkin at Riverside Studios, arranged by Blake Morrison. Arrive late as there is heavy

rain and the traffic solid, nearly two hours to get from Camden Town to Hammersmith. I am to read with Pinter, who has the beginnings of a moustache he is growing in order to play Goldberg in a TV production of *The Birthday Party*. My lateness and the state of the traffic occasions some disjointed conversation between us very much in the manner of his plays. I am told this often happens.

Patrick Garland, who is due to compere the programme, is also late so we kick off without him, George Hartley talking about Larkin and the Marvell Press and his early days in Hull. Ordering *The Less Deceived* no one ever got the title right, asking for 'Alas! Deceived', 'The Lass Deceived' or 'The Less Received' and calling the author Carkin, Lartin, Laikin or Lock. I sit in the front row with Blake Morrison, Julian Barnes and Andrew Motion. There are more poems and reminiscences, but it's all a bit thin and jerky.

Now Patrick G. arrives, bringing the video of the film he made of Larkin in 1965, but there is further delay because while the machine works there is no sound. Eventually we sit and watch it like a silent film, with Patrick giving a commentary and saying how Larkinesque this situation is (which it isn't particularly) and how when he was stuck in the unending traffic jam he had felt that was Larkinesque too and how often the word Larkinesque is used and now it's part of the language. Pinter, whose own adjective is much more often used, remains impassive. Patrick, as always, tells some good stories, including one I hadn't heard of how Larkin used to cheer himself up by looking in the mirror and saying the line from *Rebecca*, 'I am Mrs de Winter now!'

Then Andrew Motion, who is tall, elegant and fair, a kind of verse Heseltine, reads his poem on the death of Larkin, which ends with his last glimpse of the great man, staring out of the hospital window, his fingers splayed out on the glass, watching as Motion drives away.

In the second half Pinter and I are to read, with an interlude about the novels by Julian Barnes. Riverside had earlier telephoned to ask what furniture we needed, and I had suggested a couple of reading-desks. These have been provided but absurdly with only one microphone so both desks are positioned centre stage, an inch or so apart with the mike between them. This means that when I read Pinter stands silently by and when he reads I do the same. Except that there is a loose board on my side and every time I shift my feet while Pinter is reading there is an audible creak. Were it Stoppard reading or Simon Gray I wouldn't care a toss: it's only because it's Pinter the creak acquires significance and seems somehow *meant*.

We finish at half-past ten and I go straight to Great Ormond Street, where Sam is in Intensive Care. See sick children (and in particular one baby almost hidden under wires and apparatus) and Larkin's fear of death seems self-indulgent. Sitting there I find myself wondering what would have happened had he worked in a hospital once a week like (dare one say it?) Jimmy Savile.

Apropos Pinter, I thought it odd that in the *Selected Letters* almost alone of Larkin's contemporaries he escaped whipping – given that neither his political views nor his poetry seemed likely to commend him to Larkin. But Pinter is passionate about cricket and, as Motion reveals, sponsored Larkin for the MCC, so it's just a case of the chaps sticking together.

This must have been a hard book to write, and I read it with growing admiration for the author and, until his pitiful death, mounting impatience with the subject. Motion, who was a friend of Larkin's, must have been attended throughout by the thought, by the sound even, of his subject's sepulchral disclaimers. Without ever having known Larkin, I feel, as I think many readers will, that I have lost a friend. I found myself and still find myself not wanting to believe that Larkin was really like this, the unpacking of that 'really', which Motion has done, what so much of the poetry is about. The publication of the *Selected Letters* before the biography was criticised but as a marketing strategy, which is what publishing is about these days, it can't be faulted. The Letters may sell the Life; the Life, splendid though it is, is unlikely to sell the Letters: few readers coming to the end of this book would want to know more. Different, yes, but not more.

There remain the poems, without which there would be no biography. Reading it I could not see how they would emerge unscathed. But I have read them again and they do, just as with Auden and Hardy, who have taken a similar biographical battering. Auden's epitaph on Yeats explains why:

Time that is intolerant
Of the brave and innocent
And indifferent in a week
To a beautiful physique

Worships language and forgives
Everyone by whom it lives;
Pardons cowardice, conceit,
Lays its honours at their feet

Time that with this strange excuse
Pardoned Kipling and his views,
And will pardon Paul Claudel,
Pardons him for writing well.[4]

The black-sailed unfamiliar ship has sailed on, leaving in its wake not a huge and birdless silence but an armada both sparkling and intact. Looking at this bright fleet, you see there is a man on the jetty, who might be anybody.

From the *London Review of Books*, 25 March 1993, pp. 3–9.

## NOTES

[Alan Bennett's essay first appeared in the *London Review of Books* as a review of Andrew Motion's *Philip Larkin: A Writer's Life*. It was subsequently reprinted in *Writing Home* (London, 1994), a collection of Bennett's prose writings. This review was one of the most candid and forthright responses to Motion's biography, and it has deservedly become one of the most popular bio-critical essays on Larkin's life and work. In his inimitable comic style, Bennett singles out those episodes in Larkin's life which seem outrageous and ridiculous, and yet he maintains a sympathetic, enquiring perspective throughout. Pursuing a steady line through Larkin's detractors and defenders, the essay wins the support of many readers in 'not wanting to believe that Larkin was really like this'. Bennett's response to the distasteful revelations in Motion's book is unabashed and vigorously discerning, but it also registers an uneasy sense of betrayal in finding such a sharp distinction between the seemingly self-deprecating, quiescent persona in the poems and the disagreeable character who inhabits the biography. For an entertaining account of the earlier affinity Bennett felt with Larkin, see the essay 'Instead of a Present' in which he comments on 'I Remember, I Remember': 'It isn't my favourite among his poems, but it's the one that made me realise that someone who admitted his childhood was "a forgotten boredom" might be talking to me.' See *Larkin at Sixty*, ed. Anthony Thwaite (London, 1982), pp. 69–74. Ed.]

1.  Andrew Motion, *Philip Larkin: A Writer's Life* (London, 1993), p. 28. Further references will be abbreviated as *WL* and included in the text.

2.  *Selected Letters of Philip Larkin 1940–1985*, ed. Anthony Thwaite (London, 1992), p. 547. Further references will be abbreviated as *Letters* and included in the text.

3.  W. H. Auden, *The Dyer's Hand* (London, 1963), p. 12.

4.  W. H. Auden, *Selected Poems*, ed. Edward Mendelson (London, 1979), p. 82.

# Further Reading

## BIBLIOGRAPHICAL SOURCES

B. C. Bloomfield's bibliography remains an interesting and useful source of information on the publication history of Larkin's poems and includes an appendix of critical writings on Larkin's work up to 1976. Mike Tierce provides a helpful supplementary listing of secondary materials up to 1984. Stephen Regan has produced a comprehensive annotated bibliography of criticism which will be updated periodically on Cd-Rom. R. J. C. Watt's *Concordance to the Poetry of Philip Larkin* is a tremendous contribution to scholarship; it reveals Larkin's changing stylistic habits between 1938 and 1983, and also 'some of the secrets of the genesis of poetic ideas, images, and even whole poems'.

B. C. Bloomfield, *Philip Larkin: A Bibliography 1933–1976* (London: Faber, 1979).

Stephen Regan, 'Philip Larkin and the Poetry of the 1950s', *Annotated Bibliography for English Studies* (Lisse, Switzerland: Swets & Zeitlinger, 1997).

Mike Tierce, 'Philip Larkin: Secondary Sources, 1950–1984', *Bulletin of Bibliography*, 43:2 (1986), 67–75.

R. J. C. Watt (ed.), *A Concordance to the Poetry of Philip Larkin* (Hildesheim, Zürich, New York: Olms-Weidmann, 1995).

## BIOGRAPHICAL SOURCES

Andrew Motion's biography and Anthony Thwaite's edition of the letters have had a profound effect on critical perceptions of Larkin's poetry. Some of the controversial reviews of these two books are mentioned in the Introduction to this volume.

Jean Hartley, *Philip Larkin, The Marvell Press and Me* (Manchester: Carcanet, 1989).

Andrew Motion, *Philip Larkin: A Writer's Life* (London: Faber, 1993).

Anthony Thwaite (ed.), *Larkin at Sixty* (London: Faber, 1982).

Anthony Thwaite (ed.), *Selected Letters of Philip Larkin 1940–1985* (London and Boston: Faber, 1992).

## BOOKS ON THE POETRY OF PHILIP LARKIN

There is now a considerable number of books on Larkin's work. This section includes those which are most frequently cited and which are likely to be of most value to readers studying modern poetry.

James Booth, *Philip Larkin: Writer* (Hemel Hempstead: Harvester Wheatsheaf, 1992).

Alan Brownjohn, *Philip Larkin* (London: Longman for the British Council, 1975).

Roger Day, *Larkin* (Milton Keynes: Open University Press, 1987).

Lolette Kuby, *An Uncommon Poet for the Common Man: A Study of Philip Larkin's Poetry* (The Hague: Mouton, 1974).

Guido Latré, *Locking Earth to the Sky: A Structuralist Approach to Philip Larkin's Poetry* (Frankfurt am Main, Bern, New York: Peter Lang, 1985).

Bruce K. Martin, *Philip Larkin* (Boston: Twayne, 1978).

Andrew Motion, *Philip Larkin* (London: Methuen, 1982).

Simon Petch, *The Art of Philip Larkin* (Sydney: Sydney University Press, 1981).

Stephen Regan, *Philip Larkin* (Basingstoke: Macmillan [Critics Debate Series], 1992).

Janice Rossen, *Philip Larkin: His Life's Work* (Hemel Hempstead: Harvester Wheatsheaf, 1989).

Andrew Swarbrick, *Out of Reach: The Poetry of Philip Larkin* (Basingstoke: Macmillan, 1995).

David Timms, *Philip Larkin* (Edinburgh: Oliver and Boyd, 1973).

A. T. Tolley, *My Proper Ground: A Study of the Work of Philip Larkin and its Development* (Edinburgh: Edinburgh University Press, 1991).

Terry Whalen, *Philip Larkin and English Poetry* (London: Macmillan, 1986).

## COLLECTIONS OF ESSAYS AND STUDENT GUIDES

The three collections of essays listed below contain a vast range of material on a diverse range of topics, from Larkin's interest in jazz to his 'religious beliefs'. Andrew Swarbrick's 'Master Guide' is an excellent student introduction to Larkin's poems. Two special journal issues on Larkin are strongly recommended: *Phoenix* 11/12 (1973/74) and *Critical Survey* 1:2 (1989).

Linda Cookson and Brian Loughrey (eds), *Critical Essays on Philip Larkin: The Poems* (Harlow: Longman, 1989).

George Hartley (ed.), *Philip Larkin 1922–1985: A Tribute* (London: Marvell Press, 1988).

Dale Salwak (ed.), *Philip Larkin: The Man and his Work* (London: Macmillan, 1989).

Andrew Swarbrick, *The Whitsun Weddings and The Less Deceived* (Basingstoke: Macmillan, 1986).

## LARKIN CRITICISM BEFORE 1975

The items listed below will give readers some understanding of the critical debate on Larkin's work that persisted until the mid-1970s. Positive appraisals of Larkin's 'clear-sighted realism' are weighed against the familiar charges of 'gentility' and 'parochialism'.

A. Alvarez (ed.), *The New Poetry* (Harmondsworth: Penguin, 1962; 1966).

C. B. Cox and A. E. Dyson, 'At Grass', in *Modern Poetry: Studies in Practical Criticism* (London: Edward Arnold, 1963).

Donald Davie, 'Landscapes of Larkin', in *Thomas Hardy and British Poetry* (London: Routledge and Kegan Paul, 1973).

Colin Falck, 'Philip Larkin', in *The Modern Poet: Essays from 'The Review'*, ed. Ian Hamilton (London: Macdonald, 1968), pp. 101–10.

Charles Tomlinson, 'Poetry Today', in *The Pelican Guide to English Literature, Vol. 7: The Modern Age*, ed. Boris Ford (Harmondsworth: Penguin, 1973), pp. 471–89.

## NEW CRITICAL PERSPECTIVES

The essays listed in this section helped to establish a more searching and appreciative response to Larkin's poetry than had been evident before 1975. The emergence of this new critical mood coincided significantly with the publication of *High Windows* in 1974. Critics began to perceive in Larkin's work a previously unacknowledged range of thematic and stylistic concerns, including symbolism. Larkin's writing had begun to move in new directions, but so too had critical standards. Among other things, these essays register a changing horizon of expectations among Larkin's readers.

James Booth, 'A Room Without a View: Larkin's Empty Attic', *Bête Noire*, 12/13 (1991/92), 320–9.

Barbara Everett, 'Larkin's Edens', in *Poets in their Time* (London: Faber, 1986), pp. 245–57.

Clive James, 'Don Juan in Hull: Philip Larkin', in *At the Pillars of Hercules* (London: Faber, 1979), pp. 51–72.

Grevel Lindop, 'Being Different from Yourself: Philip Larkin in the 1970s', in *British Poetry Since 1970: A Critical Survey*, ed. Peter Jones and Michael Schmidt (Manchester: Carcanet, 1980), pp. 46–54.

Edna Longley, 'Poète Maudit Manqué', in *Philip Larkin 1922–1985: A Tribute*, ed. George Hartley (London: Marvell Press, 1988), pp. 220–31.

Edward Neill, 'Modernism and Englishness: Reflections on Auden and Larkin', *Essays and Studies*, 36 (1983), 79–93.

Michael O'Neill, 'The Importance of Difference: Larkin's *The Whitsun Weddings*', in *Philip Larkin 1922–1985: A Tribute*, ed. George Hartley (London: Marvell Press, 1988), pp. 184–7.

John Osborne, 'The Hull Poets', *Bête Noire*, 2/3 (1987), 180–204.

J. Reibetanz, '"The Whitsun Weddings": Larkin's Reinterpretation of Time and Form in Keats', *Contemporary Literature*, 17 (1976), 529–40.

Richard Rorty, 'Philip Larkin: "Continuing to Live"', in *Contingency, Irony and Solidarity* (Cambridge: Cambridge University Press, 1989).

John Powell Ward, *The English Line: Poetry of the Unpoetic from Wordsworth to Larkin* (Basingstoke: Macmillan, 1992).

J. R. Watson, 'The Other Larkin', *Critical Quarterly*, 17 (1975), 347–60.

John Woolley, 'Larkin: Romance, Fiction and Myth', *English*, 35 (1986), 237–67.

## CULTURAL POLITICS AND POSTCOLONIAL CRITICISM

This section gathers together those critical approaches which might loosely be identified as 'historicist' or 'materialist', including essays which are concerned with questions of national identity and postcolonial perspectives in Larkin's poetry. For an extensive historicist appraisal of Larkin's poems, see Part Two of Stephen Regan's *Philip Larkin* in the Macmillan Critics Debate Series (listed above).

Nigel Alderman, '"The life with a hole in it": Philip Larkin and the condition of England', *Textual Practice*, 8: 2 (1994), 279–301.

Joseph Bristow, 'The Obscenity of Philip Larkin', *Critical Inquiry*, 21 (1994), 156–81.

Neil Corcoran, 'A Movement Pursued: Philip Larkin', in *English Poetry Since 1940* (London: Longman, 1993), pp. 87–95.

Andrew Crozier, 'Thrills and frills: poetry as figures of empirical lyricism', in *Society and Literature 1945–1970*, ed. Alan Sinfield (London: Methuen, 1973), pp. 199–233.

David Gervais, 'Larkin, Betjeman and the aftermath of "England"', in *Literary Englands: Versions of 'Englishness' in Modern Writing* (Cambridge: Cambridge University Press, 1993), pp. 185–219.

John Goodby, '"The importance of elsewhere", or "No man is an Ireland": self, selves and social consensus in the poetry of Philip Larkin', *Critical Survey*, 1: 2 (1989), 131–8.

John Goode, 'A Reading of Deceptions', in *Philip Larkin 1922–1985: A Tribute*, ed. George Hartley (London: Marvell Press, 1988), pp. 126–34.

Seamus Heaney, 'Englands of the Mind', in *Preoccupations: Selected Prose 1968–1978* (London and Boston: Faber, 1980), pp. 150–69.

Graham Holderness, 'Philip Larkin: the limits of experience', in *Critical Essays on Philip Larkin: The Poems*, ed. Linda Cookson and Brian Loughrey (Harlow: Longman, 1989), pp. 106–14.

Blake Morrison, *The Movement: English Poetry and Fiction of the 1950s* (Oxford: Oxford University Press, 1980).

Tony Pinkney, 'Old Toads Down Cemetery Road', *News From Nowhere*, 1 (1986), 37–47.

## LINGUISTIC CRITICISM AND DISCOURSE ANALYSIS

The essays listed in this section are concerned mainly with the language of Larkin's poems, though the study of 'rhetoric' and 'discourse' inevitably raises questions about the 'society' in which poetry is written and read. A strong revival of interest in stylistic analysis is evident in some of the more recent essays listed below. See Guido Latré's book (listed above) for a full-length structuralist approach to the poems.

Jonathan Raban, *The Society of the Poem* (London: Harrap, 1971).

Graham Trengove, 'What Happens in "Whatever Happened?"?', in *The Taming of the Text: Explorations in Language, Literature and Culture*, ed. Willie Van Peer (London: Routledge, 1988).

Graham Trengove, '"Vers de société": Towards Some Society', in *Reading, Analysing and Teaching Literature*, ed. Mick Short (Harlow: Longman, 1989).

David Trotter, *The Making of the Reader: Language and Subjectivity in Modern American, English and Irish Poetry* (London: Macmillan, 1984).

Peter Verdonk, 'Poems as Text and Discourse: The Poetics of Philip Larkin', in *Literary Pragmatics*, ed. Roger Sell (London: Routledge, 1991).

Katie Wales, 'Teach yourself "rhetoric": an analysis of Philip Larkin's "Church Going"', in *Twentieth-Century Poetry: From Text to Context*, ed. Peter Verdonk (London and New York: Routledge, 1993), pp. 87–99.

H. G. Widdowson, 'The Conditional Presence of Mr Bleaney', in *Language and Literature: An Introductory Reader in Stylistics*, ed. Ronald Carter (London: George Allen and Unwin, 1982).

## LARKIN'S INFLUENCES AND INTERTEXTUAL CRITICISM

Some of the most stimulating criticism has been preoccupied with the textual relationships between Larkin's poetry and that of his predecessors. Some excellent work has also been done on Larkin's 'legacy' to a younger generation of poets. In addition to the essays that follow, see the chapter on Larkin and Betjeman in David Gervais, *Literary Englands* (listed above).

Douglas Dunn, *Under the Influence: Douglas Dunn on Philip Larkin* (Edinburgh: Edinburgh University Library, 1987).

Seamus Heaney, 'Joy or Night: Last Things in the Poetry of W. B. Yeats and Philip Larkin', in *The Redress of Poetry: Oxford Lectures* (London and Boston: Faber, 1995), pp. 146–63.

Peter Hollindale, 'Philip Larkin's "The Explosion"', *Critical Survey*, 1: 2 (1989), 139–48.

Edna Longley, 'Larkin, Edward Thomas and the Tradition', *Phoenix*, 11–12 (1973/4), 63–89. Reprinted as '"Any-angled light": Philip Larkin and Edward Thomas', in *Poetry in the Wars* (Newcastle: Bloodaxe, 1986), pp. 113–39.

## OTHER RECOMMENDED READING

The books listed below include chapters on Philip Larkin and discuss the poetry in the broad context of modern literature. These books also provide an insight into the changing critical reception of Larkin's work, especially across the 1970s and 1980s.

John Bayley, 'The Importance of Elsewhere', in *The Uses of Division: Unity and Disharmony in Literature* (London: Chatto & Windus, 1976), pp. 171–82.

Calvin Bedient, *Eight Contemporary Poets* (London: Oxford University Press, 1974).

Merle Brown, *Double Lyric: Divisiveness and Communal Creativity in Recent English Poetry* (New York: Columbia Press, 1980).

Martin Dodsworth (ed.), *The Survival of Poetry* (London: Faber, 1970).

John Haffenden, *Viewpoints: Poets in Conversation* (London: Faber, 1981).

Ian Hamilton, *The Modern Poet: Essays from 'The Review'* (London: Macdonald, 1968).

Jerzy Jarniewicz, *The Uses of the Commonplace in Contemporary British Poetry: Larkin, Dunn and Raine* (Lodz, Poland: Wydawnictwo Uniwersytetu Lodzkiego, 1994).

Peter Jones and Michael Schmidt (eds), *British Poetry Since 1970: A Critical Survey* (Manchester: Carcanet, 1980).

John Lucas, *Modern English Poetry from Hardy to Hughes* (London: Batsford, 1986).

Neil Powell, *Carpenters of Light: Some Contemporary English Poets* (Manchester: Carcanet, 1979).

Christopher Ricks, 'Philip Larkin: "Like something almost being said"', in *The Force of Poetry* (Oxford: Clarendon, 1984), pp. 274–84.

Geoffrey Thurley, *The Ironic Harvest: English Poetry in the Twentieth Century* (London: Edward Arnold, 1974).

# Notes on Contributors

**Alan Bennett** read history at Exeter College, Oxford. Among his many stage plays are *Forty Years On; Habeas Corpus; The Old Country; Enjoy; The Madness of George III; Kafka's Dick*; and an adaptation of Kenneth Grahame's *Wind in the Willows* for the National Theatre. He has also written many television plays, including *An Englishman Abroad; A Question of Attribution*; and the highly popular *Talking Heads* series.

**James Booth** is Senior Lecturer in English at the University of Hull. His publications include *Writers and Politics in Nigeria* (London and New York, 1981) and *Philip Larkin: Writer* (Hemel Hempstead, 1992). He is also the author of *Northern Museums: Sylloge of Coins of the British Isles* 48 (London, 1996). He has recently completed two essays comparing the writings of Philip Larkin and Seamus Heaney.

**Steve Clark** is Visiting Professor at the University of Osaka in Japan. He is the author of *Paul Ricoeur* (London, 1990) and *Sordid Images: The Poetry of Masculine Desire* (London, 1994). He is the editor of *Selected Poems of Akenside, Macpherson and Young* (Manchester, 1994), and co-editor with David Worrall of *Historicizing Blake* (Basingstoke, 1994).

**Barbara Everett** is Senior Research Fellow at Somerville College, Oxford. Her publications include *Donne: A London Poet* (London, 1972); *Eliot's Four Quartets and French Symbolism* (Oxford, 1980); *Poets in Their Time: Essays on English Poetry from Donne to Larkin* (London, 1986); and *Young Hamlet: Essays on Shakespeare's Tragedies* (Oxford, 1989).

**Seamus Heaney** was Professor of Poetry at Oxford University from 1989 to 1994. His *New Selected Poems* was published in 1990, and two new collections have since appeared: *Seeing Things* (London, 1991) and *The Spirit Level* (London, 1996). He has written a play, *The Cure at Troy* (1991), and three books of critical essays: *Preoccupations: Selected Prose 1968–1978* (London and Boston, 1980); *The Government of the Tongue* (London and Boston, 1988); and *The Redress of Poetry* (London and New York, 1995). In 1995 he was awarded the Nobel Prize for Literature.

**Graham Holderness** is Professor of Cultural Studies and Dean of the School of Humanities and Education at the University of Hertfordshire. His publications include *D. H. Lawrence: History, Ideology and Fiction* (London, 1982), and books on *Wuthering Heights, Women in Love* and *Hamlet* (Milton Keynes, 1985, 1986, 1987). He has written extensively on Shakespeare's plays, including *Shakespeare in Performance: The Taming of the Shrew* (London, 1989), and the Penguin Critical Studies of *Richard II* (London, 1989) and *Romeo and Juliet* (1991). He has edited *The Shakespeare Myth* (London, 1988) and *The Politics of Theatre and Drama* (1992). He is currently working on the series *Shakespearean Originals*, new editions of the plays based on the original printed texts.

**David Lodge** is Honorary Professor of Modern English Literature at Birmingham University. He is a novelist as well as a critic. His critical works include *Language of Fiction* (London, 1966); *The Modes of Modern Writing* (London, 1977); *Working with Structuralism* (London, 1981); and *Write On: Occasional Essays 1965–85* (London, 1986). He is the editor of *Modern Criticism and Theory: A Reader* (London, 1988). His novels include *Changing Places* (London, 1975); *Small World* (London, 1984); *Nice Work* (London, 1988); *Paradise News* (London, 1991); and *Therapy* (London, 1995).

**Andrew Motion** is Professor of Creative Writing at the University of East Anglia. His work as a critic and biographer includes *Philip Larkin: A Writer's Life* (London, 1993); *Philip Larkin* (London, 1982); and *The Poetry of Edward Thomas* (London, 1980). With Blake Morrison, he edited *The Penguin Book of Contemporary British Poetry* (Harmondsworth, 1982). His *Dangerous Play: Selected Poems 1974–1984* was published by Penguin in 1985, and among his recent collections of poetry are *The Price of Everything* (London, 1994) and *Salt Water* (London, 1997). His biography of John Keats will be published in the autumn of 1997.

**Tom Paulin** is a Fellow of Hertford College, Oxford, and G. M. Young Lecturer in English. He is the author of *Thomas Hardy: The Poetry of Perception* (London, 1975); *Ireland and the English Crisis* (Newcastle Upon Tyne, 1984); and *Minotaur: Poetry and the Nation State* (London, 1992). He is also the editor of *The Faber Book of Political Verse* and *The Faber Book of Vernacular Verse* (London, 1990). His *Selected Poems 1972–1990* was published in 1993, closely followed by a new book of poems, *Walking a Line* (London, 1994). A new selection of critical essays, *Writing to the Moment*, appeared in 1996. He is currently working on a critical study of the writings of William Hazlitt.

**Janice Rossen** is a Visiting Scholar at the University of Texas, Austin. She is the author of *Philip Larkin: His Life's Work* (Hemel Hempstead, 1989) and *The World of Barbara Pym* (London, 1987). She is the editor of *Independent Women: The Function of Gender in the Novels of Barbara Pym* (Hemel Hempstead, 1988).

**Stan Smith** holds the Established Chair in English at the University of Dundee, where he co-directs the Auden Concordance Project with R. J. C. Watt. His publications include *Inviolable Voice: History and Twentieth-Century Poetry* (Dublin, 1982); *W. H. Auden* (Oxford, 1985); *Edward Thomas* (London, 1986); *W. B. Yeats: A Critical Introduction* (Basingstoke, 1990); *The Origins of Modernism* (Hemel Hempstead, 1994); and *W. H. Auden* [Writers and their Work] (Southampton, 1997). He is General Editor of the Longman Critical Readers series and Longman Studies in Twentieth-Century Literature.

**Andrew Swarbrick** is Head of English at the Royal Grammar School, Worcester. He is the author of *Out of Reach: The Poetry of Philip Larkin* (Basingstoke, 1995) and editor of *The Art of Oliver Goldsmith* (London, 1984). He has also written books on Philip Larkin (Basingstoke, 1985) and T. S. Eliot (Basingstoke, 1988) for the Macmillan Master Guides series.

# Index